Charleston Conference
Proceedings 2001

Katina Strauch, Editor

LIBRARIES
U N L I M I T E D
A Member of the Greenwood Publishing Group

Westport, Connecticut • London

Libraries Unlimited
A Member of Greenwood Publishing Group, Inc.
88 Post Road West
Westport, CT 06881
1-800-225-5800
www.lu.com

ISBN 1-59158-073-0

Introduction

Keynote Address

Serials

Digital Enviroment

Table of Contents

Collection Development

Books and Publishing

Consortia

Personnel Development

W e are honored to publish this series of papers from the 2001 Charleston Conference, the 21st Charleston Conference: The Trends They Are A'Changing, November 1-3, 2001. We have many people to thank for this publication. First, Rosann Bazirjian of Penn State University and Vicky Speck of ABC-Clio, whose attention to detail and content has assured us of producing a seminal work in the library literature.

Second, we would like to thank EBSCO Subscription Services for their layout, typesetting, and monetary support. The proceedings Website www.ebsco.co/home/charleston is also maintained by EBSCO. Thank you.

And, last but not least, thanks to Martin Dillon and Libraries Unlimited who have graciously arranged to publish and distribute the proceedings for the 2001 Charleston Conference and succeeding conferences! Thank you one and all!

See you at the 22nd Annual Charleston Conference: Issues in Book and Serial Acquisition: Two Faces Have I: One for Books and One for Bytes to be held October 31-November 2, 2001. See you there!

Cordially,

Bruce Strauch
Publisher

Against the Grain Press
MSC 98, The Citadel.
209 Richardson Ave.
Charleston, SC 29409
843-723-3536 (phone and fax)
strauchk@earthlink.net
www.against-the-grain.com
www.charlestonco.com
www.cofc.edu/library/conference

The Charleston Conference continues to be a major event for information exchange among librarians, publishers, and other vendors. Every year more people tell us how much of a learning experience the conference has been for them. After we put together the 2000 proceedings, we received such a favorable response that we, and the other Conference Directors, thought we should repeat the experience so that those who were not able to attend could have a taste of the topics that were addressed.

The theme of the 2001 Charleston Conference was "The Trends They Are A'Changing." While not all presenters prepared written versions of their remarks, enough did so that we are able to include an overview of such subjects as serials, the digital environment, books and publishing, collection development, consortia, and personnel development. These topics are always of high interest and provide opportunities for multiple perspectives and observations.

Katina Strauch, founder of the conference, continues to serve as an inspiration for us. Her enthusiasm for the project was infectious. We hope you, the reader, find the papers as thought-provoking as we did and that they encourage the ongoing dialogue between librarian, publisher, and vendor that can only make the learning experience for the ultimate user better.

Signed,

Co-Editors of the 21st Charleston Conference proceedings

Rosann Bazirjian, Assistant Dean for Technical and Access Services, Pennsylvania State University

Vicky H. Speck, Editorial Director, Serials, ABC-CLIO

Tom Sanville from OhioLiNK was the keynote speaker. He set the stage for a wonderful conference by addressing this year's theme: The Trends They Are A'Changing. He spoke about OhioLiNK's goals as an explanation for their practices. He spoke about empowerment, integrated versus segregated access, leveraged spending and progressive cooperation. He spoke about old rules and new rules. He spoke about OhioLiNK's "big deal" and the need to be better buyers of information. He ended with a plea to librarians to not be afraid of evolution but to embrace it and live with it.

Keynote Address

THE TRENDS THEY ARE A'CHANGING

Tom Sanville, Executive Director, OhioLINK

Slide 1 Wow, what a crowd. I hope to keep you awake. I'm glad this is an informal conference because I'm not much of a formal speaker. I accepted the invitation to be here this morning with a degree of trepidation knowing that I was supposed to give the keynote speech. I do good "this is how we do it good" speeches; but I don't know about doing keynote speeches because I always think there's an expectation from the audience that somehow I'm going to tell you something that you don't already know. That's probably not true anytime you've ever heard a keynote speech. And it certainly won't be true today much to your chagrin maybe, but I'll be honest about that. Maybe I'll give you some questions to talk about and maybe crystallize some of your thinking or maybe uncrystallize some of your thinking but I don't think in today's world, given all the uncertainties, that it's likely that any of us are going to walk up on the stage and "part the waters" with some new piece of information. So don't get your expectations too high. I will try to give my remarks in a way that will give you something to think about and raise some questions in your mind for the next few days while you are together.

This is how I've titled this, regardless of what is in the program. This is what I'm more or less going to talk about; that the rules of the game have got to change and how to provide adequately for our needs.

The Rules of the Game have got to Change

Providing Adequately for Journal Needs

"Before I refuse to take your questions, I have an opening statement." Ronald Reagan

Slide 2 These are Katina's marching orders in an e-mail to me. These are the things she told me I had to do — so we'll see how successful I am in doing this. She characterized some of the things the OhioLiNK program was doing as against the grain, off the wall, leading edge. But from the inside looking out, you don't think it's that way, if you're doing things you need to do to survive and build your future.

Katina's Marching Orders
- Stir the Pot
- Be Outrageous
- Don't Be Conventional
- Get people thinking
- Address the against the grain/off the wall/ Bleeding edge unique approaches of OhioLINK

"You can't build a reputation on what you are going to do." Henry Ford

Slide 3 Before we start I want to get realistic about a few key points. One is this second bullet that reminds me of the world's oldest lawyer joke — how do you know a lawyer's lying to you? -- when he moves his lips, right? Well, now anytime that any of us talk to each other about what we ought to be doing tomorrow, I think you ought to keep that in mind because we have so many things in flux, in evolution that I think it's impossible for us to really know what we're doing. We are simultaneously in a

Before we start, let's be Realistic
- We, You, Publishers, Authors don't really know what we are doing
- BECAUSE EVERYTHING IS EVOLVING
- Technology
- Publishing roles
- Pricing
- User Needs
- Every solution has a dark side

"Change is constant." Benjamin Disraeli

revolution with technology, publishing rules, pricing and user needs. Now, how in the world you're ever going to change all those variables simultaneously and claim that you know what you're doing, is beyond me. You have to do something, but to claim that you know what you're doing is a stretch for me, so I hope we all have an open mind in that regard.

And the other thing I want to be realistic about is that every solution, OhioLINK solutions, or SPARC solutions, or anybody else's solutions in this area all have a dark side. Everything that people are doing is predicated upon what they think the consequence is going to be. But nobody can really accurately predict what the consequences will be given all these things changing simultaneously. So every solution has a dark side with the sequence of events that you think will happen, that in the end won't happen quite that way. So I'm not throwing out any solutions. I'm not talking about the OhioLINK perspectives as being the gospel. I don't anybody else has the single answer either. Every possible thing our community is trying has a downside to it.

Slide 4 So another title for this could be Ohio's Approach: Against the Grain or Necessity? Or, Questions and Hypotheses in Action. What we're trying to do amidst all of this uncertainty is put things in motion, put actions in place, and we're testing as we go. We are doing this by trial and error based on our best estimates of what we think is a reasonable approach to solve some of our problems.

> OhioLINK's Approach:
> Against the Grain or Necessity?
> or
> Questions and Hypotheses in Action
> • Our Compelling Goal and Philosophies
> • Collecting: Old Rules vs. New Rules
> • Objectives
> "Necessity is the mother of taking chances." Mark Twain

So what I'm going to talk about are our compelling goals and some of our philosophies. We'll talk about some of the collection issues that we face, some of the old rules, and some of the new rules that we'd like to create for collection materials. We'll talk a little about our objectives as we try to put those new rules in place, and then we'll talk about risks rewards outcomes, possibilities, what ifs, and so forth.

Slide 5 This is essentially what the OhioLINK community sees as its objective. There is a lot of rhetoric written starting back in the mid-1980s that is still valid to this day, that when it's distilled says this is our goal — economically sustainable, increased access to information as a consortium. Because the conclusion reached way back then (the 1980's) was that we did not have any system that was economically sustainable, let alone that provided increased access to information and that was going to lead us to success. So this is our goal, our mission, in a nutshell. If what we're doing doesn't contribute, doesn't advance, doesn't evolve towards this, then we're not moving forward. The underlying last words, "as a consortium" are critical. The notion that we could do this as individuals is an obsolete one.

> "One of the most dangerous forms of human error is forgetting what one is trying to achieve." Paul Nitze
>
> • Economically sustainable, increased student and faculty access to and use of library provided information to support and improve instruction and research...as a consortium

Slide 6 As we approach that goal, we are looking at ourselves as realistically as possible. We're only Ohio. We're not somebody else. We have to look realistically at who we are, what we need, and when do we need it based on our community. And that was the conclusion of the people that preceded me. I got there in 1992, long after what I'm talking about now was already essentially thought out and laid out in the late 1980s as a philosophical approach. But looking at Ohio's needs, whatever we did had

> *"At times it is folly to hasten, at other times to delay. The wise do everything in its proper time."* Ovid
>
> - We're only OHIO
> - Make a major impact on access NOW
> - Deal with the world as it is – we must start where the money is
> - Make changes NOW that improve our long term prospects and foundations

to have an immediate impact. We couldn't necessarily say, "I hope three generations from now that what I'm doing will create a different world." We said we needed it now. We had to put something in place that would have immediate impact, which meant that we had to deal with the world as it is. We have to take the pieces of the puzzle as they exist and try to reformulate them. We can't necessarily look strictly at the long-term issues, but we have to look at where the community is right now in terms of how libraries spend their money, where is the money being spent, and how do we make modifications to that. In doing that though, we certainly look at our goal, economically sustainable increased information access, and realize that's a long-term goal. It has to be good for the long term, so whatever we do, even as we are trying to press for immediate or near term results, we have to look at it having validity as a building block to the long term.

Slide 7 High expectations are a key to everything. I think this is a very, very important issue and I think in OhioLINK's case the community established very, very high expectations relative to what they were experiencing. And these are some of the philosophies that I think the OhioLINK community works very hard to translate into a new world, looking beyond the restrictions or obstacles of our current practices and saying how can we change these to put these new philosophies into place.

> *"High expectations are the key to everything."* Sam Walton
>
> - User Empowerment rather than Mediation
> - Abundant rather than Rationed Access
> - Universal rather than Selective Access
> - Immediate rather than Delayed Access
> - Integrated rather than Segregated Access
> - Leveraged Spending rather than Less Efficient Spending
> - Progressive, vested interest Cooperation rather than parochial orientation

User empowerment was a philosophy that was put into place from the very start. From the day that the OhioLINK community decided that there was going to be a patron-initiated online borrowing system, they set the philosophical stage for everything that we do- which is get out of the way of user maximum access and let them decide what they want to do. And I think that if you look at everything that we've done since then, it really has pushed that envelope in terms of maximizing the opportunities. Get out of the way, give the user the opportunity to do what they want to do to maximum effect. Therefore, we've always looked at abundant and universal access over rationed and restricted access.

One of the things that I like to say in presentations on this topic is that I like to provide information to our libraries whether they need it or not. And I say that because in today's world, given all the things that are in motion, we really don't know what people need or what they will use. Why try to pre-judge to the extent that we've had to do that in the past? And what do we find out if we provide maximum access? That it's amazing what people will use if you give them the opportunity. So when we look at decision-making, we always lean towards more rather than less or let's let the user decide what they need given the maximal opportunity.

Integrated versus segregated access; that's one reason why we do so many things ourselves, because we got tired of working with vendors with their vertical solution when we were building a multi-vendor horizontal solution. Some of those things are changing, I'm glad to say and this gives us better opportunities in the future. But when we got going horizontal integrating was not something that was happening outside of our own system.

Leveraged spending and progressive cooperation. Leveraged group spending versus less efficient spending. I've probably mentioned this concept multiple times throughout this talk as one of the things that drove OhioLINK into formation. The fact was that every year our library directors, individually, got to go to their provosts and vice presidents and say "I want more money so I can buy less information. Please give me more money so I can buy less information." And with the pressures that higher education faces, is that going to carry the day? So in OhioLINK we are looking at ways to change this so that we can now say to our administrators, "If you give us more money, we will buy much more for the dollar because we are working cooperatively in our own vested self interest." And that's the critical issue for the OhioLINK program and what we're doing and why we're doing it. As Director, I have to try to fashion our direction, but in the end, I only want to do the things that the libraries feel good about doing. Same with Henny Youngman — "doctor, it hurts when I go like this; — well then, don't go like this." We don't do things that don't feel good, that don't have positive results at the library level. Sometimes this causes us to have to give up some of our old notions, but once we realize what's happened, we're realize going forward.

Slide 8 Well, what practices, or old rules, got us into this mess and what are we trying to do get out of it? It's a situation that if you don't change you're going to rot anyway, so you might as well do something.

The old rules that you lived by in the past certainly are based on libraries as individual economic units of purchase. Everybody was an island; they had their collections and they had a focus on what that selection should be. The way in which information could be used was really based on where you were relative to that collection. It was based on the mentality of use based on a static media — print. Everybody knows how useful print can be, how portable it is, how rapidly it can be consumed; how much you can consume; how fast you can get it if you don't have it. All those things are well known, very static approaches to information use that have created an idea of what people need based on how much they could actually consume based on this dominant form of media: print.

> "Why not upset the apple cart? If you don't, the apples will rot anyway." Frank Clark
> • OLD RULES
> • Based on individual library as economic unit of purchase and and use
> • Based on a mentality of use and need built on the STATIC limitations of print
> • Based on a mentality of forced physical and economic rationing
> • Based on a "library in the vise grip" model

We've developed a mentality of forced physical and economic rationing — a vicious circle, so to speak, that creates our own prison. And I call it the "library in the vise grip" model. With the faculty and students as consumers and the faculty as information producers, on the one hand, and, on the other hand, the publishers where we have to go to buy that information, and you're caught in the middle. Being in that vise grip has forced us to be very, very, very, very, very, very short-term oriented. Required to supply what my people need right now, what can't they live without. As a library, I can't cut this because my faculty member has to have it today, they will not let me think long term with the intent of managing my economic resources.

Slide 9 This chart shows what the old rules got from major universities in Ohio in terms of how much of the published material might they could afford to collect. This is a set of print inventories that we have made of journal publishers over time. This covers about 5,600 titles from a lot of different publishers, societies, commercial publishers, you name it. Our major universities average under 25 percent in print subscriptions for the titles that these publishers put out in journal form. You see how many of our schools have less than 25 percent. We only have one school in the state that has more than half. And, of course, these percentages are getting worse. So we see this as being as not the way to run a railroad. This is not the way for us to be relevant partners in the educational process on our campus with our instructors and teachers.

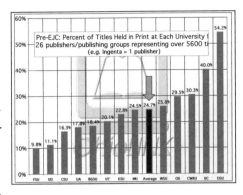

Slide 10 So the old rules got us a level of print journals that did not and do not meet our patron needs and the knowledge that we're losing ground every year. We know that as individual libraries, given the current state of affairs, an individual library cannot leverage significantly greater access on limited funds. You can pull a few rabbits out of your hat but you cannot dramatically change this 25 percent average for individual libraries. It's impossible to do this under the current way in which the market is structured. It will not happen. And every year we get less and less effective. Every year prices have gone up and, as we all know, at rates greater than our budgets.

> *"Bad business practices, if left uncorrected, will drive out good business practices."* Ralph Nader

- Ohio libraries DID NOT, DO NOT and WILL NOT have all the journals their patrons need. We are losing ground.
- Journals are priced such that individual libraries cannot leverage significantly greater access on limited funds
- Every year, in the here and now, we are less effective

Slide 11 So, what kinds of new rules are we trying to put in place? New rules are based on the group as the economic unit of purchase. You need to be a bigger gorilla. Be a gorilla. Be a force that can negotiate a better equation for the information resources that you need. Get rid of notions that we know what the level of use we'll be able to expect and let's talk about the mental-

> *"Rules are made for people who aren't willing to make up their own."* Chuck Yeager

- NEW RULES
- Based on the GROUP as economic unit of purchase and use
- Based on a mentality of EXPANDING and EVOLVING USE via electronic information which is highly elastic based on ease of access
- Based on a delivery and economic model that allows for EXPANSION over RATIONING.

ity that is based on expanding and evolving use of electronic information, whose use we know by experience is highly elastic. You know what happens when you put things on the desktop rather than ask somebody to get them two days later, a week later, or whenever. You know how much can be consumed from your own experience. We certainly experience this even with physical materials. We started delivering post patron initiated borrowing, where they got to push the button and ask for it. We can deliver it relatively fast and use is going through the roof. Based on our executing economic models that allow for expansion over rationing, we don't live within the old constructs of yesterday's world. Again, coming back with that desktop delivery, what a dramatic difference that makes over any type of delayed delivery.

Slide 12 If this is the information age, as everybody says it is, or at least the dawn of the information age, we need to get more information value for each dollar spent. Let's take money that's going to spent anyway and instead of spending it poorly, let's spend it together and spend it more wisely and get more information, more value, per dollar spent. And it's not just getting access to the information, but getting the use of the information, so in the end you get a lower cost per user of the information that you buy. That's a key issue that has to be understood not only by us as buyers but from the publishing side; that the unit cost of information has to go down if this an information age where you use a lot of information. This is the same thing that happened in the Industrial Revolution. We don't have all the physical, wonderful consumer products that we have because they sell at high prices. We have them primarily because they produce and sell them at low prices that we can all afford in much higher numbers. From my early, early career days, having worked with Coca Cola Company, I'm always thinking high volumes. And why not in the information age as well?

Begin to gain control over costs; stabilize the equation. This comes back to our position that we have to deal with the real world as it exists right now. To do that we have to go after the places where we actually spend the money. Until we get those under control, we can't possibly hope to build a better foundation for the long term. So our focus at the beginning was to go after the places where we have the most money involved and where we need to get the most control. This then will enable us to look beyond.

And very, very, very, very important is let's learn a little more about how information is really used. Let's quit making assumptions about what people use, what they need, and how much they can consume. One of the nice advantages of electronic information is that it opens up some doors to measuring what use really means, not necessarily in a complete sense, but certainly in a much more comprehensive sense than we had in the past.

Slides 13/14 So, how have we gone about putting the new rules to work? Let me just run through the basic steps of what a "big deal" is, how are we going about trying to achieve some of these goals and objectives. For a given a publisher we basically start

"What isn't tried won't work." C. McDonald

• Determine statewide current print
The BIG DEAL
• Guarantee collective spending level
• Purchase all titles in electronic form
• All schools access all titles
• Archive and integrate locally
• Measure usage levels (downloads)
• Re-negotiate to achieve more

by looking at how much money we have in print so we know where our investment level is. We know what their material has been worth to us based on the realities of the money that we've had in our pockets and the material that they've had to offer. Then we have a starting point. From that starting point, we try to negotiate a multi-year collective group-wide license that guarantees some level of collective spending in return for which we will purchase all titles in electronic form. Now, of course, the equation for doing that varies widely from publisher to publisher based on the circumstances involved. In return, all of our schools get access to all the titles. We archive and we integrate this material into our own electronic journal center to maximize use. So far we have over 4,000 titles in it; it's got over 2.7 million journal articles in it, and it's a one-stop shop for the patrons at this point.

"What isn't tried won't work." C. McDonald

• Determine statewide current print funds
• Negotiate multi-year collective license
• Guarantee collective spending level
• Purchase all titles in electronic form
• Measure usage levels (downloads)
• Re-negotiate to achieve more sustainable expanded access
• Re-negotiate to achieve more

And now we've got something that you can use to measure usage levels. Downloads are obviously the primary thing we measure to begin with, but we are looking beyond that to see what can we measure beyond that in terms of the qualitative use of the downloaded text. What do users do with all those downloads? We now have empirical starting points that we did not have, and most importantly, now we can use these to negotiate access on a more rational basis. These last points are important to consider when I read what's been written about the big deal, in terms of what's wrong with it. I don't think people are giving enough credit to the fact that this is not a big deal forever. This is not in concrete. It is not without a thought or a plan that we will learn from every step that we take. So the big deal is a place to start. Let's put everything on the table and see what's used. Also see what isn't used? Not only does that have a dramatic impact on what we should do specifically as a group, but I would hope through access by our broader community to electronic journals usage, that this would begin to say something more fundamentally to the whole industry about what should be produced, why it should be produced, at what cost. Do we need it or don't we need it, and what adjustments should be made. So I think, the big deal is a big stepping stone, it's a big enabler to where we might want to go next, and we're going to learn from our experience by first opening up the gates, and now let's see what really makes the most sense in the longer term. We're not pre-judging how big the big deal should be long term. We think it should be as big as possible to begin with, and let's use it for our own purposes tactically as well as to help drive the industry forward in terms of what does it really say about the system of information production.

Slide 15 What are some of the issues about the big deal that have been raised? Are we abdicating selection? Are we rewarding about bad guys, whoever they are? Are we making the bad guys stronger and more powerful in this equation? Are we going to the good guys? Who are the good guys? And what about the small new guys? Are we jeopardizing serial agents? Well, the answer to all these questions is no, no, no, no, yes, no. With respect to selection, we are changing what we think the definition of selection ought to be. We're saying it ought to be longer term. It ought to be more in user driven. We're not abdicating selection, we're just saying we're not going to pre-select and we're going to get more use information in hand before we decide what kind of selection decisions we want to make. We're not abdicating, but we are, to a certain extent, foregoing it for the opportunity to see what our users might really use beyond what the limited collections we have delivered in print. At this point, I'd simply reference that I've written about some of our user statistics, several times and several places over the last couple of year. Every time a new year rolls around, I put out another updated version of how much use we're getting on campuses. I know that David Kohl will probably talk about some of that on Friday morning. We've seen a dramatic expansion in usage that is going to drive a different sort of selection decision.

> *"If you want to make enemies, try to change something."* Woodrow Wilson
>
> - Are we abdicating selection?
> - Are we rewarding the bad guys?
> - Are we making the bad guys stronger?
> - Are we ignoring the good guys?
> - What about the small and new guys?
> - Are we jeopardizing serial agents?
>
> OhioLINK

We don't think we're abdicating selection but we are changing the way selection ought to be done. Are we worried that deals with the bad guys will eliminate opportunity for the good guys? We are not sure who is wearing the white and black hats. We have executed these new deals with for profits, not for profits, from big to small, and will do a lot of different deals with a lot of different people but it has to have a basis in reality. I've specified where we're coming from in terms of what we think the reality is.

The other thing is, we don't think we're giving anybody any extra leverage in terms of who will be stronger or weaker in the marketplace. What we're doing is enabling ourselves to have as much information as possible to negotiate with anybody on the most rational terms necessary to deliver what we think our users need. We're not ignoring anybody. We are obviously are starting with some of the big publishers because, as I said, we're going to start where the money is. And we've got to get that under control before we can make anything else happen. But we've also licenses with variety of other publishers, so we're going to spread our eggs around but we have to do it in the most realistic way possible.

Are we jeopardizing serial agents? I think the Charleston Advisor published our paper on what we think the answer to that is and how all the changes that we're talking about can balance everybody's interests. In the short term and the long term, we're all in jeopardy. Every single one of us in jeopardy. Serials agents, no more or less than anybody else, have to have something of value in the delivery of electronic information to our users.

We don't think, in the end, that we are ignoring any of these issues, but as I said, every solution has a dark side. And if we don't see the consequences of what we're doing progress the way we think they should, then there could be bad consequences. And if there are, then we'll stop doing what we do. We'll change what we do. But if we keep evolving the way we think we are, then we think that we will be addressing a lot of the concerns people have.

Slide 16 But, I have other concerns about what other people want. Why are some so happy to have more journals created? The first thing that comes up when we sit around the table with the library directors in Ohio and we look at some of the new publisher initiatives, the first thing that comes out of the lips of the directors, not out of my lips, out of the director's lips, is, "there's just one more journal I can't afford to buy." That doesn't make the new journals bad. It just means that, notwithstanding the consequence people think will happen from these new initiatives, in reality it could be good or it could be bad. I think we better keep our eyes open and be sure that we are looking at the consequences and being sure that we don't go down a path that users or libraries really don't want to go. At least it should be a question that should be on people's minds.

> *"Those who have the answer have misunderstood the question."* Anonymous
> - Why are more journals seemingly, inherently better?
> - Is there really a free lunch?
> - Who are the good guys?
> - Isn't time of the essence?
> - If this is a crisis are we really being radical enough?
> - Are we really empowered to be radical enough?
> - Are we trying to solve a problem that's not ours too solve by and large?
> - Why not more focus on negative impact of the

Is there really a free lunch? I know nothing in my life experience that says there is. And so when we see a lot of talk about the ability to produce all the information that we all would like to see with no cost to anybody, I begin to wonder when the other shoe is going to fall. I at least question when the economic realities are really going to set in — if and when that might happen. At least we have a wonder about that.

Who are the good guys? There are a lot of analyses that define who the good guys are, the bad guys are, whose prices generate high use, the right cost per use, the right cost of production and so forth and so on. I think it's a real muddy playing field in that regard. For example, I think we have people who are playing catch up. I characterize the industry in two camps: we have the over-capitalized publishers and the under-capitalized publishers. The under-capitalized publishers are continuing to aggressively advance prices since they are realizing they have to catch up to get in the game. I think there are many ways to look at good guys and bad guys. If someone continues to raise their prices eight to nine percent every year, does that make them a good guy or a bad guy? A lot of issues come into play but it's not just prices and price increases. There's a whole series of factors and I'm not satisfied with the characterizations of who the culprits are in all this. OhioLINK can't necessarily do good, reasonable realistic group deals with a lot of publishers that people would characterized as good guys because they have unrealistic expectations about what kind of money we have in the state of Ohio for their information.

Isn't time of the essence? In our case, we think it is. We think that so much has happened in the electronic information world that we feel some sense of urgency. There are a lot of things that are happening that I think will serve generations beyond us but we also need to make sure that we're doing things are working for the here and now.

If this is a crisis, are we being radical enough? Some things that are in place will take years and years and years and years to be effective, to have a real impact. Are we being radical enough to really make ourselves effective both now and in the future? And are we really empowered to be radical enough? You know the Public Library of Science? Most people probably have read or glanced at it. You know the thing that's missing in it for me? It doesn't say at the end, "and we authorized our libraries to make the best purchase decisions in our long-term interests." Why doesn't it say that? Why doesn't it empower us to say no, in the short term, if we think that it is necessary for our long-term economic sustainability? That's the missing ingredient. We're not empowered. It doesn't say anything about what they'll let us do in response to what they might do. And I wonder, are we trying to solve a problem that is not ours to solve by and large? We beat ourselves up, we agonize over all this when, in fact, most of the variables are not under our control. And I don't want to go there, but that's a whole other long topic for someone to talk about.

I really wonder why we don't talk more about the negative impact of the scholar's reward system on what we're doing? Are we being honest enough with the people that really control how much information we really have to buy? These are all questions that I think people should have in mind in as well.

Slide 17 So, in conclusion, let me close with a few remarks. One, don't underestimate user demand. Our experience is that user demand always exceeds their expectations and the few libraries that want to hold back and stay in a traditional limited selection model are under-estimating the demand and the opportunities. Look at selection longer term, more user driven. Again, I think this comes back to some extent are we empowered to do that? We must become better buyers. We must get "No" in our vocabulary. I've said as part of the big deal, to make the big deal legitimate, a step forward, within our own Ohio community, that if necessary we must walk away from a big deal. If we do so, if we undo a big state license for all the Elsevier material for example, we will know so much more about what we really need than we knew before we got into the big deals. We can't help but be ahead of the game, not as far as if we can keep managing the big deals in an effective manner, but we should be willing to walk away and undo that approach if necessary. We'll be better buyers and they'll become better suppliers.

> *"It is easier to be wise for others than for ourselves."* Aleksandr Solzehnitsyn
>
> - Don't under estimate user demand
> - Selection- longer term and more user driven
> - We must become better buyers
> - Reform the old as well as build the new
> - Trial and Error – 2 steps forward, 1 step back
> - Evolution
> - Evolution
>
> OhioLINK

We must look across the spectrum of options we have. I think that in the end it can be much cheaper and more effective to rebuild what already exists than to try to recreate an entirely new model. And let's all realize that this is, in fact, trial and error as I said at the beginning. There are too many things in motion to know what any one of these solutions might mean to us and how it will really work out.

And, finally, evolution, evolution, evolution. Don't be afraid of it. Embrace it. Get on with it. Live with it or you're going to watch it run over you.

That's all I have to offer this morning. I hope I've given you something to think about for the rest of your day. Thanks.

Serials continue to be a major focus of the Charleston Conference. This year, many of our speakers addressed the importance of linking. It is so important that we provide our users with easily retrievable information, and linking provides the answer to this. Using many of the new linking tools that are available, users are able to click on citations in a journal and immediately access a cited article. In many instances, through our on-line catalogs, users can click on a journal title and automatically be taken to a journal rather than an aggregators' web page. The article economy is also very important, and speakers addressed the issue of cost efficiencies as they relate to subscriptions versus access to journal articles via document delivery.

Serials

CROSSREF: STATUS UPDATE, NEW DEVELOPMENTS

Amy Brand, Cross Ref, Director of Business Development

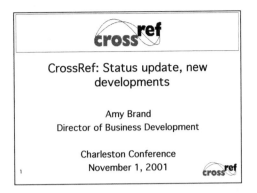

This presentation was part of the lively lunch on CrossRef: The Citation-Linking Backbone. I was asked to provide current statistics on the CrossRef system, along with a preview of future functionality.

Background and current status

I began by addressing some of the common misconceptions surrounding CrossRef, particularly in the library community (see slide 2). Among other things, CrossRef is not a plan by publishers to push researchers and libraries to purchase individual articles. The majority of online journal publishers do not currently offer pay-per-view. Publishers and libraries share concerns about transitioning from subscriptions to an article-based transaction model.

CrossRef is the only DOI registration agency whose mission is to implement citation linking and serve the scholarly and professional community. It is also a not-for-profit, independent membership organization, with a board of directors composed equally of commercial and non-commercial publishers. (See slides 3 and 4).

The two key benefits of the CrossRef system, as given in slide 5, are the persistence of the DOI link, in contrast to URL-based links, and the fact that a single agreement with CrossRef serves as a linking agreement with all participating publishers. This point is illustrated in slide 6. Secondary publishers can also forego having to sign numerous bilateral linking agreements with publishers by linking through CrossRef.

Two key benefits of the CrossRef/DOI system

- A DOI link is a persistent link, unlike a URL
    - *No stale links in citations or database records*
    - *Gives publishers flexibility to update URLs as needed*
    - *CrossRef so far has seen about 40% of URLs in its database change*

- A single agreement with CrossRef serves as a linking agreement with all participating publishers
    - *No bilateral linking agreements needed*

Slides 7 through 9 feature CrossRef from the end-user perspective. The user sitting at a computer terminal and encountering a CrossRef link in an article citation or in an A&I record experiences linking to the target/cited article as a one-click process. In fact, behind the scenes that DOI-based link is sent to the DOI directory for resolution to the appropriate online location. It is this added level of indirection that keeps the DOI link from going stale.

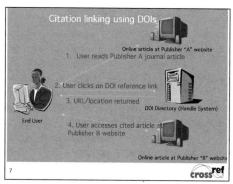

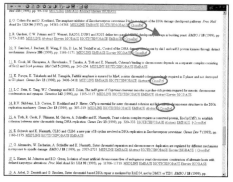
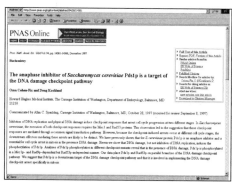

By participating in CrossRef, publishers can affect both inbound and outbound links (slide 10). For inbound links to their content, publishers must deposit basic article-level metadata with CrossRef, including a DOI and up-to-date URL. For outbound links to other publishersÌ cited content, publishers query CrossRefÌs metadata database to find the DOI that matches the reference from which they want to link out. If there is a match, they retrieve the DOI and insert it in their electronic publication. The overall matching rate is improving daily as more content records are

What do publishers have to do?

- For INBOUND links...Publishers deposit metadata for online articles with CrossRef, including a DOI and URL.

- For OUTBOUND links...Publishers query the central metadata database to find the DOI matching the citation from which they want to create a link. If there is a match, they retrieve the DOI and insert it in their electronic publication.

added to the database, including more journals titles as well as more back-file content from participating publishers.

Slide 11 outlines some basic operational policies. Unlike primary and secondary publishers, who must pay 10 cents for each DOI retrieved, on top of membership fees, libraries are permitted unlimited access to the CrossRef system for a small flat fee of $500 per year. There is never any fee associated with clicking on a DOI link. The DOI usually resolves to an abstract, but at a minimum always resolves a full bibliographic citation. Terms of access to the full text are controlled by the publisher; subscribed users are typically IP-authenticated.

> ### Policy and operations
> - A DOI must resolve to, at minimum, a full bibliographic citation
> - Terms of access to the full text are controlled by the publisher
> - There is <u>no charge</u> to the user for following a CrossRef link
> - Publishers fund the system by paying for deposits and retrievals; affiliates also pay for retrievals
> - Libraries have unlimited access for a nominal annual fee of $500/year
>
> 11

> ### Is it working? – yes!
> - Metadata deposited for over 3.7 million articles from over 5,500 journals
> - 90 member publishers – 60% non-profit
> - 27 libraries, affiliates, and agents
> - 80% of members actively depositing metadata; 35% creating outbound links
> - 1-2 million new content items per year
>
> 12

> ### Participants
>
> **Publishers**
> - American Chemical Society
> - Institute of Physics
> - BioMed Central
> - New England J. Medicine
> - Wiley
> - MIT Press
> - Sage
> - etc.
>
> **Publishers' Agents**
> - Allen Press
> - BioOne
> - American Institute of Physics (as pub. mem.)
> - Catchword/ingenta
> - HighWire
> - MetaPress
>
> 13

CrossRef has come very far in its first 18 months of operations (see slides 12-14). To date, we have 90 publishers on board, half of whom are non-profit, 80% of whom are actively depositing for inbound links, and 35% of whom are retrieving DOIs to create outbound links. Twenty-seven libraries, affiliates, and agents have also joined. We have metadata from over 5,000 journals and over 3.7 million articles, with the expectation that up to 2 million new

> ### More participants
>
> **Library Affiliates**
> - Korea Advanced Institute of Technology
> - Indiana/Purdue University
> - Boston College Library
> - Lund University Libraries
> - Max-Planck-Institute Stuttgart
> - Toshiba
> - University of Nevada, Reno
> - Illinois University
> - University of Rochester
>
> **Other Affiliates**
> - Cambridge Scientific Abs
> - Openly Informatics
> - FIZ-Karlsruhe
> - VA Center for PTSD
> - Dialog
> - EBSCO
> - IFIS
> - iGroup
> - Korea Info-Net Service
> - Information Express
> - Maruzen
> - Swets Blackwell
>
> 14

article records will be added on a yearly basis. The number of end-user clicks on DOI links now averages close to one million per month (slide 15).

> ### More participants
>
> **Library Affiliates**
> - Korea Advanced Institute of Technology
> - Indiana/Purdue University
> - Boston College Library
> - Lund University Libraries
> - Max-Planck-Institute Stuttgart
> - Toshiba
> - University of Nevada, Reno
> - Illinois University
> - University of Rochester
>
> **Other Affiliates**
> - Cambridge Scientific Abs
> - Openly Informatics
> - FIZ-Karlsruhe
> - VA Center for PTSD
> - Dialog
> - EBSCO
> - IFIS
> - iGroup
> - Korea Info-Net Service
> - Information Express
> - Maruzen
> - Swets Blackwell
>
> 14

What does this mean for libraries?

Because CrossRef is a citation linking infrastructure, and not a customizable software product, it cannot on its own address the article-level linking needs of individual libraries. Slide 16 outlines the disconnect between a possible future world in which CrossRef would automatically get the institutional user to the appropriate full text, and the real world in which libraries currently function.

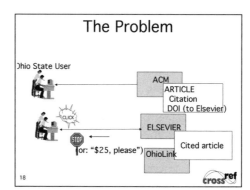

Because not all appropriate access can or necessarily should be controlled by IP-authentication at the publisher website, libraries need to implement local linking solutions that take all of their holdings into account. Slides 17 and 18 illustrate the appropriate copy problem, or how to keep the library user from following a citation link to a page that requests pay-per-view, when in fact that user has subscription rights to the content in question.

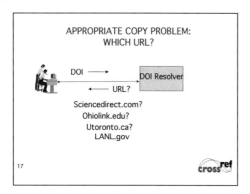

In order to address the appropriate copy problem, CrossRef has developed a local linking prototype in conjunction with the parties listed in slide 19. Because there is some confusion about the relationship among CrossRef, SFX, and OpenURL, slide 20 offers a definition of terms. The prototype itself is outlined in slides 21 through 23. When the user in a library environment clicks on a DOI link, the DOI server can redirect the link to the local server for resolution. The local linking server can get the article-level metadata it needs from CrossRef in a process called "reverse metadata

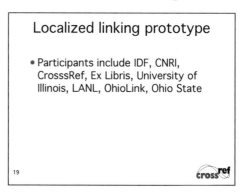

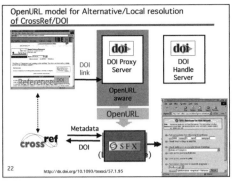

look-up." In effect, CrossRef automatically makes all of its member publishers OpenURL-compliant for the purposes of localized linking.

As summarized in slides 24 through 28, CrossRef allows library users to navigate at the article level, even though most library journal catalogues do not contain article-level information. CrossRef is thus a key piece of the puzzle in localized linking solutions for library digital collections, even though it can't solve the appropriate copy on its own. User navigation at the article level leads to increased usage of acquired electronic resources. DOI links have the added benefit that the user has facilitated access to content not owned by his or her library.

Linking from the library perspective

- Library users want to navigate directly from citations or database records to journal articles

- Libraries want users to access local holdings but their records do not contain article-level information or links

- Localized linking solutions such as SFX use OpenURL to get metadata and create links based on library holdings

24

CrossRef from the library perspective

- CrossRef facilitates *article-level linking* for libraries because publishers are implementing CrossRef links and libraries can use them

- With reverse metadata look-up, CrossRef will make it easy for publishers to be OpenURL compliant

- CrossRef is a key piece of the puzzle in localized linking solutions for library digital collections

25

Why can't CrossRef solve the appropriate copy problem on its own?

- Because only the library knows what it owns and has rights to – IP authentication at the publishers' websites doesn't account for all access

- Because CrossRef is not a commercial, customizable software product

26

Review: 2 possibilities...

- Your institution subscribes, so DOI link takes you directly to the publisher's site where you are authenticated... or to an intermediate page where other access options are presented
- Your institution does not subscribe, but the DOI link takes you directly to the publisher's site where you see an abstract and are offered pay-per-view
  - More than user might see otherwise
  - Appropriate for user with individual subscription

27

Review: How CrossRef benefits libraries

- Increase usage of acquired electronic resources
- Expand access to content not owned, or "just-in-time" content
- Improve patron efficiency and satisfaction
- Enrich locally held databases with links to full text
- Address the "appropriate copy" problem
- Article-level metadata coming soon

28

New developments

New developments underway at CrossRef are shown in slides 29 through 33. In order to enable citation linking into and out of other content types, and to facilitate access to online proceedings and book chapters, CrossRef will soon be registering metadata for a wide variety of content types including books and conference proceedings.

Linking from the library perspective

- Library users want to navigate directly from citations or database records to journal articles

- Libraries want users to access local holdings but their records do not contain article-level information or links

- Localized linking solutions such as SFX use OpenURL to get metadata and create links based on library holdings

24

crossref

CrossRef from the library perspective

- CrossRef facilitates *article-level linking* for libraries because publishers are implementing CrossRef links and libraries can use them

- With reverse metadata look-up, CrossRef will make it easy for publishers to be OpenURL compliant

- CrossRef is a key piece of the puzzle in localized linking solutions for library digital collections

25

crossref

Why can't CrossRef solve the appropriate copy problem on its own?

- Because only the library knows what it owns and has rights to – IP authentication at the publishers' websites doesn't account for all access

- Because CrossRef is not a commercial, customizable software product

26

crossref

Review: 2 possibilities...

- Your institution subscribes, so DOI link takes you directly to the publisher's site where you are authenticated... or to an intermediate page where other access options are presented

- Your institution does not subscribe, but the DOI link takes you directly to the publisher's site where you see an abstract and are offered pay-per-view
  - More than user might see otherwise
  - Appropriate for user with individual subscription

27

crossref

Review: How CrossRef benefits libraries

- Increase usage of acquired electronic resources
- Expand access to content not owned, or "just-in-time" content
- Improve patron efficiency and satisfaction
- Enrich locally held databases with links to full text
- Address the "appropriate copy" problem
- Article-level metadata coming soon

28

crossref

Publishers will also soon be able to associate a single DOI with multiple elements or actions. For instance, the DOI could point to multiple URLs for geographically dispersed mirror sites, to more information about the author, to sub-parts of an article, to different article formats (PDF or HTML), or to rights information.

Finally, we are actively exploring the possibility of a cross-publisher search capability, wherein a user could search the full-text of all participating publishers from a single search interface. This would offer a new way for researchers to navigate deep-web, proprietary, peer-reviewed material, assuring both breadth of search and authoritative search results.

CrossSearch is another step in harnessing the power of collaboration among publishers. We believe this continued cooperation, with the involvement of libraries and others in the information chain, is needed to ensure the vitality of the scholarly communication process. As we like to say, don't be the missing link.

UNLOCKING THE POTENTIAL OF YOUR ELECTRONIC COLLECTION THROUGH LINKING

Chris Pierard, Principal & Co-Founder, Serials Solutions, LLC

When linking from items such as indexes, abstracts and citations to the full text one should really consider three main areas. First, database aggregators and publishers need to facilitate open linking technology such as Open URLs in order to link out of their databases. And they need to have a system in place to be able to link into their content. Second, you need a link server to create links that carry all of the pertinent information it needs to direct the link. Third you need an accurate list of titles to populate the link server with the library specific information it needs.

That is what I'm here to talk about. As you know, Serials Solutions specializes in providing customized A-Z lists of titles that are available to institutions via various subscriptions to database aggregators, publishers and associations. Creating these lists can be achieved two different ways. You can either create these in house or outsource the project to a third party. Either way two issues are present that should be considered. First, tracking the title changes that occur each month in aggregated databases. Second, standardizing all the variations of titles that exist in separate databases.

Let's start off with the title changes that occur each month in aggregated databases. Everybody is aware of the volume of title changes that occur every month.

A library will subscribe to a package of journals generally based on the combined content of these journals knowing that the individual titles that are present in these databases are going to change as licensing agreements start and end throughout the year. However, libraries can feel pretty good that the combined content will remain about the same throughout their subscription. Given the fact that we realize this is the nature of the industry and will most likely always be present it gives us the incentive to go out and creatively find ways to deal with this.

Title changes are going to continue to occur, therefore, how do we create a system to track all of these changes across several databases? First, you need to create a database to hold all of this information. This requires hiring the technical expertise, if you don't already have it, to design a database. Access, File Maker Pro and SQL are some databases we've seen that coupled with cold fusion can be very effective solutions. Realistically this is the easiest part. There are lots of examples to follow and plenty of colleagues to reference for guidance.

The next piece is to gather all of the titles to populate your database and set a system in place to continually maintain this information. This requires you to first identify which databases that you subscribe to and to identify which titles you have access to in select databases. For some of our clients this in and of itself was a somewhat arduous task. Actually gathering the titles is the most difficult part since titles lists are in so many different formats, sometimes they are very hard to find and it is difficult to find the time to maintain this. One of our clients has over 70 separate databases that contain at least some full text. As you can image it would take them an enormous amount of time to maintain one comprehensive list of all of the titles contained in this database. If you don't update this information on a regular basis your list can quickly become antiquated. Let's say you're titles haven't been updated in 6 months. You may show the *Harvard Business Review* as being available through a few different sources when in fact it's only available through one. We believe this is the most important piece of the puzzle. What good is all of this technology if your patrons aren't getting to the proper content because the underlying data is inaccurate?

There are several different methods you can use to gather all of this information. Some of the ways that Serials Solutions uses is to work with companies, like EBSCO Publishing, to have FTP sites set up where their titles lists are in a format that is consistent with our database. Other companies we work with have sent us Excel spread sheets, some have given us access to non-public sites and in several instances we gather the data off their web pages which can be very difficult and time-consuming. I would recommend contacting your rep. They may have some good ideas for you. To give you an idea of just how burdensome gathering and organizing all of this data can be here's an example. We know of one institution that currently has three full-time employees tackling this problem and is considering hiring a fourth. In all fairness, they are also cataloguing this data but I wonder how many of you here have it in your budgets to hire four full-time staff this year. I would venture to guess not many.

So I've giving you a little background on what may be required to obtain all of this data from so many different sources. Once you have gathered all of the data there's still more work to do. How do you organize it into a format that makes sense? Standardizing these journals is a must. What I mean by standardizing is accounting for all of the different title variations and missing information such as ISSNs.

A natural place to start when trying to standardize these titles is the ISSN. For the most part it's a unique indicator that works very well. Just sort all of the titles by ISSN and group them together. As you know it isn't that easy for a few reasons. The ISSN isn't always unique even though it is supposed to be. Some periodicals just don't have ISSNs. The ISSN is not always present in title lists provided by database aggregators and publishers.

Without an ISSN you can consolidate all of the titles using the title itself. Unfortunately, titles can vary among different database aggregators and publishers. Serials Solutions' database has 65,000 unique representations of titles and approximately 25,000 unique titles. That means we have 40,000 variations of the same titles. A good example is *The Journal of the American Medical Association*. It's important to note that we didn't introduce these variations this is just the data that we have to work with. It's understandable how these variations occur. Some database aggregators will use titles that they think are the most clear to the patron. These titles can still be consistent with titles found in CONSER MARC records since there are multiple title fields present in these MARC records.

There is another factor that compounds the difference in titles even more, human error. In dealing with lots of data, errors are inevitable. You have thousands of pieces of data that at some point were entered in with human hands. You have a journal title, ISSN, first date available electronically, last date available electronically, publications ID, embargo periods and URLs. You have any number of pieces of information that are important to libraries and patrons. All of which have to be correct for the system as a whole to work properly. There will be somewhat of a reoccurring theme in my presentation. The underlying data has to be correct in order for all of this great technology to be of value.

If you know using the ISSN is the best method to consolidate these titles, ISSNs aren't always present, there are many different variations of title names and errors may sometimes be present, what do you do about it? You normalize your journals. You take every possible variation of a journal title and associate it to a known title. To say this is an excruciating process would be an understatement. It is very difficult and is also a task that Serials Solutions is currently undertaking. Once normalization has occurred you then have the capability to insert missing data such as ISSNs. You can use any number of sources as a benchmark such as Ulrich's, OCLC, or Library of Congress. This is the benchmark that Serials Solutions uses since we can use CONSER MARC records from their retrospective file as the benchmark.

OK, so where do we stand? You've created a database to hold all of this information, you have a system in place to maintain it and you've normalized all of the journals and inserted missing information. What you have is a list that is worth its weight in gold. You can use this list to populate link servers, you can create HTML pages that your patrons can use to easily find and access this content, you can populate existing databases that you've created, you can work with your ILS vendor to integrate this information into your OPAC or you can even produce MARC records. This is a definitely a challenge and however you choose to attempt to address this is issue whether it's with an in-house solution a third party or a combination of both, it is definitely a challenge worth tackling. You really begin to realize the value of these resources and all of the technology you may have invested in. In the end you get what you're paying for.

THE ARTICLE ECONOMY

Jay Schafer, Coordinator of Collections, University of Massachusetts - Amherst

In his keynote address yesterday, Tom Sanville hit the nail on the head for me when he said, "We [librarians, publishers, vendors, authors] don't really know what we are doing because everything is evolving."

Mary Reichel this morning almost said it when she remarked something to the effect that, "Print on paper may not be capable of portraying the interactive electronic world of data sets and images." Much of what I have heard over the past two days is mostly talking about changing our paper world into an electronic version or not. What I believe we need to be discussing is how to take advantage of the capabilities offered by networked digital information technologies to change and improve our current system of scholarly communication.

I drive about 50 miles to get to UMass in Amherst, so I have lots of time to read audio books. Last month, I was listening to one entitled, *The Renaissance: A Short History*, by Paul Johnson. My ears pricked up when I heard him talking about printing and libraries, "By 1500, less than half a century after the first printed book, there were printing firms in 60 German towns, and Venice alone had 150 presses." He goes on to say that the quantitative impact was "overwhelming."

> *Before printing, only the very largest libraries contained as many as 600 books, and the total number of books in Europe was well under 100,000. By 1500, after 45 years of the printed book, the total has been calculated at nine million.*

Mr. Johnson's text compliments another that talks about this same image of the invention of the printing press. It is a RAND Report (#P8014) by James Dewar entitled *The Information Age & The Printing Press: Looking Backward to See Ahead.* "The design of a scientific periodical, far from primarily aiming at disseminating knowledge, really seeks to reinforce property rights over ideas; intellectual property and authors were not legal concepts designed to protect writers — they were invented for the printers' or stationers' benefits."

Obviously, the advent of networked digital information can be depicted in a similar manner. Today, keeping track of the number of Web pages searched by Google is very much like keeping track of the number of hamburgers sold by McDonald's.

Growth of the Web

- 1991 the first browser released to the high energy physics community via the CERN program library

- By late 1993 there were over 500 known servers

- By the end of 1994, the Web had 10,000 servers and 10 million users

- In 1997, with more than 650,000 servers and 1,000 new ones appearing every day

---

To me, the comparison of the invention of the printing press and the advent of networked digital information is how we as a profession should be thinking. The printing press is credited with many events of unintentional consequences. The Reformation and our current system of scholarly communication are two of these. Isn't it quite reasonable to believe that what we know as librarianship at this moment in history will radically change as the unintended consequences of networked digital information come to pass?

Jean-Claude Guedon wrote an excellent piece entitled, "In Oldenburg's Shadow: Librarians, Research Scientists, Publishers, and the Control of Scientific Publishing." In it, he does an admirable job of tracing the history of scholarly communication, from the invention of the printing press into the current world of networked digital information. Let me share a few pertinent quotes with you.

> ...research scientists treat articles and published journals exactly as Oldenburg had anticipated, i.e., as registers of intellectual property whose functions are close to that of a land registry.

> A scientific journal does not act only as a public register; it also labels, or, even better, it brands. Colleagues note whether your latest article appeared in a journal like _Cell_ or _Nature_, or whether it appeared in a less prestigious journal

> As science goes through various phases—research investigation, giving credit, validation—it relies on different documentary units. Short- and long-term scientific memory really relies on articles, authors' names, and keywords; journals are of secondary importance in this regard. However, in the validation phase, the journal counts more than anything else because evaluation procedures rely very strongly on them, especially since the introduction of the impact factors.

> "After Gutenberg, it took about two and a half centuries to devise a relatively stable copyright law; correspondingly, we may expect at least several decades of legal wrangling to reshape or perhaps even dismantle copyright laws as we presently know them."

And so, back to the topic ..._The Article Economy in Libraries_. I don't need to beat this poor horse too much more. You all know that libraries have been dealing with the article economy for a very long time in different ways:

- Interlibrary loan and the borrowing of "nonreturnables"

- Copy machines that allow users to carry articles away with them

- Full text aggregated databases that are collections of articles

- Full text electronic journals, with much emphasis placed upon accessing or linking articles within those journals

For about a decade, librarians like me have been standing up in front of audiences like you and showing how the article economy can save libraries a considerable amount of money. I have the requisite slides showing how two separate document delivery projects at UMass Amherst produced considerable savings.

The first example is the "classic" use of the UnCover SUMO product to provide unmediated document delivery services directly to faculty:

> **SUMO**
> **(Subsidized UnMediated Ordering)**
>
> - 3 months use
> - 40 journals - 88 requests
> - SUMO cost — $1,430
> - Cost to own journals — $33,359 +

Next, we have the results of a cooperative document delivery program set up between UMass Amherst Library and the Health Sciences Library at UMass Worcester:

> **Worcester Expedited ILL**
>
> - 11 months use
> - 24-hour turnaround — 2,123 requests
> - 803 journals
> - Expedited ILL cost — $21,230
> - Copyright fees — $6,305
> - Cost to own journals — $509,515
> - Savings over purchase — $475,740

> **Worcester Expedited ILL**
>
> - *Clinica chimica acta* (cancelled 1989)
> - $3,643/yr.
> - 7 uses (cost - $70 - no CCC fee)
>
> - *Journal of clinical psychopharmacology*
> - $239/yr.
> - 7 uses (cost - $70 ÷ $20.26 CCC fee = $90.26)
>
> - *European Journal of Pharmacology*
> - $6,876/yr.
> - 41 uses (cost - $410 ÷ $303.60 CCC fee = $714.60)

I'm sure most of you have similar stories. But mine is particularly timely. On September 26, I learned that the Acquisitions Budget at UMass Amherst was being reduced by 20% this fiscal year. We knew some reduction was coming so we had not yet returned our serials renewal invoice. Obviously, we did not anticipate a 20% reduction. There was a vetted cancellation list lying around from a proposed cut in 1999. This was a traditional across the board cut involving all departments. The average cost of these 434 titles is $700. To create an additional list in the amount of $600,000, we looked to titles costing more than $2,000. We found 205 titles of relatively low use. These average $3,000 per title. Not surprisingly, these titles are all in the sciences and engineering.

And so, UMass Amherst is on the cutting edge. We are not participants in the Big Deal so we can cut deeply where others of you may not be able. We are cutting with a firm belief that our faculty will be well served by an investment in the Article Economy. There is some question about how well served our graduate students will be, but that will play out.

I for one am looking at this cataclysmic reduction as an opportunity. It is an opportunity to see if it is really possible to move out from under the yoke of oppressive journal subscriptions, mostly in the traditional paper format. With this in mind, I look forward to hearing more about my new mantra...the article economy.

REVOLUTION OR EVOLUTION?
DIGITAL MYTHS AND JOURNAL FUTURES:
SIFTING FACT FROM FICTION

Michael A. Mabe, Director, Academic Relations, Elsevier Science LTD

[Text of a plenary presentation made on 1 November 2001 at the 2001 Charleston
Library Conference]

Digital Myths

Exactly two weeks ago today, Carol Tenopir and Donald King wrote the following in the New Journals issue of Nature in an article entitled "Lessons for the Future of Journals." [1]

The mistaken belief persists that new technologies can easily remedy any weakness in the system... The journal system is at a critical stage — poor judgement could mean its deterioration or destruction. We believe that insights from the past can provide constructive evidence for innovators and the scientific community alike...If we discard the functions performed by librarians and publishers, we will surely need to reinvent them. There is a tendency to promote an innovation as the only solution to a problem... Publishers, scientists and librarians need to base their actions on facts, not emotion.

This is a manifesto position that I most strongly support and it is the advent of such evidence-base publishing research, which can give us all a fresh perspective on old debates.

This is a key objective of the newly formed interdisciplinary research collaboration called CIBER, the Centre for Information Behaviour and Evaluation of Research at City University in London, which I'm proud to be associated with. And this bringing together of qualitative and quantitative user studies, sociology and bibliometrics forms a key subtext in what I want to say to you this morning.

Now we need to be very careful if we're going to talk about the future. We need to understand the past and the present even to be able to anticipate it. In the wise words of Forest Gump "if you don't know where you're going, you're probably not going to wind up there."

But we also need to be wary of technical over optimism. Walt Crawford, a former President of the American Library Association and a member of the Research Libraries Group, has summed this up well in numerous articles, especially one on 'the persistence of paper' [2]. Crawford warns us that we must be wary of the technological hand wave, that substitute for clear thinking which allows technical "ifs" to become "whens" and allows these "whens" to be always just around a forever retreating corner. He also advises that when the technological hand wave is used in conjunction with the word "inevitable" we should be particularly cautious. Frequently "inevitable" means "never." This is wise advice if we consider what happened earlier this year with the dot.com collapse.

Most importantly, we need to beware of mythology reported as fact. One of the most consistent elements of the study of the scholarly communication system has been the tendency of people to write persuasive, but ultimately fictional things about it. The fable or myth I am about to sketch has never been explicitly outlined, as I will here, but comes behind any number of so-called Îanalyses' of the journal system.

The myth goes something like this:

Once upon a time ...

Before the 1960s the system was in balance, scholars and librarians had everything they needed, all publishing was done by learned societies.

Then...

Research and education expanded, the number of journals grew, published for gain by both societies and commercial publishers.

Libraries began to have difficulties in the 1970s, leading to an endless spiral of cancellations and cost rises.

And this analysis leads the mythmakers to conclude two interesting outcomes: that traditional publishing models have to be jettisoned and that all the answers lie in technology.

Now, tone deafness and jetlag prevents me from singing you the correct response to this fictional story, but a chorus from Gershwin's opera *Porgy and Bess* is most appropriate:

It ain't necessarily so,
It ain't necessarily so,
The things that you're liable
To read in the Bible,
It ain't necessarily so

Let us look at aspects of the fable in turn seeking some facts to back it up.

Pre-1960s: Fact versus Fiction

The mythmakers would have us believe that the pre-1960s was a veritable Eden for the scientific communication system. Lots of funds, a system in balance, academic societies fulfilling scholarly needs. No commercial lion to lie down with the learned lamb. However, let us look at some facts.

Henry Oldenburg started the world's first scientific journal, Philosophical Transactions of 1665, as a private commercial venture. It took nearly a century before the Royal Society finally assumed full responsibility, both financial and intellectual in 1752. Taylor and Francis, who still publish it today, have published the world's first physics journal in English, Philosophical Magazine of 1798, commercially since its inception. The first clinical journal published in English, *The Lancet* of 1823, was started as a commercial venture and is now published by Elsevier. Macmillan has published the world's first general science journal, Nature, commercially since its launch in1869. Clearly the contention that everything pre-1960 was done by the learned societies is false.

So what about the pre-1960s balance in the myth? Let us first look at journal growth. Whenever I go to conferences, people are always saying, "Too many journals!" This is an example of this phenomenon in the reviewing literature. Here, another is reviewing one new medical journal.

> This is truly the decade of the journal, and one should seek to
> limit their number rather than to increase them, since there can
> also be too many periodicals.
>
> [Review in *Neues med. Wochb. F. Aertzte*] [3]

Interestingly, this remark was published in 1789. There is nothing new under the sun.

Earlier this year a colleague and I published an article [4] looking at journal growth in some depth. Figure 1a is taken from our results and shows the growth in the number of refereed academic journals as recorded in *Ulrich's Periodicals Database on CD-ROM*. We used the search terms "active", "scholarly", "scientific" and "refereed". As you can see there has indeed been a significant rise in the number of journals over the 20th century. It is worth noting, however, that the total number of active refereed academic journals is around 11,000 not the 70,000 plus of many other commentators [5].

If we look at this same data on a logarithmic scale (Figure 1b), some interesting patterns develop. The graph is characterised by three straight-line episodes. The first of these, from 1900 to 1945 is a period determined by low or absent government funding of science, two World Wars, and the learned societies as the major (but not the only) publishing force. For this period, the number of journals increased at a steady 3.3% per annum. The second straight line occurs from about 1945 to 1978-9, the period of the post war boom, the space race, unparalleled defence spending and the Cold War, which terminated in the oil price crisis of the 1970s. Here the number of journals increased at 4.7% per annum. Yet, from 1979 until the present day, well into the crisis for journals, a period characterised by a mixed commercial and society market for journal publishing, the growth rate was smaller. It returned to exactly the same growth rate the system had from 1900-1945, 3.3% per annum. This is highly suggestive of a self-organising system where the rate of specialisation of knowledge is the driving force, not economics, publishers or librarians.

What could be the cause of this? The strongest candidate, stronger than money, grants, *etc.*, is sociological. It is the growth in the number of scientists in the world. Data is not available for the early period, but in the 1980s and 1990s, as you can see in Figure 2, the number of scientists in the USA rises at exactly the same rate as the number of journals. There are more journals because there are more scientists.

Given that this has been true for at least half a century, what is it that individual researchers are reacting to? I believe we are dealing here with information anxiety. The ratio between the number of researchers and the number of papers in the world has been relatively constant for most of journal history, but this does not prevent any individual from feeling overwhelmed and thinking this phenomenon is new. As Faraday laments:

> It is certainly impossible .. to read all the books and papers that are published..; their number is immense...[6]

... and in <u>1826</u>!

Library Difficulties

What about other aspects of the supposed pre-1960s balance? The mythmakers tell us that problems for libraries started in the 1970s. Yet the evidence suggest otherwise:

> libraries are suffering because of the increasing volume of publications and rapidly rising prices.
> [*Association of American Libraries Report* 1927][7]

Clearly things have been going wrong, or however we care to describe it, for a lot longer than the mythmakers have suggested.

In the late 1960s some people had already correctly identified part of the problem: relative funding. In the UK, the Great Britain University Grants Committee, Report of the Committee of Libraries, chaired by Parry and published in 1967 [8] recommended that ideally a fully supported university library would require 6% of total university expenditure.

So, are we dealing with a 'serials crisis' or a 'crisis of priorities?' The mythmakers are not entirely inaccurate; after all, most myths contain grains of truth. But their diagnosis of the problem and its solution seem wide of the mark. From the 1970s libraries have increasingly been unable to stock all of the materials that they would like. Cutting or freezing library budgets has always been seen (if only by administrators) as an easy option. Despite learned reports like that of Parry in the UK, library funding as a percentage of university funding has fallen dramatically: it has never reached its 6% ideal. A recent survey of the top 100 US research universities showed that the current average expenditure on the library was 2.5% of the university total. Yet, throughout this period, there has always been more money for research. So, if output growth — that is to say, the number of researchers, journals and articles — always sees growth, while support funding — the purchasing power of libraries for those same journals and articles — is being cut, there will always be a problem. This comes out clearly in Figure 3, where the rate at which R&D funding has increased in the US is compared to the funding of the average ARL library [9].

Are Traditional Publishing Models Still Valid?

The response of the mythmakers has been to suggest that there is a fundamental flaw in the traditional models of publishing and that everything can be cured by the application of technology. There are two claims that lie behind this argument. The first is a claim about technology change: publishing is essentially all about production technology, so if the technology changes then so does publishing. The second claim is about economics: the web is essentially free, therefore publishing on the web is essentially free.

1. The Technological Claim

Technology Shift and the Journal

To examine the technology claim, we need to look at what it is that the journal does and what users say they want.

So, what does the journal do? The research journal has been called the "minutes" of science. Most research [10] on this topic has come up with four information functions:

- Registration: the establishment of the priority and ownership of research work by a particular author.

- Evaluation — certification: quality control through peer review and rejection, so that the better papers are published. Appearance of a paper in a particular journal stamps that paper and by implication rewards its author as being of the same quality level as the journal.

- Dissemination: the broadcasting of authors' claims to like-minded peers around the world through the channel that the journal represents

- Archiving: the establishment of a permanent record in the scientific literature for the work that was undertaken.

These functions are deeply embedded in the professional practice of research and do not seem to have changed over time.

We can see evidence of this in the correspondence of Henry Oldenburg [11], the creator of the first scientific journal in 1665. Writing to Sir Robert Boyle in November 1664 regarding what procedures the new publication should follow, Oldenburg says [my emphases]:

> [Huygens] hath been written to, to communicate freely to ye Society, what new discoveries he maketh, or wt new Expts he tryeth, the Society being **very careful of registring as well the person and time of any new matter, imparted to ym, as the matter itselfe**; whereby the honor of ye invention will be inviolably preserved to all posterity.

This is the first recorded instance of the function of registration, that is to say, Oldenburg felt it was important not only to publish what scientific work had been done but also when it was done and who did it. In a further letter, also sent to Boyle, in December 1664, Oldenburg says:

> [If we adopt this procedure] all Ingenious men will be thereby **incouraged to impart their knowledge** and discoveryes, as farre as they may.

Here Oldenburg is making the point that a system that protects peoples' intellectual rights will encourage authors to share their discoveries, that is, to disseminate knowledge around the scientific community. In 1665, Boyle, in replying to Oldenburg who had previously requested from him some papers for Philosophical Transactions, says:

> I might justly be thought too little sensible of my own Interest, if
> I should .. neglect the opportunity of having some of my
> Memoirs preserv'd, by being incorporated into a **Collection, that
> is like to be as lasting as usefull.**

Here Boyle is clearly establishing the principle of the archive, that is, that the journal should represent a permanent and enduring record of the work undertaken by scientists.

On 1 March 1665 the Royal Society Council voted to allow Henry Oldenburg to commence publication of *Philosophical Transactions* (at his own expense and risk), recording in their Orders in Council that it:

> ... be printed the first Monday of every month, ..; and .. licensed
> under the charter by the Council of the Society, **being first
> reviewed** by some of the members of the same. [12]

These formal minutes establish not merely the periodicity of the journal but also emphasise the need for its contents to be filtered. This is the very first instance of peer review as one of the key functions of the journal.

We have here then, in 1665, the very first scientific journal with the four basic functions of the modern journal. You will note that these functions are completely independent of the technology required to achieve them. They relate to the needs of the researcher as a human being for personal recognition and reward and a little bit of immortality. Human beings have not changed significantly since 1665 and we should not expect them to in the near future. These same functions will be important for future journals, and publishers and others must take account of them too.

Technology and the Scientific Method

If this were not enough evidence for the disconnect between technology shift and publishing shift, we need look no further than the role of the modern journal in science, a rhetorical engine for turning private observations into publicly accepted fact, an exercise in what philosophers might call practical epistemology [13].

Figure 4 expands and extends the work of Arthur Smith of the American Physical Society [14, 15]. It places communication vehicles into a space defined by the extent to which those vehicles are private or public and the extent to which they are about preliminary observation by one research group or ultimate generalised acceptance and integration into the public canon of knowledge. The diagram has four regions. The first region is that of the semi-private communication of research and its discussion with colleagues. The second region is the communication of results to the other members of the scientific community. The third region is that of the formal, public, critical evaluation of research. The last region is where discoveries have been accepted as part of Îthe facts of the world' and not regarded as potentially challengeable.

When we overlay the various stages of scientific work and their communication vehicles into these regions (Figure 5), we can see the rhetorical progress of an initial observation from the semi-private domain of researcher and co-workers, via seminars workshops and conferences, to its first formal public statement in a peer reviewed journal. It is worth noting that the role of the semi-public drafts of work for comment (sometimes called preprints) overlap with conference presentations but rhetorically have a very different position from the formal peer reviewed paper. The formal paper is like the presentation of evidence under oath in the Court of Scientific Opinion. It is public, sworn testimony that is unretractable and forms the basis for determining the value of the witness and the evidence he or she has given. Preprints and conference presentations, however, have no such status. They can be withdrawn and disavowed without harm to their originator. They exist to generate comment (to help improve the authors' arguments) and to stake preliminary informal claims to areas of investigation.

The publication of testimony will often provoke other workers to publish their observations, which may differ or contradict the original. These subsequent publications in peer-reviewed journals are further witness testimonies in the trial of a scientific idea, with the journal acting as the record of the Court of Scientific Opinion. It is in the journals that these rival interpretations of the world battle it out (often over a number of years) until consensus builds around a particular scientific theory. At this point we move from the critical, evaluative region to that region of confirmation and acceptance, the writing of history and textbooks, the awarding of Nobel Prizes. Again, it should be noted that the role of the journal as rhetorical engine has nothing to do with technology.

What Researchers Think

So what do the research community say that they want to see in the future? How does that relate to publishing technology shift? Figure 6 summarises the results of an Elsevier Science/University of Twente study into the views of researchers about the nature of the communication system by 2010. This research project interviewed around 3,000 academics at various levels of seniority worldwide.

As authors, researchers felt that they would want to publish more (even though statistically they are actually publishing less). They felt that all authors would have access to electronic networks, that peer review would remain important, and that the journal remained attractive as an intellectual package. They also wanted the widest possible dissemination. The same researchers, as readers, said that they wished for an integrated system, one that allowed for browsing, where the quality of information was important, and one which allowed them to read less (even though statistically they are reading more). Clearly authors wanting to publish more and readers wanting to read less create some difficulties for publishers! Nevertheless it is instructive that satisfying these desires lies behind most of the thinking about electronic journal platforms such as ScienceDirect, which attempt to deliver these contradictory requirements to authors and readers.

Here for the first time we see some technology effects, but they are superficial. The technology of the internet is harnessed as a delivery mechanism; it does not overturn the fundamental requirements for researchers from their communication system. Based on these three examinations, of what the journal does and what researchers want we can conclusively state that the first claim of the mythmakers, that publishing is about technology and will change with technology, is unsubstantiated.

2. The Economic Claim

What then about the second claim, the economic one, that technology (that is, the internet) makes publishing essentially free?

We have already seen that researchers clearly regard the World Wide Web as a reproduction and distribution medium. Publishing costs are made up of two components: origination or the cost to create the first copy; and copying and distribution, the cost to duplicate and send out to customers.

Copying and distribution become virtually zero in an electronic environment but the other aspects of cost become much more complicated, particularly as the system moves away from standard subscription models towards licensing of content. Every customer will have a unique licensing arrangement. Management of unique contracts for every customer and the complications of authentication and electronic archiving eat up most of the savings that are achieved by duplicating and distributing online. But whatever is done, in most cases the first copy costs remain unchanged, and these historically have always been the single largest cost component.

It is possible to estimate the current first copy costs of the publishing system. This has been done by a number of researchers, most notably Andrew Odlyzko [16] and Tenopir and King [17]. Odlyzko has estimated the first copy costs for a number of journals and gets values ranging from $1000 to $8,000 per article. Tenopir and King estimated about $4,000, which agreed with the median figure of Odlyzko's range. These first copy costs are made up of several components. The first of these is the peer review cost, which is a cost for **all** submissions, not just the published ones. On average about 35% of papers are rejected after peer review. This means that the journal must bare 135% of the review costs of the *published papers*. Although refereeing is done as a *pro bono* activity by the scholarly community, its administration, that is the support of one (and frequently more) journal editors and editorial offices, selection and communication with referees, is a significant component, often 15-20% of the total first copy cost. The other costs relate directly to those papers that are actually published and include typesetting, proofing, web mounting, journal list management, marketing and organisational overheads. But the conclusion we ought to draw is that if users want the functions included in the scholarly journal, and they seem to, the first copy costs, no matter how we publish, have got to come from somewhere.

Last month I attended a conference on digital libraries [18]. Mike Keller of Highwire Press gave the opening plenary talk "Digital Libraries — Panacea or Recreational Chemical" where he proposed three dot.com fallacies:

- No. 1 — early innovators will predominate;

- No. 2 — business models built on the hope or unusual pricing schemes will define the economy;

- No. 3 — consumers' behaviour will change rapidly.

Fallacies 2 and 3 are particularly relevant to our concerns here today.

Fallacies No. 1 and 2 have already been shown to be false earlier this year with the pricking of the dot.com bubble. In the scholarly communication world, unfortunately, models based on Fallacy No. 2 still abound.

One approach is the otherwise sound idea that authors should pay for publishing and reading should be free. Unfortunately the amounts that they are being asked to pay are usually in the order of about $500 per article while the estimates of first copy costs are around $4,000 per article. It is clearly not enough, and even these small amounts tend to put authors off submitting papers.

The second idea, originally adopted by BioMed Central and others but already abandoned, is that you can raise all the money needed through advertising. The reality is that most research journals do not generate a lot of advertising. The exceptions are those that are more in the nature of professional magazines and sell to individuals rather than institutions — *Nature, Science, British Medical Journal* — where advertising revenue could in theory support the publishing operation. The vast majority of research journals, however, generate barely half to one percent of their income through advertising sales. So advertising supported research journals are not an alternative either.

I have demonstrated the futility of Fallacy No. 3 already — the idea that consumer behaviour will change quickly. Well, here we are 336 years on and the journal model invented by Oldenburg remains as strong as ever. So overall, the second great claim of the myth-makers, that the internet will lead to an essentially free journal future, also seems to be false.

Evolution not Revolution

Clearly some things are going to change, but what? I think we're dealing here with an evolutionary process not a revolutionary one. The fundamental journal functions will remain. They don't seem to change over time or with technology. Any future system must deliver these functions if it is going to be accepted and used by authors and readers. These functions do not come for free. The first copy costs are still there and have to be recouped somehow.

So what about the future? I think the primacy of established behaviour is a very important principle. What behaviours we see now we're going to see in the future. New technology will be adopted for certain tasks, but only where it really helps productivity and where it is easy to use. The one commodity that none of us have enough of is time, and that is where the future lies, in delivering time-saving enhancements.

The future will also see the continued existence of older technologies in parallel with the new. Even paper may continue to be around for a very long time to come. But we will see the development of new, electronic value-added services that save time for readers and authors, such as new approaches to search engines, cross-referencing tools and automated templates to try to make the act of authoring easier and faster.

In the world of libraries we're already seeing the consortia solution as one approach to the thorny economic problem of offering readers ever greater access and functionality for decreasing marginal cost, but there will need to be others.

This paper may be seen by some as a paean to complacency. It is not. We must continue to experiment with new models to provide the access and services that researchers want. But we must never forget that they must be realistic.

There will be choices and they will have consequences. The research and library communities will have to make those choices. But, in doing so, we must stop our ears to the siren voices of the myth-makers and their easy "solutions" from the slick, technological box of tricks. We owe it to all those who have come before us and to our colleagues to choose wisely using hard evidence as our guide, otherwise we are selling everybody down the road.

REFERENCES

1. Carol Tenopir and Donald W King Lessons for the future of journals. *Nature*, 18 October, 413.672-3, 2001
2. http://www.onlineinc.com/onlinemag/OL1998/crawford1.html
3. D A Kronick *A History of Scientific and Technical Periodicals*, (ed. 2) Scarecrow Press, 1976, p171
4. M Mabe and M Amin Growth dynamics of scholarly journals *Scientometrics* 51(1).147-62, 2001
5. A J Meadows *Communicating Research*, Academic Press, 1998, pp15,16
6. M Faraday (1826) quoted in J G Crowther British Scientists of the Nineteenth Century, Vol. 1,Penguin, 1940, p113
7. Quoted by Bob Campbell in *Newsletter on Serials Pricing Issues* No. 175, 23 March 1997
8. Great Britain University Grants Committee, Chair Thomas Parry, Report of the Committee on Libraries, HMSO, London, 1967
9. For an earlier version of this chart see: M Mabe Challenges and responses *Advanced Materials* 4(10).609-11, 1992
10. J M Ziman Public Knowledge, CUP, 1968; J R Ravetz Scientific Knowledge and its Social Problems, Penguin, 1973; A A Manten in A J Meadows (ed.) *Development of Science Publishing in Europe*, Elsevier, 1980
11. A R Hall and M B Hall The Correspondence of Henry Oldenburg, Vol. II – VII, University of Wisconsin Press, 1966 – 1970
12. R K Bluhm in *The Royal Society, Its Origins and Founders*, The Royal Society, 1960, pp183-98
13. A G Gross *The Rhetoric of Science*, Harvard UP, 1996
14. Arthur P Smith the journal as an overlay on preprint databases. *Learned Publishing* 13(1).43-8, 2000
15. M Mabe Digital dilemmas. *ASLIB Proc.* 53(3).85-92, 2001
16. Andrew Odlyzko Tragic loss or good riddance? *I. J. Human–Computer Studies* 42.71-122, 1995; The economics of scholarly journals *First Monday* 2(8), 1997
17. Carol Tenopir and Donald W King Trends in scientific scholarly publishing in the US *J Scholarly Publishing* 48(3).137-70, 1997
18. 5th European Conference on Digital Libraries, Darmstadt, Germany, September 2001, chaired by Panis Constantopoulos and Ingeborg Solvberg

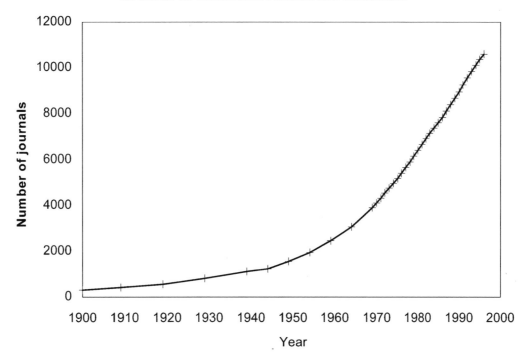

Growth of Refereed Academic Journals

Figure 1a

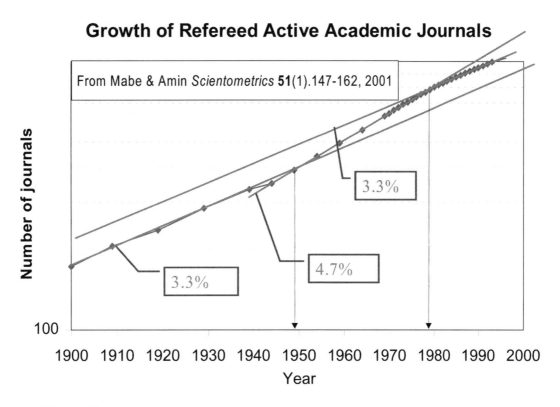

Growth of Refereed Active Academic Journals

From Mabe & Amin *Scientometrics* **51**(1).147-162, 2001

3.3%

4.7%

3.3%

Figure 1b

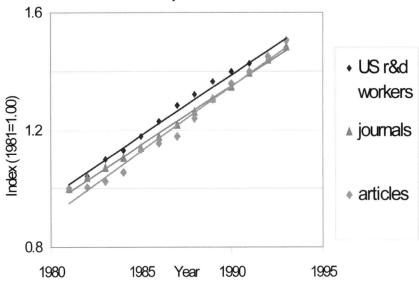

Figure 2

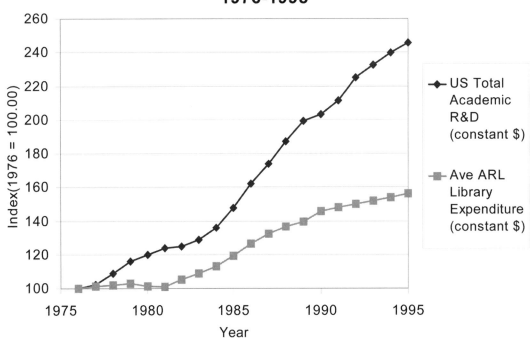

Figure 3

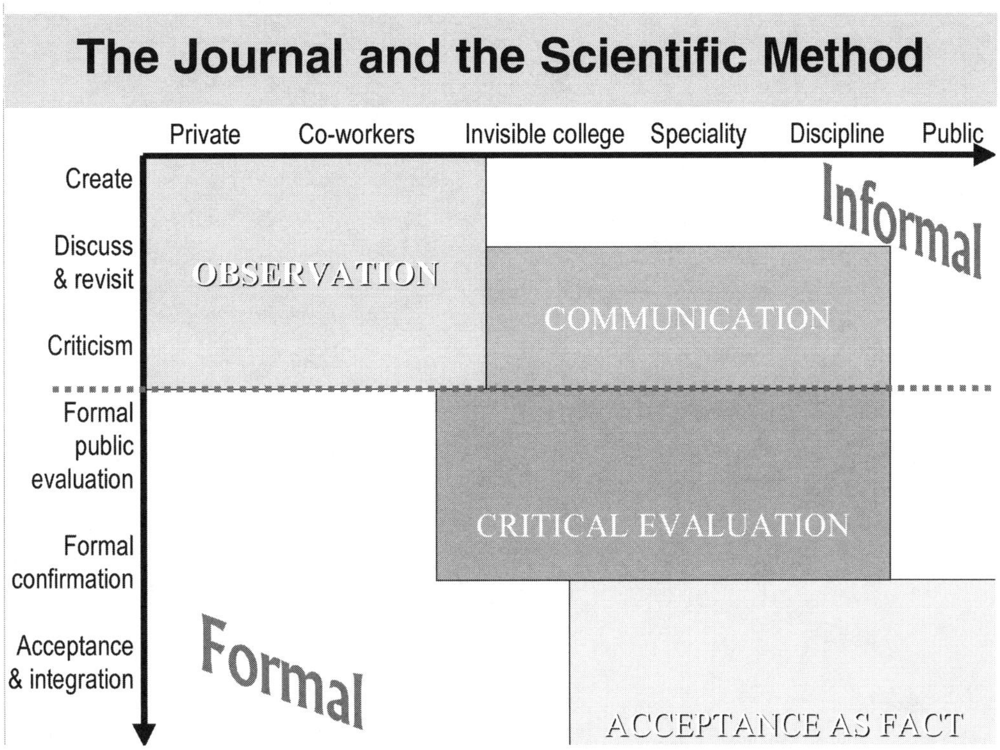

The Journal and the Scientific Method

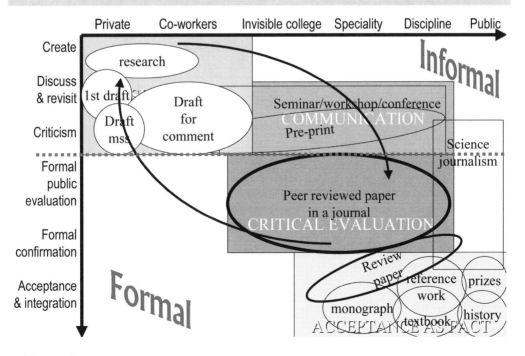

Figure 4

The Journal and the Scientific Method

Figure 5

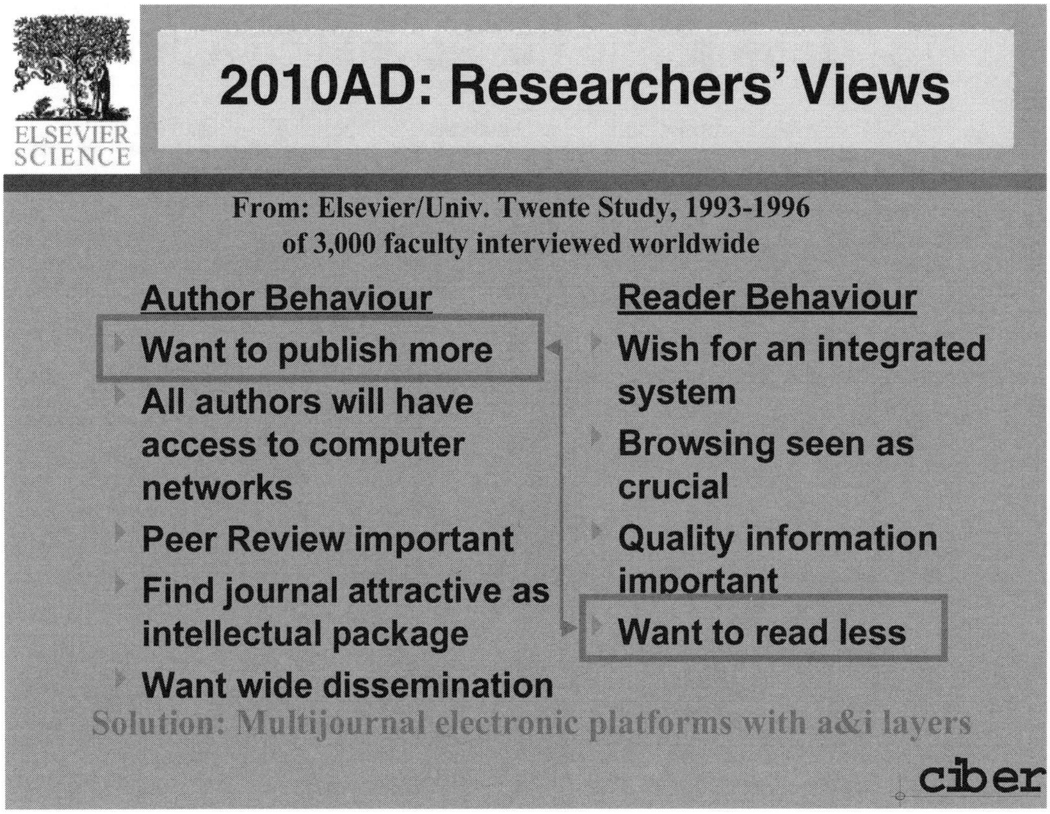
2010AD: Researchers' Views
ELSEVIER SCIENCE
From: Elsevier/Univ. Twente Study, 1993-1996
of 3,000 faculty interviewed worldwide
Author Behaviour
Want to publish more
All authors will have access to computer networks
Peer Review important
Find journal attractive as intellectual package
Want wide dissemination
Reader Behaviour
Wish for an integrated system
Browsing seen as crucial
Quality information important
Want to read less
Solution: Multijournal electronic platforms with a&i layers
ciber

Figure 6

SEEING SERIALS FROM BOTH SIDES OF THE FENCE

Karalyn Kavanaugh, EBSCO Information Systems (with Deb Van Petten, Valdosta State University)

This is a low-tech presentation. There are no graphics or Power Point outlines to follow along. Deb Van Petten and I worked with each other for a few days. These are our observations from that time.

I'm Karalyn Kavanaugh, an account services manager with EBSCO Information Services for the past 10 years. I spend much of my time in libraries working with librarians to make the service we provide as useful as possible. Part of my job is to help with transitions from another serials vendor to EBSCO.

Preparing for this program was like playing that game you play sometimes at a party or personnel development workshop where you're introduced to a person, you ask them questions about themselves and you listen to them tell you everything they know about themselves in five minutes. Then you tell the group all you learned about that other person. This program is like that. But I spent a lot more than 5 minutes with Deb Van Petten. We'll talk about the high points of each of our jobs but it's not the whole picture.

Deb Van Petten is Assistant Professor/Acquisitions Librarian at Valdosta State University's Odum Library. She's served in that capacity for the past three years. She's been at Valdosta State for 11 years. Deb's a member of ALA and she represents the Odum Library at South Georgia Associated Libraries (SGAL). She's primary owner of the SGAL-L discussion list. She's currently on the Georgia Integrated Library (GIL) Subcommittee for Catalog Holdings Statements, and she won the President's Award for her work on cataloging the book collection at the Lowndes County Historical Society.

Deb is responsible for all of acquisitions, both books and serials. Library acquisitions has five basic elements: coordinating the selection of materials; administering the funds for buying them; keeping statistics; coordinating the procedures with other departments; and keeping positive relationships with the vendors, donors and other material sources. For this program we'll concentrate on the serials.

Valdosta State did a brave thing; it switched integrated library systems at the same time they switched to a new serials vendor. The decision to use EBSCO as their serials vendor came in the summer of 2000 to start with the year 2001 subscriptions. At the same time it was to join the other Georgia public colleges and universities in the use of Endeavor's Voyager System. Valdosta was part of the third phase of libraries to implement the new version of Voyager.

Deb sees change like she's encountered a fence. She says..."Don't let a fence stop you. Find a way over it, under it or around it. Change is inevitable. Find a way to work with it." Her motto played out well this past year as she handled the transition to EBSCO while implementing a new library system. We found that the best-laid plans didn't always materialize and that there were stumbling blocks along the way. In this case the production data for the migration of catalog records wasn't ready when it should have been, which slowed down the progress the staff hoped to make to get ready for the new serials module. In the midst of this and other plans that didn't materialize, Deb remembered that her maternal grandmother's last name was Murphy...maybe it was Murphy's law in action.

I worked with Deb at Valdosta State for a few days in February, helping the staff enter vendor data into the order records of Voyager, to get ready to interface with EBSCO. In that time I saw the high points of her job and how much there is to be done. I observed a lot and learned a lot.

One of my library jobs back in the late 1970s, before I became a librarian and before I began working for EBSCO, was to check in periodicals and claim them for the art and architecture library at the University of Cincinnati. The main library actually placed the claims with the vendor. I knew about periodicals and I knew about claims. That had been my introduction to serials.

Deb has three and one-half staff members devoted to periodicals; two of them had just started working at the library. The library has 1,460 subscriptions on order with EBSCO and some titles are ordered directly from the publisher. I not only saw staff check in serial issues, but saw them struggle with learning a new system.

Deb participated in training on the new system with other unit heads at Odum Library in October. She then taught herself enough of how it works to come up with procedures for teaching the staff how to start working in the system. The production delay in migration of the records delayed the staff training until February 1-2, so when I arrived on February 5, they weren't much more familiar with Voyager than I was.

There were boxes and boxes of periodical issues sorted by frequency setting on any available desk or cart. All the dailies were together, as were all the weeklies, all the quarterlies, etc. If a student or faculty needed something that was not checked in yet, they filled out a form, requested the issue and the staff person found it from one of the boxes and gave it to them. After they were finished using the issue they brought it back to be placed in the box with others of that frequency.

Deb showed me how to create serial records from the instructions she prepared, which included using the barcodes based on the subscription titles on order with EBSCO. The barcodes were arranged by frequency; they had the ISSN, the vendor title number and the subscription identifier for each title. The Subscription ID is the match point for EDIFACT invoice loading and claiming in Voyager. We scanned that data into the appropriate field in each serial record in the system. The barcodes also included the start dates, the frequency and the subscription term that were used to help in setting up each of the 1,460 records.

While I was creating serial records I observed some of Deb's responsibilities. She manages book acquisitions, serials and binding. As many of you know, that's a lot of stuff. One day there were two calls from vendors hoping to sell her new products; one was a school media association vendor with an AV product, another one was a book jobber wanting her to try its approval plan. Both times Deb listened graciously and then answered that she wasn't interested at the moment.

During the other times Deb trained all four of us on creating records and then spent much of her time answering our individual questions and concerns. She patiently walked us through errors and helped us get back to where we should be when we got lost in the system. It took us lots of trials and errors that first day to get it right. To help us she had created workflow procedures using "Screen Seize," a screen capture program that made it easier to follow the directions because we could see which screen we should be on to enter the data.

There were also 40 hours of time from student assistants who had been trained to help out at the periodical service window who were around some of the time. They work at the periodical service window, check in newspapers, shelve issues or pull the newspapers off the shelf when the microfilm arrives. Deb met with them too, to discuss any problems or concerns and that took some of her time.

Deb meets weekly with her supervisor, the associate director, to discuss staff issues and any acquisitions projects. The serial cataloger came in a number of times to find out how to handle a new serials setup. Deb dropped what she was doing to handle the concern. New ideas were discussed, old procedures were reiterated or processes adjusted to accommodate the situation — a constant challenge.

There were questions at the periodical service window, faculty calling for their requests, or to place an order — the rush one, of course. Or they wanted to to find out when their book order would be in, which meant stopping what she was doing and tracking down the order to see where it was in the process. Purchase orders also needed to be signed.

And there was e-mail, always e-mail including discussion list messages to read or answer. Those discussion lists came in handy when a system question came up; she'd query the members for suggestions on how to handle an issue concerning Voyager purchase orders or EDI invoicing. During the same time another staff person needed training on another project, so there were questions and follow-up times.

I'm not sure when Deb slept.

I observed the things I've spoken about and I was reminded of these things both from my experience with Deb at Odum Library and in the years I worked as a librarian and during my employment at EBSCO.

The price of journals has changed — while there are still some for $15.00 a year, quite a few at are at $500.00 per year. Some cost in the thousands. Until working so closely with Valdosta State's subscriptions I didn't know the individual costs of many journals. Of course, I am well aware of the rising cost of periodicals and the resulting budget crunches, but not so much the individual costs of journals.

I was again made aware of how people resist change—I know no one likes change, but that was reinforced. Staff expressed their reluctance to embrace what was being taught. I saw the inability of staff to grasp the full picture or the new way of doing things. For some, their confidence was shaken and their sense of security in knowing their jobs was threatened. Deb worked really hard to assure them they were doing fine, that the learning curve was a real thing, that the change was going to be OK. She'd made the decision to keep the workflow the same, as it had been as much as possible, until the staff was comfortable with working in the new system. They had that as a constant, but the new system threw them somewhat, still. I realized that even well trained staff members need attention sometimes and that Deb's role in the day-to-day activities was demanding.

I saw again that transitioning from one vendor to another required flexibility in dealing with new terminology. Items such as quotes versus proformas, different title numbering systems from one vendor to another, and figuring out which vendor is responsible for what, especially when it comes to standing orders and continuations, were challenging. The payment and arrival for these publications are the most difficult to capture and streamline.

I saw how in Voyager a purchase order (PO) is really a line item that in other systems is called an ID number. The PO refers to a line item for a title that is on order. I actually learned more about the Voyager system, enough to help other EBSCO customers work with setting up their serial records.

I learned a lot about hierarchy -- computer system hierarchy and personnel hierarchy, such as the division of labor in a technical services department, the chain of command required to work within a department, and the layers of communication required (i.e., Deb with staff, Deb with associate director and faculty, etc.)

I saw how it was for an acquisitions librarian to build confidence with her staff -- Deb taught the staff how to do it and gave it to them to work on, encouraging them along the way and trusted that they would grasp it.

I learned about the reports that an acquisitions librarian has to prepare for the administrators and faculty. Deb showed me the statistics she keeps and the data she uses to predict next year's budget expenditures for books and serials. She'll find that reports generated by EBSCO will help with serials data for next year.

I saw the struggle that working with a new system and a new serials vendor creates. It took a lot of planning and foresight. It requires a lot of collaboration and camaraderie.

The hardest part of doing this talk was talking about myself. But after working with Deb, I can tell you I learned that I like my job. I'm glad not to be in Deb's shoes. I'm glad not to have the personnel issues; not to have someone challenge my decisions at every turn; not to have to learn a new procedure and create training materials; and not to train staff over and over again, then follow up on their progress.

While I observed Deb doing her job, again, I was reminded that the services vendors provide to libraries and the work that librarians do to make it all come together really do make both of our jobs easier. And the fence between us is not nearly as tall.

THE DIGITAL INFORMATION PLAYER: WE HAVE THE DATA BUT NOT YET THE UNDERSTANDING

David Nicholas and Anthony Watkinson, CIBER, Department of Information Science, City University, London, United Kingdom

Abstract

The ubiquitous digital library provides us with enormous amounts of real-time data on use but we don't seem to know what to do with it (apart from making the occasional broadcast that we have X million 'hits' etc). Clearly the data does not seem to have improved our understanding of what people do with these systems or how satisfied they are with them. This understanding is unlikely to come until librarians everywhere — and especially those in academe — think long and hard about the terminology that they employ to describe information users, use and information seeking in the digital environment. Existing (largely print) terminology is proving an impediment to understanding what happens when people go online to communicate and/or retrieve information, as they are doing in droves. It also produces wildly false readings and prevents us establishing what really determines user satisfaction with information services. This paper, based upon wide-ranging research into the behaviour of the digital information consumer, undertaken by City University's CIBER Research Group (http://www.soi.city.ac.uk/is/research/ciber/), considers the term and some related ones — intermediary and end-user, in the light of our emerging knowledge of the new information order. A more suitable term - the information 'player', is presented for consideration and its significance is explained. It is argued that the new term will enhance our understanding of what goes on in the digital information environment and help correct the singularly one-dimensional stance with which we are viewing events. Without these mental and conceptual changes information professionals are in danger, especially in the academic world, of failing to recognise that what they are essentially serving is a consumer, a player. And you can bet your bottom dollar that the likes of Amazon will not be guilty of making this mistake.

Introduction

This paper arises out of the frustrations of many years of attempting to portray and evaluate information seeking behaviour in digital environments — and never really being able to do this accurately or to our own satisfaction.[1] Increasing sample sizes — something that is relatively easy to do thanks to Web logs, or changing the methodology — focus groups being the latest flavour of the month, never seemed to do the trick. What really seemed to be needed was a change in terminology -the kind of change that the Web brought with it. This would in its turn bring about a new way of looking/thinking and hence produce more apt and understood descriptions of the information seeking process, which in its part would lead to better information systems and services. The terminology currently used represents that of another age, and is proving an impediment to understanding and functioning in

---

1 This became most notable during the senior author's most recent project looking at digital health information for the consumer. The Web, the kiosk, digital TV and the changing face of consumer health information provision: a national impact study. April 2000 — January 2002

this one. In many respects the information profession is imprisoned by a Renaissance vocabulary, which represents a largely print-based and mediated world, yet increasingly works in a virtual world. New metaphors and a new language are required if we are to service needs in the digital environment. There is a pressing need for a new vocabulary for evaluating networked services like the Web, Intranets and mobile devices. Without it there is a danger that information systems will develop a life of their own, irrespective of the actual needs of information consumers and this will result in growing disenchantment with all things digital. Some would argue that this has already happened but is being camouflaged by the huge rollout of one digital platform after another — Web, kiosk, Digital TV and mobile device. We are in a digital fog. To be absolutely honest the previous generations of information systems really took little cognisance of the user — despite the widespread employment of the dreaded phrase 'user-friendly' (a distinctly self-justifying systems-based phrase). But that has to change as we ready ourselves for the huge leap towards personalised information delivery, as we surely will. We have moved to a dynamic, interactive and sophisticated information environment and our terminology, practices and thinking need to reflect this. Unfortunately, they don't.

You might ask, but what is there in a name, a word or a phrase? The answer must be, in today's communication-rich environment, everything. Words are a vehicle for our thinking and the search for accurate terminology should drive our thinking. Terminology determines the perceptions of the people we serve and the questions they ask of us. Consider, for instance, the extent of professional soul-searching associated with the term librarian and the large number of articles and dissertations that have been written on the topic. We of all professions should know be aware of the negative associations words have.

A Holistic Approach to Information Seeking Behaviour

Our argument assumes that the information seeker scanning, for example, an online newspaper for the football results or the television schedules is behaving in much the same way as the academic researcher finding out who has done something new in a specialist area of study. In the print environment, we could be talking about the same person but they would be in a different physical situation. They will certainly be taking up and putting down today's print newspaper before looking for, finding, and opening the issues of an abstracting journal. It is also very likely that they will have to move from one building to another to get the information they require. Researchers sitting at their screens in their offices are likely to be accessing both these sources of information, possibly at the same time. When not searching or printing out, they could be looking up train times or indulging in recreational pornography using the same techniques they have been learning and adding to since they became familiar with the Internet. And we all know what students get up to. There are no longer clear distinctions in time-frames or technique between different information seeking strategies.

The Information User

Essentially, our argument is that the profession needs to change its vocabulary to change its thinking, and needs to start with what is probably the central (key) word of them all — user. The word is employed inaccurately because it is often used to describe non-users, too. The population being described by the term user is a potential one, and an all-inclusive one. In reality it is used to describe anyone who might avail themselves of an information service. There are some hidden assumptions here that tell us much about the profession's psyche. The first assumption is that the term user embraces the majority of people — but frequently it does not. The second assumption is that it is good to use. And this partly explains the evangelical approach of many information professionals towards their 'flock'. The implication is that use is the normal state, but, of course, it is not always the case. The profession just wishes it were.

There is however a more general complaint that can be levelled at the word. User (and users), like information, has lost much of its meaning. It is a tired, over-used, cheap and misused word, which provides the information profession with a debased currency. It does not reflect the close and complex engagement that takes place between a person and today's interactive information systems. The word users paints a picture of a featureless mass, a homogenous body - people who are accustomed to being fed information in batch-processing model (as they were not so long ago). It is too passive and too mechanical for today's dynamic information environment. Users are in reality fast-moving individuals whose needs are constantly changing, depending on the problem, time, place and mood. Neither does the term recognise the fact that digital information systems create much greater information diversity than print-based systems. It is the wrong word, in the wrong place, at the wrong time. But we go on using it, and as a consequence, fail to see the massive changes that are going on information seeking behaviour.

The Information player

Too much professional time has been spent complaining about the word user. There has been more than enough hand wringing. The time has come to abandon it, or maybe better, to prescribe closely its meaning (to those who passively receive our products). What we really need is a more active and accurate term to denote the digital user. The concept of individuality referred to above leads us to the term we need — *information player*. *I-player* would appear to be a powerful — and very American — abbreviation. It is a term much richer in meaning, one that conveys both individuality and action. That is *player* used in the context of sport, meaning a football or baseball player. Players, of course, can be members of a team, but even then there are always the stars; or they can be truly individual, like tennis or golf players. Or we could use the term as it is used in the context or business, meaning someone whom invests in financial markets, or plays these markets after all information now constitutes a market (though some of us I am sure would rather not know this).

Player is a term that recognises that today's information seeking can be interactive, recreational, social and competitive.

❑ *Interactive.* Today's information consumer plays a much more important, complicated, creative and engaged role in the information seeking/retrieval process. The term user is one-dimensional and, if dynamic at all, that is only in a linear sense. Player on the other hand suggests a multidimensional evolving relationship — the kind of relationship that is so much a feature of modern day information systems, like the Web. A player is constantly looking for new routes to goal (success) — evaluating options (information) as they go. Feedback from players is an essential part of search success. The player is part of the system while the user was all too often the person who stood outside the system, looking in.

Using traditional information systems was rather like going into an office canteen, at a specific time, asking for items on a restricted menu, having them given to you, you eating up and someone coming and taking away your plates (sometimes, before you have finished your meal). All very orderly, all very one-way. Today's information systems are more analogous to the buffet lunch you order from an outside specialist food caterer. You choose what you like, when you like, you take it to the table and you choose whether to return the empty plate to the trolley or leave it on the table. This plainly represents a fundamental change in behaviour — and you can spot this in the transactional logs. In the latter case you are much more involved and in control of the whole process. Determining the success or otherwise of the function — in this case the provision of food, but in our case the provision of information — will require us to examine different things to determine satisfaction. That is the point being made.

❑   *Recreational.* Today's information systems are now very much an extension of our life — and this will prove to be even more so as the digital mobile phone expands its horizons into the information systems/retrieval domain. The word player very much comes from the real world. Information seeking today is no longer just about professional or academic problem solving; it can be recreational, domestic and mindless, too. Indeed, the distinction between professional and recreational searching in the serendipitous and supermarket digital information environment is becoming increasingly blurred (to the dissatisfaction of many an employer). In a sense this has already been recognised through the use of the term surfing (for information).

❑   *Social.* Information gathering is often a social — and pleasurable, activity. The social context of the term player is very important. Players play with somebody else. Players have different social roles: you have, for instance, teacher and student, politician and voter, journalist and reader. This takes us close to the concept of virtual communities. Of course, one of the best ways to build a successful information service is to create a virtual community of players. Are we as a profession doing this? The answer has to be not enough.

❑   *Competitive.* There are costs — financial and/or time costs, associated with finding - or not finding — information. You can win or lose in the information chasing and locating 'game'. Of course, players invest their time and money in every information journey or enterprise. With the migration of many communication, information retrieval, recreational and shopping activities to the Internet the investment has increased enormously. The reality is information services have to compete with each other to attract people to play.

The word player has other very important connotations. Firstly, it is a term that acknowledges the new economic and political realities of the new millennium. There has been a shift in power from information provider to information consumer. The information consumer now holds centre stage (an example of player power). This fact worries academic librarians and Media moguls alike. Indeed, anyone who manages large, centralised, inflexible batch-processing style information factories. Today's consumers have a wide choice and can quickly vote with their mice. Thus, as a patron of a university library you were always supplicants — the Inter-library Loans (ILL) librarian had particular powers to open or not the information gates to the wider world. Now the academic can go to the Web - Amazon.com etc. The ILL librarian will have to undercut the opposition now (in terms of delivery times, cost or customer care): the tables have plainly turned — users have become players.

Secondly, the word player is closely connected with the term spectacle, a term once associated with pageants and tournaments. Today the Internet is the biggest capitalistic spectacle of our times, and digital interactive television is not a long way behind. Witness how people pay fortunes for impressive Internet addresses. Witness, too, the amazing — and sometimes mythical — rise of e-commerce. There are fortunes to be had for the big players and games and adventures for the not so lucky. But do academic libraries see themselves belonging to an information pageant or spectacle — certainly not in the UK, where this would all be seen as a dumbing down.

Thirdly, the term player is very much an Internet-type word. The Internet is very much part of the liberal world economy — the word user is most certainly not, and player most definitely is. There is an urgent need to get our words in line with the vocabulary of the Internet and the millions of new information consumers. The Internet has its own rich and picturesque language for describing itself. This cannot be ignored. It is only by employing this language that information professionals can address the much larger and more powerful audience that the Internet commands. We are dealing with a post-Modernist reality.

Satisfaction and Outcomes

To its great dishonour the profession has not come up with is a term that describes success in information seeking — not simply using information, in the digital information environment. Interestingly, there really was no word for this in the print environment either. Of course, the terms references and records were often treated as synonyms for success. The more records/references the higher the alleged success levels — but the success being referred to here is really the prowess of the intermediary in finding lots of information, and not necessarily the success of the consumer in meeting their needs. Satisfaction — much beloved by questionnaire framers, is surely too remote, indirect, imprecise and passé a term. Not surprisingly, this is the problem with the term user too. In player-speak it is all about what constitutes a score, what is the information equivalent of a goal or home run? Courtesy of the Web comes the word *hits*. Certainly it has directness and energy on its side; the only problem lies in its imprecision. But the term player forces you to really look beyond the action to consider the outcomes. Pursuing the sport's analogy, the goal that leads to a side winning a game means that they will be promoted etc. So what does the receipt of information lead to — a better grade, a published paper, an argument won or, in the case of our current research study, improved health? This surely is the benchmark against which the individual measures success but I very much doubt whether the librarian uses the same benchmark. But, if not, why not — we are surely all playing in the same game, if not the same team?

Re-assessing information seeking behaviour

The concept of a player is very helpful one in illuminating how people interact with information systems — and, also, re-visiting what we have said and learnt about them in the past. Continuing the sports analogy, few goals are probably scored in a textbook manner. Thus the stars of the football world are famous for their ability to do the unconventional, the unusual, the creative. In any game of football players do a lot of things that are not in the training/coaching manuals, but plainly they have received training. Similarly, a lot of information is collected by unconventional, unusual or serendipitous means. Thus, maybe, what was first seen as minimalist and idiosyncratic information behaviour was not so odd, strange etc after all — maybe it was just creative. Too often 'end-user' searching has been compared unfavourably with that of information professionals. But would you really expect all players to function the same or do as the manager has told them. Surely not.

Of course, all players are subject to the rules of the game. The digital environment has many rules associated with it — and these rules may be broken, of course. These rules can be social — i.e. recreational searching at the office should only be conducted at lunch times or that visiting pornographic sites is strictly taboo for university students, or they may be associated with searching — Boolean or proximity searching, for instance.

Maybe, too, the term player will help bury, once and for all, the myth that searching databases is a fundamentally academic exercise, that requires high recall and is easily met by copious abstracts or bibliographic references of material (often) well past their sell by date. The time has come to finally admit that consumers in the digital information environment have long superseded academics as the star players, and should not be represented as *the* model information players. To determine satisfaction/success on the basis of the number of references found — or, for that matter, the amount of time spent online, must be wrong, but nevertheless they have been used as quality metrics for a very long time. Rapid access and speed of information delivery is surely the players quality metric. The evidence is in the logs.

Informobility

The advent of the mobile phone as an information retrieval system — connected, for instance, to the Internet and other specialist databases, will surely kill off the term user and herald the arrival of the term player. With real-time information on the move — or informobility, plainly now the stress is really on action, movement and playing. The digital mobile phone offers a highly personal information service that is a much closer approximation to real life (hence the popularity with children) — and as far away from the traditional (four-walled) concept of a library as you can get. The mobile phone represents a genuinely popular (mass) platform for seeking and finding information. We are all players now. What will surely drive the use of the phone as an information retrieval medium will be the vast and ever-increasing amounts of real-time information becoming available. Playing too is a real-time activity — and a performance indicator, but is it one of your priorities?

Other Renaissance Terms

Getting behind the word is getting behind the concept. Getting behind the concept requires us to evaluate other related, possibly, obsolete, pejorative or 'loaded' words. What then should be done about 'end-user' — another very overworked, de-personalised term? End-user is used to describe someone who searches information systems themselves — once a rare activity, now an extremely common one; indeed so common now it is only used to mask what is happening in the digital world. Its part of the information fog. The information profession is not alone in using this term; it has also become part of business-speak, too. Of course, the term is built around the concept of user — and shares all the same problems. It is also very inaccurate — many end-users (especially in the consumer health field), for instance, pass on some information to others and do not consume it themselves. The term gatekeeper — another powerful sports metaphor, is often used to describe these people. The distinction between searcher and consumer that was once so marked is now so blurred as to be meaningless — but many of our systems still persist with the distinction. But having argued for the removal of the term, it should be re-introduced, but its meaning should be severely proscribed. Its use should be reserved to describe activities that involve the consumption of information canteen or batch-processing style; although not used in a derogatory sense but in a passive, uncomplaining sense.

Information Professionals

Given that we are now dealing with a *player* then its axiomatic that the role of the information professional must be revisited as well. Has it been diminished as a direct result of player-empowerment? Are they players any longer? And plainly that has happened in places, where information professionals have retired to the back-room — processing database feeds for instance. But what of those who are still playing? Terms such as intermediary and intermediation are surely no longer appropriate — far too passive, hands-off, non-internet words. They are in synch with the concept of user but out of synch with the concept of playing. As always the real issue is how dynamic a role the information professional should play. In football parlance are information professionals strikers or goalkeepers, or, maybe, player/managers. Perhaps, as we have hinted, some information professionals are not players at all, but ancillary staff - the chief coach or the groundsman, for example. The game is the same but the roles are quite different. If information professionals are to be coaches then that assumes that they are acknowledged authorities in the field — and maybe many of them would be deluding themselves if they believed this. To be coaches they would also need to understand their players intimately and that means having player profiles — information needs assessments. Most don't, but maybe the change of vocabulary would lead to a change in their behaviour?

What then of the groundsman metaphor — someone who is responsible for the environment in which the players operate: the 'pitch' in sports terms and cyberspace in information terms. This is a plainly a back-room operation, but nevertheless still one of direct importance to the quality of playing. The involvement of many information professionals — incidentally one of the few terms that still fits, in Intranet, Web site and database developments would suggest that many are, indeed, ground staff. Traditionally the profession has very much played the role of the groundsman, but that was when much information gathering was conducted in the library, but today's pitches are found in cyberspace — and few information professionals can claim to have full territorial rights there.

The term player also helps us in the planning and marketing of information training or skills programmes — something that appears to fall more and more in the information professional's domain. For instance, the latest 'buzz' term information literacy, would be unsuitable, as it is far too judgmental, prescriptive, and one-way. All players think they can play — even if they can't. *I-coaching* would be much more player-friendly term. The concept of the personal trainer is also a useful one here. Does your library have personal trainers or coaches?

The Patron as Player

The library literature is full of comment about schemes to measure usage behaviour. Librarians need a sound metric to justify how they spend their limited budgets. They want to be able to select on the basis of what their patrons actually do want. They want rules. However anyone with only a passing knowledge of the new science of usage statistics will have realised that it is not easy to measure. Even if everyone agrees exactly what to measure, which they don't, there is an amazing amount of noise in the system. Not only that but behind the statistics, once refined, is the question — what does it all mean? Is the use satisfying? What sort of use is educational or furthers scholarship? Without a serious and realistic vocabulary to describe what users do when they use, there are huge opportunities to misunderstand information play.

Conclusions

These past few years information professionals have had to sit back and allow Internet 'nerds' to educate them in the culture of the new digital information world order. Starting from scratch as they did, carrying no Renaissance baggage, they invented a brand-new vocabulary, full of live, popular, direct and apposite words. Very few of the words used — surfing, visitors, hits, navigate etc, have their origins in the librarianship field, which of course is telling in itself. The information profession should take a leaf out of their book and put some new words to work — starting, but not finishing, with the word player. If the term user already seems outmoded in connection with the Web, just think how even more outmoded it will appear in the context of mobile digital devices. A redundant and obsolete vocabulary is likely to (further) divorce the profession from the wider information world that they surely should be a part of.

Such a change in vocabulary should help information professionals find their true role in the Information Society — and so far that role is unclear and slow coming. Clearly from we have said about increased levels of interactivity between people and information systems a major part of their role will be developing, counselling and coaching the *i-players*. The personal trainer could be a highly prized job. For that to occur the whole profession has to move closer to the players and treat them all as individuals — something that many information professionals have been historically reluctant to do. Information professionals have to demonstrate their own player credentials (most of the successful football managers have also been players) — and that is not simply about showing that they are better players, but also that they possess true team spirit.

The technology and the opportunities are there, but whether the interest and inter-personal skills amongst information professionals are there is much less certain. We shall know whether this has all come to pass when an evaluation of an information service is conducted in terms of player satisfaction and not by system performance, and when pride is shown in the quality and skills of the players and not just the quality of the systems.

Information consumerism has surely come to academe. This once self-contained, insular and monopolistic world of academic libraries has been penetrated — and boy, how. The logs show this in breathtaking detail but to see the patterns and meanings in the logs you need to put on your player spectacles.

Perhaps, the profession's much-publicised neglect of the 'user' can be explained in some way by the term itself. After all such a general and vague term hardly reminds us of the primacy of the individual and the necessity to investigate the individual's information needs. The term player demands attention and such investigation. Maybe, the solution to many of our professional ills lies with just changing one word. Now that begins to sound easy.

CHARLESTON PANEL ON USAGE STATISTICS 2001

e-Metric Initiatives in the United States

Denise M. Davis, Director, Statistics and Surveys, National Commission on Libraries and Information Science (NCLIS)

Discussions began in 1996 about the following issues:

- Identification of specific statistics that most individuals can agree on as important to standardize (in terms of definitions) and can be provided by the publishers of online and CD-ROM databases

- Identification of key issues and concerns from the library community regarding collection of electronic resource use statistics

- Review of the specific types of statistics and reporting formats provided by database publishers and vendors

Now the questions libraries need to answer are the same; what vendors are able to provide has improved dramatically.

- There is greater literacy of what data are collectable and what data are valuable to libraries

- Uniformity in statistics reporting remains a key issue

- National library surveys are beginning to adopt measures and require reporting

- National and international standards organizations are adopting electronic measures (ISO and NISO)

Lead Projects, 1998-present:

Developing National Data Collection Models for Library Network Statistics and Performance Measures (2000).
http://www.ii.fsu.edu/Projects/IMLS/index.html

Network Performance Measures Focus Group: Group Discussion #3, Summary Notes (2000-2001).
http://www.nclis.gov/statsurv/FINALRPT.NCLIS.vendor.FG.1.11.01.doc

State Library Agency Survey Steering Committee adopts core network performance measures for FY2002 national reporting (2001).
http://www.nclis.gov/libraries/lsp/StLArevised2001.html

Guidelines for Statistical Measures of Usage of Web-Based Indexed, Abstracted, and Full Text Resources (November 1998). International Coalition of Library Consortia (ICOLC).
http://www.library.yale.edu/consortia/webstats.html

ARL New Measure Initiative (2001). Association of Research Libraries (ARL). http://www.arl.org/stats/newmeas/newmeas.html

Where to find additional information:

CLIR report on vendor statistics (prepared by Judy Luther). The white paper is available from
http://www.clir.org/pubs/reports/reports.html

Library Statistics & Measures, compiled by Joe Ryan
http://web.syr.edu/~jryan/infopro/stats.html

NISO Z39.7 Library Statistics Standard revision
http://www.nclis.gov/statsurv/niso/z39.7/z39.7.html

ISO Standard 2789, Library Statistics
http://www.iso.org/iso/en/ISOOnline.frontpage

Publishers Usage Statistics

Jerry Cowhig, Managing Director, Institute of Physics Publishing

All usage statistics today exist between a single publisher and a single library or consortium. And all known initiatives on the future of statistics seem to assume this continued model. Soon librarians will pool statistics but they will come from disparate sources and will be incomplete. Comparisons will therefore be difficult

In most other media there exists an agreed universal measure, e.g. for magazine circulation, radio listener numbers, commercial websites. And there are companies that collect such figures, e.g. BPA, ABC.

I propose that the STM learned journal industry needs:

- A single measure to define a journal's readership (such as full-text downloads per article in 12 months)

- Auditing of the figure by a third party

- Publication of the information

Such headline figures and the associated detailed analyses could stand beside citation reports and impact factors, which judge a journal by its citations, to create a new recognized industry measure that judges a journal by its readership.

I am discussing this idea with auditing companies and endeavoring to gather support from publishers.

Usage Statistics — The View from the Intermediary

Helen Henderson, Consultant

Intermediaries have been working with the problems that electronic publishers now find themselves faced with since the 1960s. Early experiences with Lockheed Dialog, SDC, and Euronet show how difficult it is to interpret statistics from multiple sources for both the vendor and the user.

Intermediaries may be abstracting and indexing services, full-text aggregators, e-journal aggregators, hosting services, or linking services. The pragmatic approach says that you do have to satisfy the providers of your data and the users of your data. Sometimes it is not clear how much users use the data, regardless of how much they demand it. Experiences with ILS vendors in the 1980s showed that less than 5% of the management reports specified for library systems were ever looked at.

The important issues for vendors are:

- Communication standards: making sure that the data can be sent, received, and understood

- Entity identifiers: for content, users, and time

- Consistency

- Compatibility

The important issues for users are monitoring their end-user activity and may include:

- Sign-ons

- Searches

- Queries

- Downloads/purchases

- Linking activities

- Alerting activities

It is important that the vendors and users are very specific about what usage statistics they want, what exactly they are going to do with them, and what they think the statistics are going to tell them.

The PALS Code of Practice on Usage Statistics

Richard Gedye, Head of Journals Marketing, Oxford University Press, and Hazel Woodward, University Librarian, Cranfield University, UK

PALS stands for Publishers and Libraries Solutions Group, and the PALS Usage Statistics Working Group comprises members drawn from the Association of Learned and Professional Publishers (ALPSP), the Joint Information Systems

Committee of the UK further and higher education funding bodies (JISC), and the Publishers Association (PA). The aim of the Working Group is to develop a Code of Practice on vendor-based usage statistics with guidance on:

- Data elements to measure

- Definitions of these data elements

- Accurate, complete, and consistent measurement of user activity

- Report formats, frequency, and granularity

- Report delivery methods

Work continues at a rapid pace. So far, the Working Group has reviewed all of the major existing projects on usage statistics (of which there are a considerable number) and established dialogues with these projects to ensure that there is no duplication of effort. A major achievement was the organization of an international vendor forum at which the majority of major scholarly publishers and aggregators were represented. The one-day forum succeeded in all its major objectives, which were to catalogue areas of agreement, flush out areas of complexity and differences in practice, and identify unresolved issues needing further work. A further important outcome was the establishing of several international task forces to address complex issues such as statistics from gateways and hosts, authentication, data models, and types of reports.

The timeline for the work is ambitious. The Working Group hopes to have a draft code of practice circulated to selected reviewers in the library and vendor world by February 2002 and Version 1.0 of the code published in April 2002. The vital factors for the successful implementation and uptake of the code are seen to be:

- Start with a small core code and build out incrementally

- Build continuous development capability into the support structure

- Need for all projects to pool their collective wisdom and work together

- Compatibility is vital

- One code — parallel codes will attract minimal buy-in

For more information visit the PALS website and join the discussion listserv to be kept up to date with further development: http://www.usagestats.org

D igital resources bring with them unique needs regarding archiving and retrieval. The importance of preserving scholarship and all that it produces cannot be minimized. Yet, we still struggle with responsibility for archiving, and various libraries, with the help of grant opportunities, have responded in a variety of ways. Publishers are working with libraries to develop long-term strategies for archiving, and our speakers addressed this issue as it related to the Mellon Grant project at Harvard University and the LOCKSS project at Stanford. Portals are also a part of the digital environment and the conference featured presentations that focused on the pluses of subject-based portals and the tools that vendors are creating to make the searching of them more efficient.

Digital Environment

ELECTRONIC ARCHIVING

Craig Van Dyck, John Wiley and Sons

I only have a short time here to talk about archiving. I think from Ivy you've already heard that there are some complex issues in the Harvard project. We at Wiley as well as at Blackwell and University of Chicago Press are spending hours talking about these issues, so this is going to be a pretty short summary of them.

Why is digital archiving important? Well, it's fairly obvious that scholarship must be preserved. In the print world there is an existing paradigm, and it's really a non-issue at this point that print copies will be preserved or at least preserved one way or another. In the online world, a new paradigm needs to be made.

Another reason it's important is that we have heard from many of our library customers that they consider archiving a pre-condition for canceling print, and canceling print is something that libraries want to do if there's a good alternative available electronically.

Another imperative is preserving access. If users were able to get at it once, they should be able to get at it again and again and again, into perpetuity.

And there's some potential that the digital archive, whatever shape it may end up taking, could function as something useful for publishers as a kind of backup for publishers. I personally don't think that's going to be an issue for a publisher like Wiley, but it may be an issue for some other publishers.

So briefly, what are some of the issues? Who has the responsibility for archiving? This is not yet clear. As a publisher, I would like to propose that publishers should take the responsibility for archiving, but I'm not so sure that that is going to be the answer that we end up with at the end of the day. That's very much a question. Publishers are not necessarily trusted on this. Publishers have not done it up until now in the print world. And, as Ivy said, publishers may not be here tomorrow.

National libraries are another candidate. Again, there are reasons not to be in favor of national libraries. Not every nation's library is entirely trustworthy nor is every nation's national government. And, I think, for me at least, and some others, the idea of expecting the government to do everything for us is not the preferred option.

Or trusted third parties — which is kind of a general phrase but I think in the kinds of projects that Mellon is funding what we are seeing is the incubation of some potential trusted third parties; there are already some existing third parties, people like OhioLINK, for example.

And another possibility is a kind of distributed various network; to me this is one of the good things about the Mellon project: The different projects are different. They are taking different approaches, and at the end of the day we might not end up with one monolithic solution — here is the archiving solution. We may have three or four or thirteen or fourteen different archiving solutions with different technologies, different business models all running at the same time as a form of backup for one another.

But technological issues are really tough. I mean, trying to future-proof everything we publish for every future that you can imagine, or not imagine, is really outside the scope of what's probably achievable. You just can't future-proof over hundreds of years, or you can't feel confident that you are.

One thing that is important is for the content in the archive somehow to be validated and verified that the bits are still good. This is the argument for a bright archive, an archive that's getting usage.

Another possibility could be some kind of formal auditing process. There are people out there who make their living performing audits. Maybe a digital archive could have an auditing process.

Another question is whether the archive should include only the intellectual content or the functionality as well. I hear people talk about, well, we must archive the user experience. My view is that that's going too far; I think that's impossible. Even in the print world we're not archiving the user experience. In the print world, we are not archiving a situation where a user has four different journals open on the desk, plus two reference books, and the light that is coming through the window. We are not archiving the user experience in the print world, and I don't think we should expect to be able to do so in the digital world.

The processes for an archive are equally important. One thing that I've started thinking about, working on the Harvard project is, Okay, there are certain things that Wiley and Blackwell and Chicago can do, but that doesn't necessarily mean that every print publisher can do those things. So we have to find a kind of lowest common denominator process, and that's not going to be so easy, really. I won't be surprised if we end up with a kind of service industry around archiving. You could argue that HighWire Press is already doing that in service to its publisher clients, saying we will handle archiving as well as the electronic publishing.

A few more issues to be solved: the business model, the cost recovery. In my view the technological issues and the business issues are equally difficult; I think a good approach is being taken in the Harvard project, and no doubt in the other Mellon projects, to pursue the technology and the business on separate parallel tracks simultaneously. We have two discussions going on with actually different groups. There's a technology group and there's a business group, and both of them are moving forward through the issues. Difficulties solving one set of issues will not slow us down in moving forward on the other issues. The technical issues in some ways are easier because they're just technical. On the business side there are other kinds of things that we have to work through, and there are some snags in the discussion. I'm really confident that we're going to get through those, but it's going to take a little bit of time. Of course, the business model also relates to a certain degree to the answers to the other questions, for example, whose responsibility is archiving.

Access terms, as Ivy was saying, are something that is still not clear. Certain triggers seem pretty clear. If the publisher doesn't exist anymore, well, the publisher can't very well demand that it have any prerogatives if it doesn't even exist; or if copyright has run out and the copyright holder no longer controls the content. And since we're talking about hundreds of years of archiving, the material in the archive will eventually come back into the public domain.

And then access versus preservation. As I've participated in the archiving issue, one thing I've noticed is that when people talk about preservation, they often are really talking about access, especially librarians. I'm not trying to say that librarians are not interested in preservation, but it seems to me that the conversation always come back to access. And yes, the two things are closely linked, but I would say that when we work our way through the archiving issue, it is important to remember there's a distinction between preservation for preservation, versus preservation for the purposes of maintaining access.

Just a couple of words about the Harvard archiving project. First, we're very happy to be participating in the project. We like to work with quality partners and we are doing so in this case. Blackwell, Chicago, and Wiley are publishers that have come to know each other quite well. Somewhat coincidentally all three are on the CrossRef board of directors, so there's actually quite a bit of cooperative work going on among not only these three publishers but other publishers.

The special problems of multiple inputs, and normalization: We will look to Harvard to be able to normalize the incoming data.

And I think one of the best things that can come out of these Mellon projects is some kind of industry archiving XML DTD. As a publisher, and I'm a production person, I can tell you that if you tell us what the target is, we can deliver to it. That's what we do. We define targets, and then we make up a process to deliver to you. And if an industry DTD can be arrived it, that would work for us at the same time. Give us the DTD, we'll convert our XML to that DTD. We do that all the time.

The PDF is something that some people say is not a good archiving format, but I would say don't underestimate PDF. I think we are seeing that it is evolving; it is a commercial product although largely freely available, but PDF has been an important part of electronic publishing going back to the mid-nineties, and I think we can count on PDF to continue for some time. Whether it will continue for hundreds of years, I don't know, but I wouldn't underestimate PDF.

And then working on the business models and processes, my own view is that it's probably too early to come to firm decisions about some of the business models. We need to have some patience here and work through these issues. The solutions that come out are intended to last for hundreds of years or, as my boss for example says, to bind future generations of Wiley management. Now that's a pretty big thing to think about, so I think it's natural for us as publishers to want to be careful when we talk about binding future generations.

In summary, just a few words about a publisher's perspective. By this point it's a given that archiving is a must. It's not a question anymore of whether archiving needs a solution. Yes, it needs a solution, and yes, we're working to try to arrive at that. I think as we've gotten into the archiving issue more, we realize we really want to be a full partner in the solution. At first, frankly, I think publishers sort of kept this issue at arm's length and hoped it would go away. But now I think we recognize that it's crucial and we've got to be a full participant and full partner in the solution. Wiley is working together with leading stakeholders to resolve the issues and, as I said, I think solutions are evolving, progress is being made, but I don't think we should rush to a conclusion.

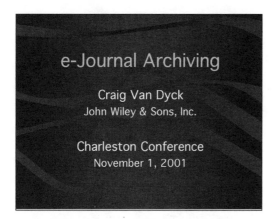

e-Journal Archiving

Craig Van Dyck
John Wiley & Sons, Inc.

Charleston Conference
November 1, 2001

The Digital Archiving Imperative

- Preserving scholarship
- Pre-condition for cancelling print
- Preserving access
- Back-up for publishers?

2

Issues to be Solved

- Who has the responsibility for archiving? Publishers? National libraries? Trusted third parties? Distributed, various network?
- Technological issues: dark vs. bright; intellectual content vs. functionality; archiving formats; "future-proofing"; etc.
- Processes

3

Issues to Be Solved, continued

- Business model; cost recovery
- Access terms
- Access vs. preservation

4

Harvard's e-Journal Archiving Project

- Wiley, Blackwell, U. Chicago Press
- The special problems of multiple inputs; normalization
- XML-based: an industry-wide archiving DTD would be good!
- PDF
- Business models; processes

5

Publisher Perspective

- Archiving is a must
- Publishers should be full partners in the solution
- Work together with leading stakeholder representatives to resolve the issues
- Don't rush; this is a very long-term matter

6

ELECTRONIC ARCHIVING: THE MELLON GRANTS

Ivy Anderson, Digital Acquisitions Coordinator, Harvard University

I am very pleased to be here this morning. It's a privilege to be leading off this session with a discussion of electronic journal archiving and its importance to the information community. I'm also delighted to be joined by Craig Van Dyck and Victoria Reich on this morning's panel.

This is my first visit to Charleston; and touring the city yesterday, I couldn't help but be struck by all of the restoration activity that is taking place in the historic district and how that serves as kind of a metaphor — and perhaps a bit of a warning as well — for the preservation work that lies before us in digital archiving.

Some of us would say that digital preservation is the biggest single issue facing libraries today. We've developed considerable expertise in other aspects of digital libraries — in digitizing objects, making them available, creating metadata, and building content and retrieval systems. But digital archiving is still a big unknown —it's the elephant in the room, if you will — and yet it is the one issue most critical to that part of the library mission that concerns itself with assuring the continuity of the historical record. And so that makes it of vital concern to all of us in this room today.

I'm going to talk this morning about some of the background that led to the Mellon Grants, and then move to a discussion of the issues that we're confronting at Harvard in our own Mellon Grant project. But first I'd like to start with a few words about archiving in what for the sake of convenience we often refer to as the paper or print era, and how that differs from archiving in the electronic era. (Of course these are not really different eras.)

The print environment is characterized by large-scale redundancy of copies in many different places. And the existence of these copies in a great many locations increases the likelihood that some of those copies and manifestations will persist over time, and so serves as an archival safeguard of sorts. The usefulness of redundancy in archiving is also a fundamental premise of the LOCKSS project that Vicky Reich is going to speak about a little later.

Another characteristic of archiving in the print era is that the access copy and the preservation copy are usually the same; and this means that some of the activities that we undertake to make materials available also contribute to their preservation. Environmental controls, binding and repair, and even reformatting, are a part of that. Although there are institutions that take on archiving as a deliberate role — national libraries and major research institutions for example —archiving also happens as the byproduct of the normal collecting activity of many different institutions with no particular archival ambitions.

But as we all know, digital is different; and one of those differences is that multiple copies are no longer held in many locations. Publishing entities or other sole content holders by and large hold copies remotely. Although there are institutions and organizations such as OhioLINK that do maintain and store local copies, that practice is fairly infrequent; by and large, today there more commonly exists a single copy, or at best a small number of copies, under single entity control.

The absence of local copies separates the service and the archiving activities that were joined in the paper world. And that leads to a different cost picture. Archiving in the electronic world now has to be undertaken as a separate, specific, conscious, and deliberate activity with its own cost imperatives separate from our other activities that support access to electronic information. And although many of us are signing perpetual licenses today for electronic content, we have no guarantee that the entities with whom we're signing those perpetual licenses are going to persist over time; and so it's not at all clear how confident we ought to be that we'll be able to exercise those rights in the absence of the old assurance of locally-held copies that existed in lots of different places.

The upshot of this is that archiving is becoming a growing problem for all of us who are by now knee deep in electronic collecting. Many of us are responding by continuing to subscribe to materials in print as well as electronically. We're paying for information in multiple formats, and we're supporting access in multiple formats. Our users, as Tom has driven home to us today, increasingly prefer and want access to information electronically; but many of us continue to purchase paper for preservation purposes if not for other purposes. Although increasing numbers of libraries are beginning to cancel or think about canceling print, quite a few of us are still collecting that paper.

This duality is causing economic strain for publishers as well as libraries. Publishers can't convert to purely digital publication while there's still a demand for paper. That demand is coming not only from the library community, but also from authors, editors, and a scholarly community that remains concerned about the persistence of the electronic record. It's hard to see how the transformations to electronic-only publication will happen until authors and scholars have been reassured that the archiving problem has been solved.

Nonetheless, the electronic copy is increasingly becoming the copy of record, both officially and informally. Several publishing organizations have indeed now made the electronic copy the official copy of record. But even where it isn't the official copy of record, we know that an increasing amount of information being published in electronic journals isn't appearing in the paper journal at all; supplementary files, longer versions of a paper that may appear in a more abbreviated form in the print journal, high resolution images that are available online but not published in print, and so on. There is an increasing divergence between the electronic copy and the print copy.

The growing urgency of this situation engendered a series of meetings over the last several years by some fairly highly placed folks in the information chain to talk about 'the archiving problem' and how we might go about solving it. Harvard participated in a number of meetings hosted by organizations such as the Society of Scholarly Publishers, NSF, the Council on Library and Information Resources, and the Coalition for Networked Information, which brought together publishers, libraries and technologists. One outcome of those discussions was a document developed under the auspices of the Digital Library Federation (DLF) entitled 'Minimum Criteria for an Archival Repository of Digital Scholarly Journals,' which outlines a set of functional areas that an entity seeking to describing itself as an archive must address. It defines an archive as an independent trusted party that has relationships with both libraries and publishers, that can provide archived content to libraries under specified conditions, that has sufficient control over the content to be able to preserve it for the long term, and that undertakes documented policies and procedures for performing these activities.

While there was some very good discussion at these meetings by leading players in the information marketplace, nothing concrete emerged from these sessions other than the Minimum Criteria document until the Mellon Foundation stepped in and said in effect: "Well, let's just try it." Dale Flecker, the Associate Librarian for Systems and Planning at Harvard and a party to many of those discussions, likes to tell a comparable story about the origins of the TULIP Project which Elsevier and other major institutions undertook in the late eighties or early nineties to study electronic information use. At that time, there were similar meetings going on at which librarians and publishers were talking about the potential of electronic journals, how people might use them, and whether publishing would actually move in that direction. But no one was doing anything to drive the process, until at one of these meetings Karen Hunter from Elsevier stood up in the room and said "I'm tired of just talking and talking; if anyone wants to do something, come over to this corner of the room and let's stop talking about it and just get started." In Dale's retelling, it's that's kind of breaking-the-logjam approach that led to the current Mellon-funded initiatives. As Tom said this morning in another context, we don't really know what we're doing yet — we're learning by doing. Even if we don't know what the outcome is going to be, it's important at a certain point to let go of uncertainty, to just plow ahead and do it.

So in that spirit, the Mellon Foundation in early 2000 invited 13 institutions to submit proposals for a one-year planning grant that would be responsive to the minimum criteria developed by DLF. Mellon recognized that we were embarking on a complex process in which there are no real models; so the planning process is designed to allow the participants to think through the issues and develop a plan. After the planning year, Mellon has agreed, or has indicated at this point, that it will fund up to four implementation projects. Those phase two proposals are due in March or April of 2002. We expect that a number of the planning institutions will step up to the plate and actually go forward.

Of the six planning projects that have been funded to date, three are publisher-based: Harvard is working with John Wiley and Sons, Blackwell Publishers and the University of Chicago Press; the University of Pennsylvania is working with Oxford and Cambridge University Presses; and Yale is working with Elsevier. These projects have as their focus working with individual publishers to develop an archiving plan and model. Several other projects are discipline-based: Cornell is working on materials in the field of agriculture and will likely be talking with a range of publishers with a focus on that discipline; New York Public Library is working with materials in the performing arts, with its performing arts library as the project locus; and MIT is working on dynamic e-journals — journals that change over time, that have interactive components, or that may lack a standard volume and issue publication format. Perhaps there are colleagues here from MIT who can tell us more about how they're construing the idea of dynamic e-journals; but the basic idea as I understand it is to address the needs of more innovative e-publications that are less like the print world than many of the more established e-journals that the rest of us are dealing with.

The Stanford LOCKSS project, also being funded by Mellon, is a little bit different from the planning projects that I've just described in that it is technology-based rather than institution-centric. I won't try to describe LOCKSS — whose acronym stands for Lots of Copies Keeps Stuff Safe — since Vicky will be telling us about it a little later in this program, except to say that it's a technology designed for large-scale replication of content across many sites. For more information about all seven

Mellon-funded projects, you can consult the web page for the projects that the Digital Library Federation maintains on its web site.

A number of basic assumptions emerged from the original discussions that are central to all of the institutionally based Mellon projects in progress. As I mentioned earlier, the DLF Minimum Criteria document has informed much of the initial thinking. The idea of very long time frames is another overarching notion. Thinking about the next century as opposed to next year raises very different issues about archiving. You have to plan for multiple, major revolutions in technology when you plan for very long timeframes. You have to think really hard about how to both structure and document the work of an archive so that its contents will be understandable to another generation a hundred years down the road.

There is also some feeling that there is value in attaching an archive to an institution that can claim an independent existence and long-term viability. Many of us in the library world have agonized over whether archiving is destined to be a role of libraries in the digital future. This project is intended to test that notion by centering its work at universities that we can generally assume will persist for a very long time, in effect attaching that activity to the persistence of those institutions.

Most of the archive projects are also designed around something called the Open Archival Information System (OAIS) Reference Model; a model for archiving that has come out of the space data community rather than the library community that articulates archiving roles and responsibilities from a high-level systems perspective. The OAIS Reference Model has generated a great deal of interest as a paradigm for thinking about the roles, functions, and systems design of an archival repository.

So Harvard has jumped into this feet first, you might say, and we're finding that there are lots and lots of issues to work through. There are no pre-existing models for how to think about what we're doing, and so we have to think very hard about a great many aspects. One problem we're confronting is the question of who will be able to use the archive. We're learning that the 'who' and 'when' and 'under what conditions' of an archive are issues that can be quite problematic in discussions with publishers. It will be very interesting to hear a discussion of some of those issues from a publisher perspective.

To start with one example: is the archive available to other institutions who subscribe to that content and, if so, does an archive have to maintain records about who subscribes and what they subscribe to, and do that for multiple institutions and multiple publishers over very long timeframes? That seems to us like a very difficult thing to do. It's not at all clear what the archive's role might be in providing access to existing subscribers and how it would know about those arrangements.

Would an archive provide access to individual subscribers, or only to subscribing institutions? Could an individual personal subscriber at an institution access material from the archive? If so, how would the archive know that that individual was authorized to use that content? Would an archive provide access to other libraries? Is there some analog to interlibrary loan for providing archived content to non-subscribers? What about third party providers? For example, a publisher might at some point want to hand off its older content to a third party service provider because the publisher itself no long finds it viable or commercially appealing to provide direct service for that content. If so, might the publisher then want that provider to be able to procure older content from the archive? These issues have to be discussed and worked through with a publishing partner.

A prior question, perhaps, is whether the archive will be dark or visible. A dark archive is generally considered to be one that securely holds content without making it directly accessible, analogous to the way microforms masters are held. While dark archiving is probably cheaper to manage —you don't have to have any kind of access system for it, for example — the question then arises of how to verify the content. How do you know that materials in a dark archive are good if they're not being used? 'Use it or lose it' is a real concern in the digital realm — the idea that if something is not used, there will not be a high level of confidence that the material is usable and viable. Not only the archive, but the subscribers and the intellectual community as a whole who are relying on that archive, must be confident that its content is, in fact, being reliably and usably preserved for the future.

If the archive is accessible in some way, then what level of access should be supported? It's unlikely that an archive can provide the kind of functionality that a publisher would provide for content that is current. Not only would that be incredibly costly, but also it's also likely to be regarded as competitive with the publisher's own business. If there is going to be a more modest level of access, what is that level and how do you control the costs?

And if there is access, when is it enabled? This isn't an either/or proposition; it might involve a particular condition. We've talked with publishers about 'sunrise' conditions for the material in our archive. Our thinking is that the archive might become accessible at some point in time or under certain conditions. For example, perhaps a subscribing institution that has a perpetual license or that has negotiated the right to procure copies can come to the archive and say "Here's my license; it says I can have copies, now hand them to me please." In such a scenario, our archive might deliver content through a batch process in which we hand off a large set of files in some format to be made accessible elsewhere. Or, perhaps we would provide direct online service to any subscriber who could demonstrate a right to that material. Yet again, perhaps the archive would make material broadly available to anyone when a particular trigger event occurred. If so, what might such a trigger event be? One such trigger might be a defined period of elapsed time, such as one year or N years after publication. The idea of opening up journal content to the world after some defined period of time has arisen in various communities, through the Public Library of Science and PubMed Central initiatives, among others. That notion — tied in part to the idea that commercial value declines over time — may be very controversial with publishers, but it's not necessarily controversial with every publisher. High Wire Press now makes content freely available on its site within one year after publication, for example. Or maybe the trigger event is a failsafe of some sort, such as when access is no longer commercially available online — because the publisher goes out of business, or sells a title to another publisher without transferring ownership of the backfiles to the new publisher.

The phrase 'no longer commercially available online' poses an interesting definitional problem. Is material in an aggregated database commercially available online, or does that only apply to availability as a distinct title, something that can be subscribed to individually? Or yet again, is 'no longer commercially available online' defined simply as 'whenever the publisher says so'? We've experienced some major pushback on this issue from some of our publisher partners. We tend to see our archival role as one that is consonant with our broader mission to make published content available to future scholarship. This is a cultural issue for libraries as well as a definitional one. Are we preserving the object, or are we preserving access to that object?

Let's now leave one sticky question — the question of access — for another: what content is deposited to the archive? When people think about electronic journal archiving, they frequently think only of articles. But when you look at an electronic journal web site, or at a print journal, you find many things besides articles. There may be supplementary materials online that are not in the print version and that are not part of the online article per se. But there are also many things that we more commonly think of as front matter —editorial boards, subscription terms, instructions to authors, and so forth. We've done a lot of thinking about these kinds of categories, and expect that handling them will be challenging. And what about advertising — is it the role of an institution that is archiving scholarly content to also archive the advertising? Advertising in print journals can be important for scholarly research, in order to study what was advertised in particular fields at a particular point in time. While having access to advertising may be important for some purposes, in the electronic realm where such information is dynamic and usually delivered by third parties, this can be a very difficult thing to archive.

This is a brief laundry list of content categories that we've identified in the journals that we've examined, both online and in print:

- description of the journal

- information about the editorial board

- instructions to authors

- copyright information

- conference announcements

- errata

- reviewer list

- editorials

- discussion for a —should we be archiving discussion fora that might be tied to a particular article?

As you can see, we're thinking about a lot more than just articles.

Then there are issues surrounding the format of the material that we're archiving. The OAIS Reference Model defines something that it calls a Submission Information Package, or SIP, which refers to the format in which content and metadata would be delivered to an archive. The model assumes that material will be ingested by an archive in a particular format and that the archive might then transform that content into another format for internal use. How many different submission formats would an archive have to support to accommodate different publishers, and how many submission formats would a publisher have to support if it were exporting material to multiple archives? Obviously this could become a very costly proposition for both sides. So, we're looking at the possibility of standardizing submission formats across publishers as a means of streamlining procedures and containing costs. We're also looking at Document Type Definitions (DTDs) for articles that are in XML or SGML. Right now many different document DTDs for journal articles exist within the publishing community. Is it possible to standardize on a single, archival DTD that might serve as a lower common denominator, one which foregoes some of the functionality of a publisher's own format but is 'good enough' for archiving? We're working with a consultant right now to examine a variety of article DTDs to determine whether there are elements of commonality that could serve as a basis for a common archival DTD.

What about the format of the articles themselves? Many journal articles are published not in SGML or XML, but in PDF, and there are other article formats in use as well. Some publishers render articles in multiple formats. Would the archive need to accept all of those formats, and what are the pros and cons of doing so? There are certainly increased costs in taking multiple formats.

If we accept multiple formats for articles and other types of material, which of those can we actually preserve? It's not clear that everything can be preserved and made usable. We think that articles in SGML and PDF probably can be made usable over time. We certainly hope so, because that is the core of the journal content that we're trying to preserve. But what about much of the supplementary material that's being deposited? Today's editors accept supplementary material of many types and in many formats from academic authors. Very few standards are imposed on an author with regard to the format of deposited material, which can range from Excel files to SPSS files to just about anything in between and beyond. Can an archive reasonably be expected to preserve and migrate an unlimited number of diverse formats? If that isn't realistic — and we think it isn't — then perhaps we need to identify the formats that a particular archive can migrate and those that the archive either can't or chooses not to preserve and migrate, and leave the latter to what we're calling 'digital archaeology' — we preserve the bits and assume that whoever wants to use that material later on will be able to parse those bits and render the material.

And, finally, the economic model for an archive is still a big unknown. We need to figure out what archiving is going to cost. Although we don't have the cost picture fully in view yet, we're working hard on it and recognize that this is going to be one of the most important ingredients in the ability of an archive to sustain itself over time. Limiting these costs would seem to be particularly important for an institution that is attaching this activity to its other activities. We've been gratified to discover that our publishing partners seem to be prepared to assume a fair amount of the cost of preparing digital materials and delivering them to the archive. Quite frankly, we weren't sure at the outset of the project whether publishers would voluntarily embrace the responsibility of converting data into a form that we could accept. I think we're making good progress in those discussions. But operating the archive will still entail substantial costs. Who should bear those costs? We've talked with some of our partners about the idea of a dowry to pay for archiving, which might come from the publisher, or from a scholarly society on whose behalf material is being published and archived. There is some precedent for a dowry approach to preservation funding among some of the publishers with whom we've been in discussions. Ultimately though, we expect that these costs will be passed on to subscribers in one form or another. We're very interested to discover whether the subscribing community will, either explicitly or implicitly, prove willing to pay for archiving.

In the brief time that we've had this morning, I hope I've managed to give you a flavor of some of the issues that Harvard has been grappling with in its planning for an electronic journal archive. We're grateful to the Mellon Foundation for supporting us in this groundbreaking experiment. The opportunity to engage in this process has been an exciting one and has taught us a great deal. It's been a pleasure to share some of that with you here in Charleston today.

LOCKSS: LOTS OF COPIES KEEP STUFF SAFE CREATING A PERMANENT WEB PUBLISHING AND ACCESS SYSTEM

Vicky Reich, Chief of Serials Department, Stanford University

(a version of this paper will appear in the November 2001 issue of the
U.K. Publication Serials)

Summary: LOCKSS (http://lockss.stanford.edu) stands for Lots of Copies Keep Stuff Safe. It is an Internet "appliance", or "easy to use" software, designed to preserve access to authoritative versions of web-published materials. The current version of LOCKSS software is restricted to electronic journals.

LOCKSS allows individual libraries to take custody of content in all formats delivered via HTTP, and safeguard their community's access it. Using LOCKSS a library can ensure that, for there readers, hyperlinks continue to resolve and content is delivered even when in the Internet those links don't work and the content is no longer available. LOCKSS ensures the locally held content maintains its integrity through a polling and reputation system; LOCKSS replicas cooperate to detect and repair preservation failures. LOCKSS is designed to run on very cheap hardware and to require almost no technical administration. The software will be distributed as open source.

Problem: Web published materials are increasingly the authoritative versions. There are no affordable, widely available techniques for preserving this "written record". The web is an effective publishing medium (data sets, dynamic lists of citing papers, e-mail notification of citing papers, hyperlinks, searching). As web editions increasingly become the 'version of record', paper versions of the same titles are merely a subset of peer reviewed scholarly discourse. Librarians need an inexpensive, robust mechanism that they control, to ensure their communities maintain long-term access to this important literature.

Requirements: The solution to this problem is in three parts:

1. The content must be preserved as bits;
2. Access to the bits must be preserved;
3. The ability to parse and understand the bits must be preserved.

There is no single approach to solving this problem. Any single solution would be perceived as vulnerable. By proposing LOCKSS we are not discounting other digital preservation solutions, other solutions must also be developed and deployed. Diversity is essential to successful preservation.

Technical Details: LOCKSS uses off-the-shelf open source software to manage aweb cache at each library for each journal the library wishes to safeguard, and to pre-load the cache with the pages of the journal as they are published. Thus pages will be preserved even if they aren't read. Through these caches each library takes physical custody of selected Web journals it purchases. Unlike normal caches, pages in these caches are never flushed; the caches grow indefinitely as the journals continue to publish. Over time, the disks holding an individual cache will fill up or fail. Librarians will be able to replace full or failed disks without interruption to the system nor will they loose access to any data previously cached.

A key innovation is the way LOCKSS caches detect and recover from failures, how the system ensures data preservation. They use a newly designed inter-cache protocol called LCAP [Library Cache Auditing Protocol]. LCAP allows caches to conduct "opinion polls" which provide assurance that the local copy of all or part of a journal matches the majority of other copies, and provide a lower bound on the number of other copies in existence. If a cache detects that its content is incomplete or otherwise corrupt it asks the publisher or one of the other caches to provide a replacement copy. LOCKSS caches respect publisher's access control mechanisms, they will only provide content to caches that have proved in the past that they had a copy. The publisher web site's access to end user "click A library's does not affect stream" data LOCKSS cache.

Depository Models: There are two approaches to digital preservation and archiving: centralized and decentralized. Key questions are - what are the costs of preserving what kinds of materials and on whom do they fall?

A decentralized system has a large number of loosely controlled repositories. Each repository or node in the system a) does some but not the whole job of preserving the content b) uses relatively inexpensive hardware c) needs relatively little technical expertise to maintain the hardware and software. The content at each repository is in constant use, under constant scrutiny, and undergoing continual repair. In a decentralized system, the publishers take little or no action to preserve the content they publish; the librarians take action to preserve access for their local communities. Librarians bear the costs of digital preservation but the costs are spread across many participants and only the participants' gain value from the system.

A centralized system has a small number of tightly controlled repositories. Each repository a) does the entire job b) requires large expensive hardware and c) sophisticated technical staff. Content is accessed after a "trigger" event (migration, publisher failure, etc.). To establish a centralized system, publishers and librarians must take cooperative legal and data management actions. The costs of preservation are borne by a few.

We predict some combination of these approaches will ultimately be implemented.

Three Perspectives: Readers, Librarians, and Publishers

The Reader's Perspective. A key goal of the LOCKSS system is to preserve a reader's access to content published on the web. Readers expect two kinds of access. They expect that:

1. When they click on a link to it, or type in a URL, the relevant page will be delivered with minimal delay and no further interaction.

2. When they enter terms into a search engine that should match the relevant page, it will be among the returned matches.

Readers who use the web are learning that if a link doesn't resolve to a page, or a search engine can't find a page, further attempts to find the information the page carries are unlikely to be worth the effort. This poses problems for those who use preservation techniques that concentrate on preserving bits; the bits may be preserved yet the reader may not know how to access them, or even that the preserved bits exist.

In contrast, the design of LOCKSS focuses on preserving the service of having links resolve to, or searches to find the relevant content. An institution using the LOCKSS system to preserve access to a journal in effect runs a web cache devoted to that journal. Readers use the cache as a proxy in the normal way. At intervals the LOCKSS cache crawls the journal publisher's web site and pre-loads itself with newly published (but not yet read) content. Just as other types of caches are invisible to their users, so are LOCKSS caches. They transparently supply pages they preserve even if those pages are no longer available from the original publisher's web site.

An institution can include the contents of the cache among the pages indexed by its local search engine, and provide its readers with searching across all the journals to which it subscribes. At present, readers typically have to search individual collections of journals separately.

The Librarian's Perspective. Librarians subscribe to journals on behalf of their readers in order to provide both immediate and long-term access. With the advent of the web, for the most part libraries are forced to lease rather than own the web-based content. Leasing provides immediate access but carries no guarantee of long-term access. Some journals provide their peer reviewed content through off line storage media (tape, CD-ROM, paper), but then links don't resolve and searching is harder to accomplish.

A major flaw with web publishing is that there has been no mechanism to implement the traditional purchase-and-own library model. The LOCKSS system is demonstrating that it is both easy and affordable to operate a purchase model for web journals. The subscribing library bears costs analogous to the costs of putting paper copies on shelves, keeping track of them and lending or copying them as needed. A library using LOCKSS caches to preserve access to a collection of journals pay for the equipment and staff time to run and manage a cache containing the full content of the journals. Unlike normal caches, the LOCKSS cache is never flushed and, over the long term, the full content remains accessible.

Because individual libraries must pay for the preservation of the content to which they subscribe, it is essential that the price they pay be as low as possible. LOCKSS software is free and open-source. It is designed to run on inexpensive hardware. The machines the LOCKSS team is using for the beta test cost less than $800 each and each machine is capable of storing the content of 5 years worth of a major journal's issues.

Running a LOCKSS cache requires so little staff time that one alpha test site complained they learned nothing about the system over the course of 10 months while running it. The low cost and democratic structure of the LOCKSS system - each copy is as valuable as any other — empowers smaller institutions to take part in the process of digital preservation.

In normal operation, an ordinary cache will only act as a proxy for, and thus supply content to, the host institution's own readers. But in a rough analog of inter-library loan, LOCKSS caches cooperate to detect and repair damage. If damage to a page is detected, the LOCKSS cache fetches a copy of the page from the publisher or from another cache. A LOCKSS cache will only supply a page to another LOCKSS cache if the requesting cache at some time in the past proved that it had the requested page. In this way, LOCKSS prevents freeloading. Those who contribute to the preservation of the journal are rewarded with continued access; those who do not contribute to the journal's preservation are not provided with replacement pages.

The Publisher's Perspective. Publishers want to maintain journal brand and image. They want material available for future society members and other subscribers. Most publishers will save money and serve their readers better if the transition to electronic-only journals can be completed. They want to encourage libraries to purchase and/or activate online versions of journals. One major obstacle to libraries purchasing online journals is resistance to the rental model with its lack of credible assurance of long-term access.

Many publishers are unhappy with a purchase model for electronic journals. They fear the journal content will be illegally replicated, or leaked, on a massive scale once copies are in the custody of others; they want their access control methods enforced. They want to retain access to reader usage data and have access to the record of the reader's interactions with their site.

The LOCKSS system solves the reader's and the librarian's problems. It enables librarians to collaborate to preserve readers' access to the content to which they subscribe, but it also addresses the publisher's concerns. Because content is provided to other caches only to repair damage to content they previously held, no new leakage paths are introduced. Because the reader is supplied preferentially from the publisher, with the cache only as a fallback, the publisher sees the same interactions they would have seen without LOCKSS caches.

The LOCKSS design has other advantages from the publisher's perspective:

It returns the responsibility for long-term preservation, and the corresponding costs, to the librarians. Although publishers have an interest in long-term preservation, they cannot do a credible job of it themselves. Failures or changes in policy by publishers are the event librarians are most interested in surviving.

Publishers could run LOCKSS caches for their own journals and, by doing so, over time could audit the other caches of their journals. A non-subscriber cache would eventually reveal itself by taking part in the damage detection and repair protocol. The mere possibility of detection should deter non-subscribers from running LOCKSS caches. Just as the publisher cannot be sure he has found all the caches, the caches cannot be sure none of the other caches belongs to the publisher.

Project Status:

The Alpha test. The LOCKSS project started in 1999, funded by NSF, Sun Microsystems, and Stanford Libraries. The Alpha software was tested in year 2000 with ~15 caches of ~160MB from AAAS Science Online. Alpha sites were Stanford, U.C. Berkeley, LANL, Tennessee, Harvard and Columbia. The basic mechanisms of the software work. The system survived a fire at LANL, network problems at Stanford, relocation of the machine at Berkeley, and flaky hardware at Columbia.

The Beta test. The worldwide beta test began 4/2001, funded by the Andrew W. Mellon Foundation, Sun Microsystems, and Stanford Libraries.

As of September 2001 48 participating libraries in five continents have signed onto the project; 54 publishers are endorsing the LOCKSS beta test (see http://lockss.stanford.edu/projectstatus.htm

The beta is testing LOCKSS security, usability, and software performance, including impact on network traffic. The publisher's web sites are simulated on shadow servers (~10-15 GB of PNAS, JBC, BMJ, Science Online) to isolate LOCKSS data streams and measure network traffic and test if the system works when the publisher "goes away". If resources allow, we plan to add to this test bed content from other publishers, particularly those who publish materials on publishing platforms not yet represented in the LOCKSS system.

Each beta site has a slightly different machine(s) and network configuration. Each one is currently running LOCKSS software version 06122001 and is participating in testing. For most libraries, the software was easy to install and is easy to maintain. This phase of testing however revealed the challenge of building a system to work easily with different international network configurations. These challenges have been met.

Formalized software testing has begun (see http://lockss.stanford.edu/softwarelbetateststatus.htm). The beta test, if funding allows, is scheduled to run to summer 2002.

DISCIPLINE-BASED PORTALS: THE NEW CONTENT MEDIATORS

By Ruth Fischer and Rick Lugg, Partners, RL Consulting

Libraries exist to discover, organize, preserve, and deliver relevant content. Subject expertise is an obvious and critical factor in the library's ability to perform well. Equally important is the library's ethical orientation towards dispassionate, balanced, and unobstructed access to authoritative information. In this confounding, increasingly digitized information environment, and as discovery and delivery tools are fast evolving, it is more important than ever that the library maintain its key role in the selection process. Commercial content mediators (middlemen in the distribution chain) can support or replace the librarian. Let's advocate for the former.

Current Model for Content Identification, Acquisition and Access

Content mediation in the current library environment is primarily format-based. The diagram below is an oversimplification of this format-based model, with the librarian at the hub maintaining relationships with materials vendors who sell content in specific digital and print formats. For example, book vendors sell in-print monographs in all subject areas, moving slowly now to include OP and eBooks. The library typically establishes a complex contract (subject profile) with one or more book wholesalers. Likewise, the library must maintain independent relationships with serials vendors, database providers, video wholesalers, eBook sellers, bookstores, and increasingly (again) with individual publishers. In each case, the library must make important decisions about the depth and breadth of coverage desired in each discipline. Beyond these traditional relationships, the library must establish a series of new relationships with web-based content providers that may or may not duplicate the content already acquired via traditional sources.

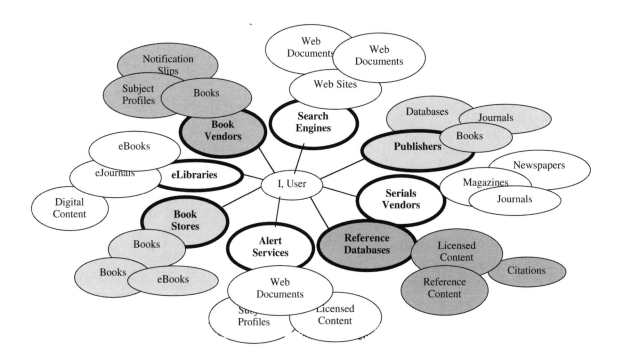

Evolving Model for Content Identification, Acquisition and Access

We examine here, in recognition of the trend, a different model for the identification and acquisition of relevant content for the library. Again the library is at the hub of the process, but instead of working with traditional format-based mediators, we observe a move toward a new kind of discipline-based mediation. Rather than book or serials vendors for example, we are curious about the possibility of **discipline-based portal providers**. If the content is consistently credible, we don't care and library patrons don't care about its original format or distribution channel. Depending on the discipline and the local user community, certain kinds of content and interface tools would be more or less appropriate and would be included in the portal according to the library's collection development policy. These subject portals could be designed at the "selector-level", meaning that collection development librarians would determine the breadth and depth of treatment necessary for each of their disciplines. As well, subject portals should be hyper linked and cross-referenced to support wide ranging interdisciplinary activity (see the cross-hatches below).

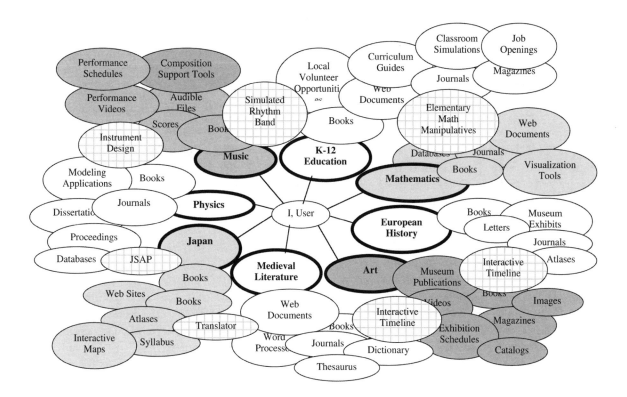

Working Definition

When we say PORTAL, we mean a web-based service, hosting digital content and/or digital metadata that has been "selected" from disparate print and electronic sources. The sources should include but not be limited to the local catalog, other library catalogs, vetted websites, locally licensed full-text databases, abstracting/indexing databases, digital images, film clips, audio files, applet archives, public domain materials, and finding aids for special and non-digital local collections. (To some extent, the degree to which the content comes from disparate sources will help us judge the true value of a subject portal. Single publisher portals should be suspect in this regard.) The content will be selected by subject specialists for use by a specific audience, and structured to provide a synoptic view. The ongoing evaluation and maintenance of the content will be as important as the original selection process.

Benefits

The benefits to this approach are significant. The end user is the primary beneficiary insofar as his/her experience of library research will be dramatically simplified by way of a single search interface which is format and source blind, and a single, integrated, ranked, hyper linked search result. Authoritative selection by experts will ensure an institutionally appropriate view of the information landscape. Apt functionality (interface tools) for each discipline can be integrated with the digital text, images, and data sets available via the portal. In addition to the assumed hyperlinks and cross-references within and between all relevant sources, these interface tools will enhance interactivity by including context sensitive help, reader software, word processors, citation support tools, course syllabi, structured discussions, various data mapping and modeling applications, simulators, and perhaps even elements of virtual reality, hereby establishing true online learning environments.

If all the material within a particular discipline was coordinated in this way, the inefficiencies of duplicated content could be eliminated. If the library were to outsource the technical development and design of their portal(s), the selector could be freed again to focus on the content rather than the various modes and costs of delivery.

Environment

Several loosely related observations lead us to believe that the environment is conducive to this approach. First, and despite the immediate lack of clarity concerning realistic business models and workable market channels, more and more content is being digitized by commercial conversion houses, publishers, and other content owners including libraries themselves. Second, students are more and more likely to **USE GOOGLE FIRST.** They expect the content they need to be available on the web, and even when it is less than adequate, they use it. Third, commercial content providers are "adding value" through links that may be richer than those provided by the library. High quality interconnectivity is critical to the scholarly endeavor, and digital connectivity has already surpassed the library's traditional (call it) organizational connectivity in terms of speed and convenience. Fourth, lots of tools and platforms are being developed to allow for the creation, operation and maintenance of discipline-based portals. Many are specific to the library and other educational environments.   Finally and most convincingly, discipline-based portals from both the commercial and scholarly sectors and are already being purchased and/or accessed through/by the library.

Examples

To a large extent, the following subject portals fit our own definition and are listed here as evidence of the trend.

- Books 24x7 provides integrated online access to monographic content related to information technology. It is designed for students and professional researchers.
- Questia provides integrated online access to books and journal articles in the Liberal Arts, enhancing its usability with integrated term paper writing software. It is designed for undergraduates with term paper assignments.
- Univ of Virginia American Civil War Collections provides integrated online access to letters, texts, images, diaries, newspapers and websites related to the Civil War. It is intended for a broad audience.
- DOE Distributed Search Subject Portals provide integrated online access to Department of Energy Reports, National Renewable Energy Laboratory Archives, and PubSCIENCE. 10-12 separate portals are each focused on a single source of renewable energy. They are designed for professional researchers.
- Columbia Earthscape provides integrated online access to books, journals, datasets, web sites, seminars, conferences, modeling systems, and teaching tools related to the earth sciences. It is designed for four discrete user groups.
- MD Consult provides integrated online access to medical books, journals, MEDLINE, drug information, clinical practice guidelines, personalized clinical updates and patient handouts. It is designed for practitioners.
- Xrefer provides integrated online access to a wide variety of general reference books from 20+ publishers. It is designed to meet basic reference needs.
- The Scholarly Electronic Publishing Weblog provides a very current, edited bibliography of resources related to electronic publishing, including citations for print books, full-text online, web sites, government documents, presentations, dissertations, listserv links and listserv extracts. It is designed for high-level researchers and professionals.
- ElementK provides online learning tools and digital resources related to Information Technology, Business, and Corporate Management. It is designed for corporate learners.
- MIT Cognet provides integrated online access to a growing number of texts related to the brain and cognitive sciences. This portal provides access to works from the MIT Press, as well as content and links to resources from other publishers, professional associations, institutions, and individuals who are willing to share public access to online work. It is designed for high level scholars and researchers.
- Knovel offers online access to several highly interactive reference books in engineering and science. It is designed for intermediate and advanced researchers.

Portal Projects

Several libraries and library "communities" have undertaken major initiatives to build their own discipline-based portals. Two are described briefly:

- Part of the development program of the Distributed National Electronic Resource in the UK (DNER), is a three year project to develop a set of subject portals. "This project aims to enhance resource discovery by developing a series of portals focused on the requirements of end-users in a variety of learning environments." (http://www.ariadne.ac.uk/issue29/clark/)

- "The ARL Scholars Portal Working Group recommends the construction of a suite of web-based services that will connect the higher education community as directly as possible with quality information resources that contribute to the teaching and learning process and that advance research. Central to the Scholars Portal service is a discovery tool that enables a user to search across certain limited but diverse and distributed websites, library catalogs, and databases of information resources to retrieve and integrate the results in a single presentation." (http://www.arl.org/access/scholarsportal/)

Technology in Support of Portals

Out-of-the-box portal solutions, discrete tools, and emerging standards/protocols have become prominent. All of the major library automation and web technology firms are scrambling to help libraries manage their digital assets. Again, examples are listed here as further evidence of the trend:

- **System Solutions**

  - Fretwell-Downing's Zportal allows the library to design the content of their portal to best suit their needs by including only the specific library catalogues, internal databases, intranet/internet web search engines, full-text databases and online services which fit their requirements.
  - Innovative Interfaces MetaFind offers a meta-search capability across the library's defined information resources, including licensed full-text or citation databases, web sites, search engines, Z39.50 databases, library catalos, and local digital collections. The grouping of the information resources is configurable by the library; different looks can be offered to different groups within the library. Innovative Interfaces has partnered with MuseGlobal to power this product.
  - ExLibris' MetaLib is a platform for managing a hybrid library environment, including digital and print resources in local and remote databases. It provides a standardized user interface and portal and is powered by two new technologies--the Universal Gateway and SFX. The Universal Gateway ensures accurate and target-sensitive searching and employs an intelligent analyzer to convert user requests into target specifications, and target data into user formats. SFX provides a host of contextual links to related information after performing an intensive, automated analysis of a document.
  - Sirsi's iBistro is an Internet access portal for library users. Its distinguishing feature is its capacity to integrate related content in a unified display through simultaneous, broadcast searching.

- Endeavor's ENCompass and LinkFinderPlus is an independent, OpenURL-enabled linking solution, which will allow comprehensive linking of all library resources, regardless of the software or information vendor. LinkFinderPlus will also integrate with the Voyager integrated library management system and the ENCompass digital organization, management and discovery tool. It will function with other linking initiatives, including CrossRef. Available in early 2002.
- Epixtech's iLibrary will allow patrons to connect to a variety of information, such as the electronic systems inside a library, integrated library systems, available databases, and community bulletins and resources, along with internet information such as e-mail, top news stories, and a variety of other information available over the internet. This product will be offered in a portal format and will provide library patrons with consolidated Internet information along with library information in a single consolidated view.
- VTLS' Virtua ILS has been developed to serve as a central library portal, providing users with a simple and intuitive interface to search and browse through merged collections. After potentially relevant items are discovered, a user can follow the links provided to go directly to the items in their source archives.
- Geac's GeoWeb provides web-based access to internal and external Z39.50 databases.
- BiblioMondo's Digital Connect is a new resource control/library portal product to allow every digital resource to be accessed and controlled from the desktop.
- Northern Light's Single Point integrates, manages, and searches content from the Web, from third-party content providers and from internal sources. It has distinctive capabilities around content integration, search, classification, and customization.

- **Enabling Tools**

  - SFX is a new server-based product that allows users to search a database and click on a resulting citation to search it automatically in other databases.

  - CrossRef is a collaborative (DOI-based) reference linking service through which a researcher can click on a reference citation in a journal and immediately access the cited article. To date, there are 88 publishers participating in CrossRef, accounting for over 5,410 journals with over 3.7 million article records in the database. There are also a number of affiliates and library affiliates participating.

  - Threaded Discussions are online, text-based discussions on a particular topic or within a particular discipline. Dozens of software packages are available now to support threaded discussions, which are specifically non-linear. A message can either kick off a new thread or serve as a reply to a thread already posted. The user can pinpoint and respond to specific messages and responses, expand or collapse threads, skip over tangential conversations, and view thread headers as a quick way to grasp the gist of a discussion.

- Web Logs are sites of personal or non-commercial origin that use a dated log format, updated on a daily or very frequent basis with new information about a particular subject or range of subjects. The information can be written by the site owner, gleaned from other web sites or other sources, or contributed by users.

- **Relevant Standards/Protocols**

  - Z39.50 is a search and retrieval protocol that integrates access to information maintained in distributed databases.
  - The Digital Object Identifier (DOI) is a proposed standard that supports the use and management of increasingly granular content.
  - Open URL is a proposed syntax for packaging metadata and DOIs, and for pointing to a user-specific resolver that can accept this packaged data, combine it with user information, and resolve the data into actual links.
  - The Open Archive Initiative is a proposed protocol, which governs the exposition of metadata, providing a framework for cross-repository interoperability.
  - Dublin Core is a fifteen element standard for cross-discipline metadata, intended to aid resource discovery on the web.
  - ONIX is the international standard for representing and communicating book industry product information in electronic form.

I, User

We patrons already know a lot about the potential benefits of working with fully integrated and immediately accessible digital content. We already choose web content over library archives. Technical solutions exist now to provide the broadcast search and consolidated retrieval services that we want, integrating content and tools from a wide variety of disparate sources. If libraries fail to take the lead here, commercial entities will step into the breach, perhaps changing the character of relevant content discovery and delivery.

Librarians should indeed step forward and remain central to the selection process, but they need not stand-alone. They need not reinvent the wheel (subject portal) in every library. The commercial tools, protocols, and taxonomies mentioned above can be well utilized to build the next generation of library-governed collections. New and inspired partnerships could emerge here, between for-profit mediators and not-for-profit scholarly and research institutions. We just all need to remember (and do) what we're good at.

Collection Development remains the backbone of the Charleston Conference. The papers in this section reflect not only the important issues relative to traditional collection development practices, but show an increased focus on new challenges including approval plans, browsing collections, disaster planning and dealing with the aftermath of a natural disaster, and new electronic formats. Responding to the needs of library users is the utmost service priority for librarians even as the perception of the library may change in the users' minds.

Collection Development

Mass Purchase Versus Selection

David Kohl, Director, University of Cincinnati Digital Press

Although the title of this session is Aggregators and Selectors, the specific question that we are examining today is the issue of mass selection versus title by title selection and how well the traditional model of title by title selection is working to benefit libraries and their patrons in today's world. As most of us know, there are two problems with the traditional model. One is economic, i.e. we can't afford it, and as a result are canceling titles across the country. The other is that it really doesn't work all that well in fully providing the materials our patrons want and need.

Perhaps the best way to begin is to quickly review how we got into this situation. As most of you know all too well, libraries and publishers have been sparring with each other for about fifteen years. Increasingly, libraries have felt under siege as they have paid more and more but gotten less and less. I think this is fairly well known and has certainly been well documented by the ARL statistics. But in addition to widespread cancellation of titles by libraries, there is a more fundamental problem that is facing us. As Figure 1 shows, the real problem with the traditional title-by-title model was that we really weren't buying that many journals to begin with.

When we did a study in Ohio, in this case of 18 core academic publishers, we looked at the potential number of titles useful to the faculties of our 13 largest universities compared to the titles from these publishers that were actually being provided by each library. As you can see, we discovered that even the largest library — at Ohio State University — was providing only a bare majority of the potentially useful titles. The University of Cincinnati was hanging in there with about 40%. But the <u>average</u> number of titles being provided out of this larger, potentially useful universe of journal titles was around 25% statewide. When you're not buying 75% of the journals useful to your patrons, canceling a few titles begins to seem like a fairly minor problem. In other words, the real problem is not that we're losing access due to journal cancellations, but that we never had that much access to begin with. And that was part of the reason why OhioLINK decided that we needed to find a new purchasing model.

The new model has three basic elements. First of all, it's a consortia deal, not a single library proposition. Secondly, the idea is that you pay a <u>little</u> more, but get a <u>lot</u> more. Specifically, as is true of all OhioLINK deals, <u>all</u> of a publisher's journals were made available to <u>all</u> members of the consortium. And the third element is negotiated inflation. Rather than let inflation be publisher-driven, we were convinced that libraries would do much better by negotiating inflationary increases. Experience has proven this to be the case as most consortia have found that negotiated inflation is usually 2 to 3 per cent lower than inflation determined by the publisher alone.

Well, there were some skeptics about this model but we think we have some pretty interesting results. Let me give you a quick pair of examples from our very first deals. (See Figure 2) When we started, Ohio academic libraries had 1,140 subscriptions to Academic Press's 150 titles. (As you would expect, this composite number includes multiple subscriptions to the same title in different libraries.) After we arranged the deal these same libraries had access to a total of 9,100 titles. The Elsevier deal had even more dramatic results, increasing the effective number of Elsevier titles in Ohio academic libraries from 3,600 to 59,800 titles.

The second point involves what happens to costs. (See Figure 3) When you look at the average cost of an AP title before we did the deal, it was running just under $1,000 per title. After the deal was in place (because we had effectively so dramatically increased subscriptions), the average cost per title dropped to just over $100. With Elsevier you see an even more striking change — from $1,900 per title to $128 per title.

Well, there were still some problems that bugged us, two in particular. One was whether all this increased access would be used. After all, getting a bargain on something no one really wants or needs is hardly a bargain. The other concern was whether these big deals would crowd out the titles from the smaller publishers. As it turned out, neither concern was warranted. Somewhat to our surprise, when we investigated the first concern about use, we found that the new titles were in fact very heavily used as a group. (See Figure 4) When you added in that additional 75%, it turned out that that formerly ignored group of titles engendered more use than the 25% that we had originally selected. While it is true that the per capita use of the 25% was higher, the sheer number of new titles, three times as many, gave this new group the edge in total use. This documentation of surprisingly heavy use of a group of formerly ignored journals has not only been replicated several times by OhioLINK studies, but we now have information from the Greek National Academic Library Consortium, HEAL-Link, which shows the same results. The Taiwanese academic library consortium, CONCERT, has also reported similar findings. It's a very impressive revelation. Clearly, selection is nice, but more is better.

The second concern, crowding out the smaller publisher, also seems to be coming into a reassuring perspective. I must be honest and say we were initially a little worried about this ourselves when we began. But the reality turns out not to be bad at all. OhioLINK has probably done more "big deals" than anyone else in the country at this point. And yet, at the University of Cincinnati, which participates in all these deals, for example, only a quarter of our collections budget is tied up in these deals. That's the total figure. And in talking with other OhioLINK libraries, they report that their experience is about the same. That leaves three quarters of the budget to still do other materials. In fact, it even gets better.

Remember that part of the "big deal" is negotiated inflation. The "big deal" almost always a multiyear deal, not only ties money up, it also frees money up. Reducing inflationary costs through negotiation can result in substantial savings. For example, the first year we had our Elsevier deal in place, the Engineering librarian at Cincinnati came to me with a kind of astonished, but pleased, look and told me that the savings in inflation for her Elsevier titles alone would be around $50,000 in the coming year. For the first time in ages she was able to begin adding new Engineering titles to the collection.

The "big deal" as modeled by OhioLINK has other flexible elements as well. Probably the most important is a rebate for canceling print subscriptions and relying on electronic alone. Typically that reduction runs about 10%. It's not just a theoretical possibility since we do have some libraries that have canceled all their paper subscriptions and lived to tell the tale. In short, the "big deal" is just not that restrictive. And when you're arguing for new funds for the library collection, it is a much more persuasive argument to show that you can add titles rather than simply slow the rate of cancellations.

But as consuming as the economic concerns are to today's librarians, I would like to elaborate a bit further on that more basic topic: Are we providing as much access as our patrons need, want and deserve? Journals aren't the only area where we in OhioLINK have found an unexpectedly strong demand for formerly unavailable materials. As some of you already know, OhioLINK has substantially increased access to Ohio's book collection. All OhioLINK patrons have access to a collection of just over 24 million volumes. Our sharing of books, however, is not a traditional inter-institutional lending; it is not done through Interlibrary Loan. Sharing materials is handled simply as a circulation function. That means a person sees a book located anywhere in the state in the OhioLINK catalog and requests it just as if they were in a branch of their own library. Because it is so convenient, reliable, cheap and quick — 80% of the books are delivered within 48 hours — we have found inter-institutional book use skyrocketing.

In Figure 5 you can see the blue is the traditional OCLC/ILL book borrowing which contrasts to the red OhioLINK inter-institutional borrowing. As you can see, this latter has become a very substantial factor system-wide. At the University of Cincinnati our inter-institutional circulation has risen from less than 1% of total circulation under the traditional ILL system to around 25% of total circulation with OhioLINK sharing. The good job we thought we were doing before OhioLINK now appears very different to us. Here too we have discovered a huge unmet demand that we had been oblivious to. Increasing access to books was as important for our patrons as increasing access to journals. Clearly, our patrons want to live in a less restricted world than we had imagined.

So what is the library role given such information? I think we're going to be working out the details for some time to come. But some basic points seem clear.

The first thing I would say is that I think the traditional library approach to collection building has been far too timid and restrictive. I think that the information above pretty clearly indicates not that we have selected the wrong journals traditionally, but that we have not been selecting enough journals. We need to shift our emphasis from fine-tuning, from detailed selection, to finding ways of increasing access.

The second point I would make is that we need to be able to approach our funding sources with a positive argument for giving libraries more money. In the long run it will simply not be a successful strategy to ask for more money to buy less. The university administration will not invest significant new sums of money each year in the Titanic. The library needs to be able to argue that it has a winning strategy, one that increases access to materials, if it is to get the new funds it needs.

The third point I would suggest for your consideration is that collection building should be done with a broad brush. The sheer volume of materials, the range of formats, and the increasingly limited time of library staff certainly indicate that bibliographers need to work smarter, not harder. But the information presented above also suggests that librarians will do a better job of meeting their patrons' needs by creating a universe of possible materials and then letting the patrons select what they need, when they need them. Rather than title-by-title fine-tuning, perhaps we should consider more selection by appropriate categories, e.g. by subject, by publisher, by language, by level.

And lastly, following from the third point, perhaps librarians should experiment with using automation to involve patrons more directly and actively in collection choices. The experiment we began along these lines at OhioLINK was with netLibrary. (Sadly, now discontinued because of their bankruptcy!) Anyway, our experiment was to have the librarians select the general universe of books using such criteria as publisher, publication date, and subject area, which patrons could use. And then as patrons selected individual titles, a mechanism was in place that automatically purchased those books for the collection. The idea was that instead of having a faculty member or student come into the library and fill out a book purchase form or talk to a bibliographer and go through all that rigermarole, we would simply streamline the process. It was kind of like an Amazon.com. You see the thing, you want it; get it, it's yours — and the library's from now on.

In summary, I have tried to argue that we have two problems. There is the economic problem that we do need to resolve and I've suggested how we might approach that solution. But as pressing as the economic problem is, we need to keep in mind that there is a bigger problem we face — providing increased access. The good job we thought we were doing really hasn't been all that good. Our patrons need and deserve more from us — and ironically, that may just be the way out of our economic problem as well. Thank you.

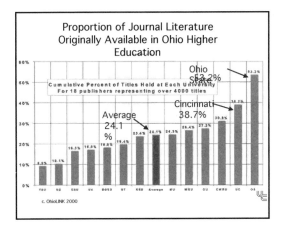

How Much Greater Access
to the Journal Literature

- Academic Press
  - Before: 1,140
    titles

  - After: 9,100
    titles

- Elsevier
  - Before: 3,600
    titles

  - After: 59,800
    titles

How Much Cheaper is the
Expanded Access

- Academic Press
  - Before: $964.91
    avg. cost per title

  - After: $132.97
    avg. cost per title

- Elsevier
  - Before: $1,944.44
    avg. cost per title

  - After: $ 128.76
    avg. cost per title

The New Titles Were
Heavily Used!

- Overall, 58% (502,000) articles were
  from journals not previously available
  at that institution vs. 42% from
  journals which were previously
  available, i.e. "selected" journals*

  - * based on 865,000 articles were downloaded
    June 1999 through May 2000
  - A second study based on 1,120,00 articles

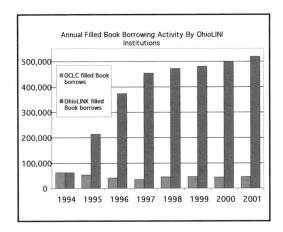

DEBATE: RESOLVED, THE ONLY REMAINING PURPOSE OF THE LIBRARY IS AS A SOCIAL CENTER

David Goodman, Biology Librarian, Princeton University and Chuck Hamaker, Associate University Librarian, Collections and Technical Services, University of North Carolina - Charlotte

Chuck Hamaker: For those of you who were here last year, or even if you weren't, if you haven't picked up the conference proceedings, one of the first pieces in there is the debate from last year between David and our good friend Anthony Ferguson who is in Hong Kong now. I consider it one of the highlights of last year. You might find it interesting to revisit and reading it this year, from a year's prospective, some things clearly Tony got right, some things David got right, and other things, we still don't know about. It is interesting reading. I'd like to quote David from last year (on page 41) — "One thing is clear from the current development of journals and electronic users of that electronic technology is that users need more guidance." That could serve as an underlying thesis for what we are about today. David and I have spent a little bit of time on e-mail figuring out what to tackle and we decided to start with:

One Catalog and One Collection for Every Library

David Goodman: I also want to mention that Barbara Winters asked me to remind you that if anyone should happen to get upset at what we say, there is a group therapy session scheduled two sessions from now.

We are not exactly having a debate in the same sense as last year because we discovered in this back and forth that there were only relatively small things that we disagreed about in to the extent of last year's debate, but this is sort of a discussion with looking at different aspects of things. Now, this first point, "One Catalog and One Collection for Every Library," which I think we both agree with to some extent, may sound like I'm a convert to OhioNet. But we should have available to everyone, and not just to everyone in the academic world, the total body of at least printed materials, not to speak of other media. We should get it, and we should control it, and it should be available to every person. Accomplishing this in a comprehensive fashion is going to take a very long period of time, but this the goal to which we are reaching and I think my disagreements there are mainly about the route to take in the immediate future. But it's clear that there's a general understanding that all academic libraries do need the basic academic journals. And I think there's a general understanding that all libraries, on some occasion, have use for almost another possible journal in the world. In addition to journals, the basic group of scholarly books and of non-scholarly contemporary books (at the least) is something that we hold in common even though we may have different pieces of it.

And I was led to this by looking over the last couple of years at how many of our users prefer to use OCLC or RLIN instead of our catalog because if we had the copy it would show up first and if we didn't, they would at least know it existed. And we're sort of proposing today that we should think this way in general ourselves. There may be a primary part of things that is local, just like there's a primary collection of books on our own personal shelves, but that this extends into the whole world of what we can make available. We realize the extension of adding titles from the aggregated databases to our catalog, many of which were not titles that in any real sense we owned, or titles from Ex Libris, meant that we were prepared to get any journal or book and therefore we should really list all of them in the catalog.

Chuck Hamaker: I had an interesting experience when I first went to UNC Charlotte. As I talked to the head of reference — we had an old basically text-based telnet session for an OPAC in 1998 — she said, "You know, in reference we don't really use our OPAC. We get more information from WorldCat than we do in our local catalog. As a result we seldom use the local catalog." That was sort of a shock to me. I thought well, maybe the answer is we just need to have a better local catalog. If we upgrade, and create a Web-based catalog they'll use it.

But from a one-catalog perspective, which is what reference was really talking, if I integrated that perspective into my local thinking, I could have less costs for shared cataloging, less staff, and support a wider range of information discovery. There may not be a future for individual OPACs. If you look at what's happening regionally and with consortia, the big push is for search the whole state with one button. This is an open enough question. If somebody's upset about me saying maybe we don't need what we're doing, please stand up and say it.

David Goodman: Right. Our intention is to have questions after every separate point as we go through and we'll spend the time where we need it. But I first want to mention, which I should have earlier, that doing this relies upon having an improved quality union catalog rather than the sort of multiple and inconsistent headings that one finds in OCLC or LC.

Chuck Hamaker: Well, if we were all working to perfect the same record, then we might have a little better chance of getting a consistent catalog. Isn't this controversial?

Audience: I think it's very interesting. You'd still have to have some piece of local control for circulation, interlibrary transport, whatever.

Hamaker: The stipulation is basically a database. You could run a separate little Oracle piece over here feeding off of that. In fact, right now, when we have to take our system down for maintenance, they crank the circulation stuff into a little handheld.

Goodman: Even in our own catalog now, we have an entry for the bibliographic item and then we have entry for copies. Electronic version, print, microfilm, copy in rare books, whatever, and the way I see this is the entry for the title including not just the Princeton copies and formats, but copies from the network, and so on.

Hamaker: You could get your own local holdings to show up first. That's no big deal.

Audience: From my local perspective, I totally agree. I find that our students prefer to go to a union catalog where they can put patron requests on any book that we don't own, get them very quickly, versus looking at our own catalog, which also tells them what the circulation state is. The only drawback for WorldCat is how fast can you get that material that you don't own.

Hamaker: As I said, when I started thinking about this in '98, I was appalled that reference librarians would rather go to a centralized WorldCat rather than to the OPAC version. But the more I thought about it, the more I tend to understand.

Audience: Well, this is just not provocative enough. I'm really disappointed with this love fest here. I'm going to say something provocative. I think the library should just shut down and the university should just contract with Starbucks for a cyber cafe and not worry about anything else.

Audience: By the way, we do have a Starbucks in our library now. It might work for some. At Texas A&M, we're maybe a little behind the times and we don't really belong to the big consortiums. Our problems is not people go to our catalog, WorldCat for everything, is that we just need to keep our OPAC up better. But we don't have a consortium that we can really go to or count on and our students use our OPAC heavily and maybe it's just our 44,000 Aggies aren't smart enough, but they just don't do it.

Goodman: Or maybe you should join one of the consortia, join RLG, for example, and there you'll be.

Hamaker: ASERL ... you know, I mentioned state and regional, ASERL -- Association of Southeastern Research Libraries, with its Kudzu system will do a search across all of the ASERL members who've agreed to be a member of the Kudzu system. They do a Z39.50 search maintained at Vanderbilt of Kudzu members to expedite ILL.

How many of you would like to see one catalog for the world? [About one-third of the audience raises hands.] Well, then, some of you do disagree with us.

Goodman: How many of you are prepared to go home and recommend doing this now? [Two or three people raise hands.]

Audience: Well, the issue isn't so much one catalog as one search for searching. I've always likened what we do when we're searching for information as like the game of Clue. In the game of Clue you can't ask a question until you get into the room where you can say was it Colonel Mustard with the rope in the billiard room and you have to actually get to the billiard room. And one of the problems with the game of Clue is that it's always supplied with one die so the longest part of the game is getting from room to room and most of us just added in another die so that we would move faster. And that's kind of what we've done now. We've added another die and we move faster. Instead of walking to the huge ERIC on print and then having to walk someplace else to use something else, we now just can move from one Silver Platter file to another except that we've made it more confusing by having all these things available on the same beige plastic box, searched different ways, done different ways. Is the talk really about one catalog or one index?

Goodman: Well, we're starting off with one catalog. The rest of it will come in the next couple of slides.

Audience: And now to argue against myself — what we do have with the individual collections is a selectivity that people will still come to us for. When one retrieves too much information, it's overwhelming.

Hamaker: You should be able to go to your local collection scoped with the one catalog approach. But with easy availability of the "one" and adding the global you've taken selection and advocacy of "your" resources and expanded them.

Audience: Selection to me is a type of advocacy. And what we found with things like aggregators, and I think this is a comparable case here, is that there are things that we like and there are things we don't like. And some of the things we've agreed to catalog and some things we've agreed not to catalog because we don't want that stuff to show up in there. And I'm afraid what you're doing is massively expanding the amount of material that you really don't want. That there's junk out there and that you have to be responsible for that in some way. And that gets back to an issue again of selection.

Tim Brown, cataloger from Wofford College: I was going to suggest that we allow a library to enhance those records in the world collection. At Wofford College we invite reference librarians, faculty and students to help us enhance records and we have much anecdotal evidence that this works in helping students find what they need. And we find too that different formats are cataloged with significant differing degrees of specificity. So to enable a student to find audio-visual materials, computer resources and books with one search we have to enhance records.

Goodman: I've added yours to my list of what we need to do.

Hamaker: The common example I always give is we had a really good focus group assessment, showed them the library home page, and their first question was where do I find the music? Sorry, you're out of luck with most library web pages, and OPACS.

Brown, Wofford: I might add to that with the help of public services and faculty members, we're bending some rules. We catalog in accordance with cataloging rules but we certainly do not hesitate to bend one.

Goodman: Our cataloging division, which has been known for decades for strict adherence to the rules, agreed last week that for electronic resources they were prepared to bend them to produce a more useful display. And what's more, they were prepared to let others than catalog librarians put records into the catalog.

Tom Izbecki, Johns Hopkins: As somebody who does a lot of reference, although I find the idea of an extended reach for our students fascinating, I also see the incredible possibility of this resembling looking for an icicle in a snowstorm. Therefore, I would like to raise the question of whether along with jettisoning MARC, we might not have to jettison our existing subject systems and develop something that works better for the subjects concerned in order to prevent the students from getting lost in the snowstorm, actually being able to get to something that works for them whether or not you're doing evaluation of these sources yourself.

Goodman: It's coming.

Izbecki: I think that's where we have to go if this is going to work.

"Bibliographic control must extend its remit, and collection management must no longer center on a locate-acquire-store-catalogue model but must move towards one which targets discover-access-facilitate (D-A-F)" [The publishing of electronic scholarly monographs and text books "Ray Lonsdale, DILS, University of Wales Aberystwyth & C.J. Armstrong, CIQM, http://www.ukoln.ac.uk/dlis/models/studies/

Hamaker: One of the slides I put up that we haven't discussed is that we have to stop centering on a locate-acquire-store and catalog model that is the one that we've been in and move to a discover-access-and facilitate model. I think that's probably part of the reason you wanted us up here.

Goodman: This is what several people have just proposed, and many of us are thinking. The role of people doing acquisitions is not to select material for the library to buy, but to select what material we want to enhance the access to and how we're going to do it. What I'm saying is not specific and the reason it's not specific is because on a broad scale, except for very special collections, I don't think we have any idea yet how to accomplish this. And, once more, I think the non-library side of the information profession may be much further ahead of us. And certainly I think all reference librarians have the same experience that the subject access which conventional library cataloging provides is even worse than the known item access. (In fact, this has been said for the whole century.)

Satisfying immediate demand--the new goal of collection dollars?
- **It's the Collection (1950's-1990's?)**
- **It's the Service (2000-?)**

Hamaker: Richard Abel has been talking about what librarians have been doing for quite a while. In fact, I think the conclusion on the book that you all picked up (edited by Lyman Newlin, Richard Abel, and Katina and Bruce Strauch) reminds us again that Dick has been saying for at least a decade that the job of librarians should be as assimilators, basically knowledge prospectors, putting things into a package that people love and specifically will look at. I think we got some of that this morning on the collaborative efforts in the scholars' workplace. We're not here talking about what is; we're talking very much where we think things are heading. And that fits into this. Does anyone want to respond to this? Actually, on one level this has always been our role. When it was in collection, that's what we were doing. Well, it's moved, and it's not the collection that's moved but the service. It's the service, it's the service. It used to be money, collection, and collections. It's now becoming service and the question of how we pay for it is another question.

Stephen Atkins, Texas A&M: I find this rather restrictive. I've been building collections for 25 years and very specialized collections. There's a lot on the Web but boy, I tell you, I can't depend on the Web. I do research and I do use the Web but I use a combination of databases, Web work, I use books, I use manuscripts, I use all sorts of things. My selectors and everything, I want them to get out and get the material and everything so that our historians and our English literature professors and everything, they're into textual criticism and things like that. That's not on the Web.

Hamaker: However, there are many libraries. I would guess there are some representatives in this room — I won't ask you to put your hand up — who will not catalog Web resources — period. There is at least one ARL library that will not permit cataloging of e-journals.

Richard Abel: I have felt for some years that libraries have turned altogether too much inward and devoted themselves too much to the organizational operational imperatives of their job and have forgotten in significant measure that what they are there to do is fundamentally to serve readers and users of information and knowledge. And that you have put together some marvelous systems that serve you marvelously well. And they serve readers, like me, very, very poorly. I really, really have to work — I'm working on another book right now, and I really, really have to dig to get the information that I need for this book and by and large, I cannot get much help from the librarians, I have to dig it up myself. And I would suggest to you people that you should be focusing much more on your audience — call it your audience, your readers, your users, whatever — those people out there, your students, your faculty, and lay people like me and what it is we require because if you do not, we are going to see a continuing growth that we already noted in the business community of so-called knowledge specialists or knowledge officers or some such name as that indicating that the corporations now have people in place who I would suggest are simply carbon copies in a corporate environment of reference librarians to whom their employees can turn to get the information you need. And you people are going to be made obsolete if you do not respond to that imperative of your users, your readers.

Hamaker: The popular phrase now is it's all about you. And I'm afraid that's where we are — it's all about you. That's the advertising lingo. We're not there.

Goodman: And we have to be there.

Hamaker: We started by interpreting the collection to you. That was my job. It wasn't my job to help you find information that you needed; it was to interpret to you how to use the collection. And in many instances we're still in that mode. It's now rapidly becoming it's all about you.

Abel: Yes. And I would like to add to that that looking beyond systems. I live in a suburb of Portland, Oregon. Near me is a little public library called Beaverton Public Library. The book I am working on right now — Guttenberg, the Renaissance and the Rise of the West — is compelling me to use all kinds of esoteric material on medieval and Renaissance history and so on. I'm getting all of that from interlibrary loan but I have to wait two and three weeks to get my hands on that material and when I do get my hands on that material, I only have it for two or three weeks before the expiration date set by the originating library says we want this book back in our library. Perfectly reasonable. I am trying to suggest to you therefore that something has to be done to deepen and broaden local collections because people like me are scattered all over this country and we need to have that kind of access when we have dug out what it is we need, that we be able to lay our hands on it and keep it and use it. I've got dozens of books that I've spent unbelievable amounts of time copying because I know that when I come to write I will not be able to have all those books sitting on my table when I write. So that's a second though.

Hamaker: I don't know about everyone else, but it's really good to see you Dick! (recognition of Richard Abel with a round of applause from the whole conference)

Goodman: Let me ask you — for the sort of thing you are doing, we have the real possibility of distributing this sort of material that you need in electronic versions on a basis where your local public library would have as much access for you as a state university library would or as the British Library would. Is this the sort of service that you would like?

Abel: If I'm going to receive the material electronically, I want it printed out. I want paper in front of me. I do not want a screen in front of me. I'm prepared to use a screen for 20 minutes to find out what it is I need, but I'm not prepared to use a screen for content and I don't believe it's just because I'm an old seventy six year old fogy. I believe it's because paper is just far too useful and too convenient and too comfortable.

Hamaker: Let me suggest to you. There is technically no reason for anything published before 1926 to ever be lent again. It could be scanned and sent to you as pdf files for you to print out any way that you want it. There is no legal reason that I know of for anything printed before 1926 not to be scanned on demand.

Goodman: There are, however, quite a lot of logistic problems that have not yet quite been solved.

Abel: I would add to that, however, that one of the things that proves very useful to me is what I was doing as an undergraduate at Reed College and that is going to the stacks and reading the stacks, not reading the catalog. I knew where the catalog was, but I preferred to go down to the stacks and start to read the stacks. I would really like to be able to do that now.

Anthony Watkinson: Bill, I want to say I had exactly the same experience. I was doing some research in an area of theology that wasn't an area I ever worked in but I had an idea and I had to give a paper. And I used the resources at Oxford that were terrible. They wouldn't let me into the theological faculty library at all. The stuff in the main body was awful. There were no bibliographical aids I could locate and they wanted me to follow through myself for the things I wanted. So I drove to Cambridge because I'm also entitled to use and I went into the stacks. And in just a day I managed to do everything because I could follow through the threads because the stuff was vaguely in the right area.

Hamaker: But actually you are in fast dwindling minority, to be honest. Graduate students don't want to go to the stacks.

Goodman: However, there are advantages to working this way at least occasionally and even for graduate students who don't, perhaps they ought to. But arranging for this on a physical basis that can be made available in every place is obviously difficult, but what I think we do need to do.— Again, I don't know how we can do it exactly, but I know we need to do it — is to provide the electronic equivalent of this kind of use as well. And, again, I don't think its librarians who are going to figure out how to do it. I think it is people working with things they're trying to sell that will figure out how to do it. But I think in maybe two years, three years, we may have this ability too. Besides an alphabetic view of the collection, we can offer, presumably, a shelf view of, let us say, the British Library. Well, that's not in classified order, so let's talk of a library which is in classified order, like the Library of Congress stacks, and where you can click on a book, open it, and if you want to, get a print out of that book.

Bill Russell, Emerald: I want to refer to two quite unexpected industries for this grouping. Just to start with a premise, everybody wants a solution to their problem and their locality whether it's their library, whether it's their state, whether it's their industry, whether it's their department. Looking at the two biggest industries in the world — the auto industry and the computer industry — both of those industries have looked to standardization to take out cost to solve their own problems. Looking at the car industry, which is one I know very well, the biggest marketplace and exchange of information. Around Ford, GM, Fiat, the big players sharing information on actual car components so they can take cost out and actually in the next five years, 3,000 parts per car will come out of the cost of the car because of that collaboration, because they're standardizing information so they're prepared to bury the hatchet, which is quite remarkable.

If you then look at Microsoft, and I don't want to get into the morals about whether Microsoft should be so big or so powerful, but as a manager, we are moving all our stuff or management information onto the Microsoft environment to take costs out and it gets our program as solving the problems that we need rather than having to create. We are therefore making the connections to solve our problems.

I'm on 18 months into the library world, but I think we're all trying to solve our own local problems, wherever that locality is. If world systems help people focus on their local connections, and their local flesh and blood connections, and getting ideas into people's brains, then I can only support what you're proposing, David and Chuck. A long answer, but good luck to you.

The Disappearing reference desk?
Reference service must be
where the user is.
the way the user wants it.
when the user wants it.
when the user needs it.

Goodman: Let me follow up your last sentence into this slide "The Disappearing Reference Desk," which is flesh and blood. We've been talking about systems. The greatest need that people using computer systems have is for personal assistance. And in the effort to save money over the last five or six years, all of the people in universities, administrators of libraries, have basically reduced this part of it. And the distinctive thing which librarians can provide, which I think human beings need in the world, at whatever level of sophistication, is the sort of service which we would categorize as reference. And my biggest concern about libraries at this point, is not that we won't be able to afford the materials, because we will contrive ways to get around it and get them as we've been talking for the last couple of days, but that funding and administrative agencies may try to reduce the amount of personal service which we give. And to me, the biggest danger of a physically disappearing library, and it is physically disappearing whether we like it or not, is that the users are leaving it for their quarters whatever we may choose to do, is the potential loss of this personal assistance. And this sort of expresses why we need the way in which it should be delivered.

Steven Atkins, Texas A&M: Now at Texas A&M we've devised a way of measuring user perceptions of the library. It's called LibQual. There are four components to it. One is place — do the people find the place a satisfactory place to work? Another component is their information needs. That happens to be the biggest component or the most important component to our users and this is from 43 different universities from around the country. They want the material to be arranged so that they can get it any way they want to but they want to do it themselves. They do not want an intermediary. They want it easy to access, but they want to be able to do it alone. They don't want any type of instruction. They want to be able to do it the simplest way possible. But they still want — down a little bit — but they still want the traditional collections. They want books, they want journals, paper and electronic. And these are still very important. I forget off-hand what the fourth one is. It's still important, but it isn't as important as the two — the access to information anyway they can get it, and the second is they still want collections.

Goodman: Yes. And, on the other hand, I hope, they do not want to give up when they have difficulties in getting it. There are going to be difficulties in the world and they presumably don't want to give up altogether. People with computer systems have formed the habit of asking for help when they run into trouble. We certainly give them help with computer systems, and are devoting considerable portions of our staff time to it. I do not see any way out of the dilemma you just raised. As the amount of the material increases, as the access to this increases, it will be more complicated to get to. And this leaves us with basically two choices — one is to restrict the effective access to material and the other one is to provide better ways of getting to it. And I do not think this can be done at this part of the century by an impersonal computer-driven model or by the best-designed non-human tools that we have the ability to design.

Jack Montgomery: I would agree with your last comment. I would also caution, Chuck, as much as I like you, to avoid making sweeping statements about people's use of research materials and who uses what. Be careful because in the minds of many people, this becomes a chorus that is not accurate. Faculty still — our faculty, outside of the hard sciences — value the monograph. They like the access to the journal but they value the monograph. We are still a monographic culture in academic in many schools. There are some exceptions — and in some departments too. It is almost discipline specific. It would depend on how the anthropologist was acculturated to use the system. Also, I'm scared that we will acculturate a whole group of people unwittingly to say there is no value beyond what I can get on my personal computer.

Hamaker: I don't think that we do that.

Montgomery: And yet we don't raise a real voice to add to that. And one other thing about service — you're quite correct. Service is our basic. I've worked in reference and I know that people still need guidance, especially — and I'm the man with the finger on the money, so I think money — I'm also Scottish — but if I'm paying $5 every time they open up an EBSCO host record, they're going to get my help because my budget goes out in April and I've got all the way until June or July to cover this, but I've got to pull money from elsewhere that has to be because none of this is going to say free.

Goodman: And the last three comments put together raise something which I think we do need to consider but which we did not put on our slides, is that people are different and use the library different ways and we have to provide for it. We have to provide for the people who will not ask for help, no matter what, as best we can. We won't be able to do it as well as for the people who are willing to ask, but we have to do something for them. We have to provide for the people who use books which technologically, in an electronic sense, has been a real challenge up to now, but we're reaching the point, we're right at the point, where it may not be much longer. We have to provide for the people in our large institutions and we have to prepare for the people who are not connected to institutions. And this makes it obviously all the more complicated and harder and we have to be prepared for the people who don't work our way and we have to be prepared in particular for those scholars who actually are scholars, who actually need to and should work with the printed objects.

Mary McClaren, University of Kentucky Libraries: Our library is one of the ARL libraries that did the LibQual. In one of the 12 main areas, we did fall below user expectations. That was one of the category rankings — and that was our OPAC. Now, I guess this both agrees and disputes your previous comments — number one is our OPAC isn't the one catalog for the collection. But the other is that the patrons do want to use it, and used it enough to know it didn't serve their needs. So it's kind of both ways.

Goodman: Yes, we provide tools and we see people using them when they should and when they shouldn't. We see people going to the OPAC when they should be going to the stacks, and people will go to the stacks when they should be going to the catalog. And people especially will be going to the catalog when they should be going to an index. We want to design the systems to try to guide them, but we're not going to do it just with the systems. We're going to do it primarily with people.

Danny Jones (Otto Harrassowitz): I think David has just made — in the past two statements he's made — he's made the point to oppose the resolution. That the library is not a social center. It is more than that, it is a place that does many things other than a place for people to go and hang out.

Goodman: What we need to do, this will work very nicely for those people who do go to the library. What we basically need and what the rest of ours was planned to be devoted to is that we need some way of providing this personal service to the people outside of the library. And as the final point, I'm going to suggest that the impersonal sort of reference service by asking e-mail questions or by telephoning people — although it is enormously useful — is not as good as the extended contact face to face with a person.

Hamaker: I have nothing else to add. (Time over)

NOBODY KNOWS THE USERS WE'VE SEEN

Marian C. Winner, Consultant and Larry X. Besant, Morehead State University

Introduction

The discussion leaders have been Library Directors for many years and have continuously explored various methods of determining user needs. Marian Winner has also done a very early study of the marketing of library services and Larry Besant has been studying the use of syllabi as predictors of the use of the library collections. (A brief introduction to this study can be found in Appendix A). Based on their years of experience and their research, they were prepared to explore a wide variety of methods of user studies employed by members of the audience in their libraries.

In order to prepare for a rewarding discussion a brief questionnaire was distributed at the beginning of each session. (A copy of the questionnaire with the results indicated can be found in Appendix B). The questionnaire was designed so it could be completed in five minutes or less. The responses were quickly tallied and the "hot" topics for a lively discussion were identified.

Results of Questionnaire

An unexpected finding was that only a little over one percent of the libraries represented in the discussions utilized the ACRL survey developed in 1990[1]. The majority of libraries have developed their own surveys and utilized the results to improve services. Most libraries rely heavily on a liaison system and other forms of direct contact with the faculty. Library Advisory Committees emerged as another tool to obtain information. Suggestion boxes in various forms are still widely used. A number of libraries found the assigned readings on course syllabi provided useful information. Other methods of obtaining user information included: reference and inter-library loan statistics; focus groups; transaction log analysis; LibQual+, a survey process[2]; user protocols; and composite measures such as gate counts and initial visits. From the automation vendors in attendance, we learned that they are designing user interfaces and new products that support the use of a combination of surveys, user groups and straw polls.

Discussion

The attendees in the sessions were interested in the topic and provided an evaluative discussion of the methods most frequently used. Marian Winner opened the discussion by citing from a publication entitled "Transforming Libraries: After the User Survey, Then What?,"[3] in which authors note that there is a persistent and widespread lack of knowledge among faculty and students about the library, even though the libraries studied used newsletters and articles in the student paper. Photocopying and parking continue to be primary concerns. The discussions confirmed these conclusions. The most effective method of securing information and informing users was found to be direct contact with users especially faculty and students using a variety of methods. The liaison system developed in the 1960s and supported by assigned subject specialists is still widely used. Library Advisory Committees composed of representatives of various user groups are still considered a viable way of contact. These methods are most effective when there are regular meetings with a prepared agenda and written documents supporting the discussions. Mary Reichel, the President of ACRL and a keynote speaker, noted that she still prefers direct contact with faculty in face-to-face meetings.

Some libraries do examine course syllabi for assigned readings. As previously stated, Larry Besant has studied syllabi over a period of time and determined a rather low percentage included library assignments. A member of the discussion group observed that there are some courses that would not benefit from a library assignment and these courses need to be excluded from the study to provide more accurate results.

In the past, librarians relied heavily on their expertise to develop collections. With the continual limitations of funding and the high cost of many publications, libraries are moving toward customer-driven selection. Various marketing methods are being employed such as focus groups, surveys developed by working with faculty in Marketing Departments, and newer methods such LibQual+. A librarian attending the Friday session reported on the successful use of a part-time student position to gain insight into student perceptions. The student employee is thoroughly trained and attends library meetings as well as student meetings, providing a continuous link between the library and the student body.

Conclusions

Technology is available for gathering a wide range of statistics for the use of library collections. Defining various user groups and their special needs still remains a challenge. Vendors are beginning to recognize the need for this information and are exploring the development of software that will provide a broad spectrum of user information. Online catalogs are currently being used to gather some statistical information. Web-based surveys are being examined but few libraries have adopted them. Access to electronic information from a multitude of sources provides users with many benefits while complicating the process of determining user needs.

Discussions exploring this topic need to continue and vendors should also be involved. As noted previously, despite continuing efforts to educate users there is still a notable lack of knowledge about libraries and library services. This long-term challenge is becoming more complex in the face of funding challenges and the increasing diversity of information formats.

Larry Besant closed the meeting by quoting John Cotton Dana's 1895 ALA presidential address and Wayne Wiegand's comments in his column in *American Libraries*. "'Has it not come sharply home to every librarian the hopelessness of the task we assume to set out for ourselves? The triviality of the great mass of the free public library's educational work? The discouraging nature of the field? The pettiness, the awful pettiness, of the results.' The problems he (Dana) complained about remain with us today and as then, are little understood. Just like Dana in the late 19th century we persist in looking at users in the life of libraries rather than libraries in the life of users."[4]

Notes

1. Van House, Nancy A., "Measuring Academic Library Performance: A Practical Approach," ALA, 1990.
2. ARL Announcement, "Texas A & M University Libraries and ARL Receive NSF Grant for Digital Libraries Assessment," see http://www.arl.org/libqual/
3. DeCandido, GraceAnne A., "After the User Survey, What Then?" in Transforming Libraries: Issues and Innovations, Office of Management Studies, ARL, 1997. (SPEC Kit # 226)
4. Weigand, Wayne, *American Libraries*, (Sept. 2001), 90.

Appendix A

A Sick Puppy:
The Tenuous Relationship between Course Syllabi and Library Use Expectations

Larry Besant, Director of Libraries
Morehead State University

Calvin Boyer, in his thoughtful essay "Faculty Client Files," notes that even a stray pet taken to the veterinarian merits a file which systematically records the professional encounter (Boyer, 1986). Unfortunately, in the 15 years since Boyer's call for client files to support library liaison work with faculty, academic institutions have yet to adopt professional standards for documenting what the curriculum expects from the Library!

Morehead State University, a comprehensive master's level public institution, offered over 1,900 courses in the Fall Semester of 2000. A random sample of 281 course sections was drawn from the directory of courses. Different sections of the same course were included in the sample if they were taught by different professors or delivered by different formats; i.e., classroom versus Internet or other distance-learning method.

Each of the course syllabi was obtained from the professors or their academic departments and was coded according to the relative intensity of required library use. Using the same scale, intensity of required (or implied) Internet use was also coded. In less than 5% of the courses did professors appear to expect intensive library use. In nearly half of the courses (47%), no library use at all was stated or implied by the course syllabi (see Table 1).

In the Fall of 2000, Morehead State offered 27 courses fully over the Internet. The number of courses using "Blackboard" classroom management software via the Internet was over 400. It was, therefore, surprising that 80% of the syllabi analyzed did not mention or imply the Internet itself as a required course resource. Heavy Internet use was a stated requirement in only 3.6% of the courses. Seventy-one percent of the syllabi did include the e-mail address of the professor, but only 17% included a URL for the course or the professor.

The results reveal a low level of curricular library use, as evidenced by course syllabi. These results confirm the findings of the relatively few other syllabi studies, which are cited below. The author of one of the earliest syllabi studies stated: "A major conclusion drawn from this syllabus study is that library resources are underused. In the university under investigation only 8 percent of the total analyzed courses make heavy use of the library, while library staff, particularly the people involved in public desk service, instruction, computer data base searching, and faculty-student liaison as a package of activities, indicate overwork, and to the observer the library in this institution appears to be busy. This indicates that the library is staffed and operated for service to well under half of the course offered by the institution. The assertion may be made that the institution observed in the study is not different from other academic institutions" (Rambler, 1982).

TABLE I
LIBRARY USE INTENSITY BASED ON SYLLABI ANALYSIS

Level 4 = Much Library Use	4's	12	4.3%
Level 3 = Significant Library use	3's	36	12.8%
Level 2 = Some Library Use	2's	51	18.1%
Level 1 = Minimum Library Use Implied	1's	49	17.4%
Level 0 = No Library Use	0's	133	47.3%
TOTAL		281	99.9%

Appendix B

NOBODY KNOWS THE USERS I'VE SEEN

What Methods For Gathering User Information Do Find Useful in Your Library?

1.   Are you using performance surveys developed by ACRL? _3_ Yes _19_ No

2.   Have you developed your own user surveys? _18_ Yes _2_ No

3.   Are you using the results of the surveys you've conducted? _14_ Yes _5_ No

4.   Are you using ongoing, web-based surveys? _6_ Yes _13_ No

5.   Have you found course syllabi informative or useful? _9_ Yes _7_ No

6.   Does your library have suggestion boxes? _17_ Yes _2_ No

7.   Do you find a library advisory committees useful? _10_ Yes _5_ No

8.   Do you find a system of liaisons with various user groups useful? _21_ Yes _1_ No

9.   Are you using other methods to learn about your users? _13_ Yes _7_ No

10.   What are some of the new or different methods that you are using?

Note: A few respondents used N/A or didn't answer a question.

COLLECTION DEVELOPMENT POLICY: THE BROWSING COLLECTION

Susan Golden, University Library, Appalachian State University, Boone, NC

Purpose

The browsing or popular reading collection serves the University community by providing literature for the general reader. The books and audiocassettes or CD's may serve enrichment, recreational, or current awareness purposes. This collection is one way in which the University Library demonstrates its commitment to lifelong learning and global education.

Description

There are several components to the Browsing Collection: McNaughton (lease) books, materials purchased for the main collection and judged to have a potential general audience, and those materials ordered specifically for the browsing collection. Materials in the Browsing Collection are comprised of current topics of interest and national discussion as well as genre fiction, "mainstream" fiction, multicultural literature, health, spirituality, business and investing, art, science, sports, biographies, adventure travel, etc.

Selection and Deselection

Important aspects of Browsing Collection selection include scanning titles to be reshelved, familiarity with subjects of current interest, and aiming at a broad spectrum of University community interests. The collection should be one of expected books, (best sellers) and of surprises. Users will find something of interest in their favorite areas and perhaps try a book that will lead them to new interests and authors. Categories presently in demand include multicultural titles, science fiction, romance, mystery, personal finance, popular science, and spirituality.

Best sellers are in great demand and occasionally multiple copies will be leased through McNaughton or firm ordered so that hold lists are not unreasonably long. Best sellers are selected on a case-by-case basis, according to expected popularity and reasonable quality. Many are anticipated by McNaughton selection lists and do not have to be added to the general collection when popularity wanes.

McNaughton books are leased books of a popular nature, although more literary fiction has been available in recent years. The vendor selects forthcoming publications predicted to be of high interest to general readers and offers them in a monthly annotated brochure, three months in advance of publication date. For more information, see http://www.brodart.com/books/mcn/mcnhome.htm

The Browsing Collection bibliographer scans book receipts selected for the main collection by other bibliographers. Those books with unusual potential interest are selected for the Browsing Collection. A blue browsing flag is placed in those items and they are rushed through cataloging. They are deselected and placed in the general collection as interest in them decreases and space is needed for other books in the Browsing Collection.

A small number of books are chosen to circulate in the browsing collection before being added to the general collection. The bibliographer reads reviews in *Booklist,* and scans the book review sections of the *New York Times* and the *Washington Post* and orders titles thought to be important and/or of general interest but not likely to be offered on the McNaughton plan or to make best seller lists. Examples of this selection are multicultural fiction and nonfiction, international authors, books from the annual ALA Notable Books list, and requests from patrons and staff that seem worthy of eventual space in the permanent collection.

For the past several years, the Collection Development team has decided to allocate a small amount of money each year to develop a very popular audiocassette/CD collection, located in the browsing collection. Sources used to select additions to the collection include and *Booklist* and *Audiophile*. In 2000-2001, the Collection Development team decided to support a trial annual subscription to Recorded Books' Griot collection of African-American popular authors on audiotape. We are planning to collect more on CD because of the extensive time needed to replace damaged audiocassettes and the increased accessibility of CD players in automobiles.

Some thoughts on Browsing Collections in Academic Libraries: Discussion Starters

Benefits of Browsing Collections:

- Helps fulfill lifelong learning mission of University
- Helps fulfill goal of spotlighting literature of diversity to the University community
- Spotlights current national and international issues and books with a "buzz"
- Takes strain of large university population off local public library
- One stop shopping for our patrons

Audience

- Seems to be mostly faculty and staff
- Regular, avid users
- College students appear to check out mostly science fiction and romance categories
- Audience for audiotapes: commuters, runners, and travelers before college breaks

Faculty resistance to funds for browsing: none!

Location of Collection:

- Specific "reading area" with comfortable chairs, wood bookcases
- Audiotapes are shelved there too, but the two are not interfiled

Funding Ideas

- Friends of Library were particularly receptive to funding audio books
- Friends groups may like to fund something specific such as multicultural literature, popular science, travel books, etc.
- Try to designate a small portion of general library funds for a lease collection (such as McNaughton or Baker and Taylor)

Selection Sources

- Useful sources: Starred reviews in *Publishers Weekly* and *Booklist*, *New York Times* bestseller lists, *Washington Post Book World*
- *Publishers Weekly Online* - a free, daily email containing news of books, authors, and bookselling. Especially useful for information on books and authors receiving media attention, and bestseller lists from around the country. http://publishersweekly.reviews.news.com/newuser --click on sign up today at left

Most popular selections

- Bestsellers
- Romance
- Mysteries and thrillers
- Spirituality and religion: Kathleen Norris, Karen Armstrong, Dalai Lama, etc.

Maintenance and Weeding

- When circulation of multiple copies of blockbusters by Grisham, King, etc. wanes
- Lack of room on shelves — send back batches of lease plan books periodically
- Weed purchased books periodically to be placed in main collection (every few months)
- Maintenance of audio books is a problem: constant replacement of missing and damaged tapes, as well as lack of room. Moving toward acquiring audio books on CD

Things we can improve

- Complete and administer survey of reading interests of user of collection and satisfaction with collection (in progress)
- Increase publicity: weekly faculty and staff campus newsletter, student newspaper

AFTER THE STORM: COLLABORATING TO RESTORE LIBRARY COLLECTIONS AND FACILITIES COMPROMISED BY DISASTER

Susan E. Parker, Associate Dean, University Library, California State University, Northridge

The Delmar T. Oviatt Library at California State University, Northridge, like many other buildings on the campus, suffered structural damage in the Northridge earthquake of January, 1994. The Library's collections were thrown from their shelves but were mostly unscathed; the building itself, comprised of a central core and two wings, sustained enough damage to force the closing of the facility for several months.

Even after the Library was returned to service, only the core of the building was available for use. The wings remained the subject of intense scrutiny by engineers and other experts until the 1997discovery of previously undetected and fatal structural damage promoted the decision to raze both wings of the Library and rebuild them. It was during this process of rebuilding that the Library's collections sustained the damage that would result in our need to hire outside help to address the situation.

In order to understand the events that constituted our disaster following the disaster, it is important to know a little bit about the construction of the Oviatt Library and the operation of the facility.

The Oviatt Library was completed in 1973, a square concrete box five stories high, with 137,896 square feet for library use within the top four floors and part of the lowest level, below ground.

In 1991, an east and a west wing were completed, bringing the Library's size to a net square footage of 234,712. The construction was state of the art, earthquake-resistant concrete-reinforced steel. Installed in the lowest two levels of the east wing was an Automated Storage and Retrieval System (ASRS), with a capacity to hold over one million volumes, a little bit less than the Library's size at the time of 1,030,000 volumes (by 2001 the Library had grown to 1,220,000 volumes).

The ASRS answered the future storage needs of the Library, even though the system had been installed in only one other academic library by 1991. Built by a company now called H.K. Systems, it is utilized primarily in industrial applications for inventory control. Because it permits random storage of items with immediate on-demand retrieval, it presents a perfect storage environment for any inventory that can be barcoded, including library books.

The Northridge ASRS installation includes over 13,300 steel bins coated with rust-proof enamel paint, occurring in 5 different sizes to maximize the use of cubic footage available. The bins are stored within a two-story tall rack system and are delivered to an operator and returned to their designated location by means of a robotic mini-load crane. The CSUN configuration has six aisles, each served by its own crane and two operator stations. The six aisles of the ASRS and its rack system are situated within their own mini-building, a separate and independent concrete box existing within the overall structure of the east wing itself.

The Oviatt Library faculty and staff devised a program for the use of the ASRS. Monographic volumes would be stored there based upon their circulation statistics;

following this protocol, books with low to no circulation would be identified and removed from the stacks and stored in the ASRS every several years, assuring that only the most frequently used items would be on the shelves. Serial and periodical bound volumes would be pulled and stored on a regular basis as well, based on date of publication. In addition, archival and special collections materials would be included in the storage facility, as designated by the faculty and staff managing those areas.

The Northridge Earthquake hit at 4:30 a.m. on January 17, 1994. It was a magnitude 6.7 earthquake, and the epicenter was near the campus of California State University, Northridge. The devastation on the campus and in the nearby areas of the San Fernando Valley and the west side of Los Angeles was severe and crippled the area for days. The early hour and the fact that the date was a holiday probably saved thousands of lives, as most people were at home asleep when the earthquake began.

CSUN was also in its January intersession and two weeks away from the beginning of the Spring semester. The campus leadership acted to assure that school would resume on time despite the many wrecked or severely damaged campus buildings and infrastructure. While the Library was also damaged, it would soon return to service without the use of the twisted east and west wings. Except, that is, for the ASRS, which did not sustain any significant damage as a result of the earthquake. Existing within its own separate building within the east wing, the ASRS had safely sheltered almost half of the Library's collection and was ready to operate once again with only minor adjustments to account for some shifting of the rack.

The rebuilding of the University became the largest FEMA-funded disaster recovery project in history, holding that distinction until September 11, 2001. The reconstruction of the Oviatt Library was one of the many FEMA projects on campus. After it was determined that the wings would be razed and rebuilt, the project was turned over to the supervision of an engineering group called DMJM/JGM, the entity contracted to oversee all FEMA-funded building projects on the campus. The wings project was designed, demolition was completed over the summer of 1997, and the rebuilding was slated to start in late December 1997 or early January 1998.

The west wing was razed entirely; the east wing was taken down to the level of the ceiling or roof of the ASRS. A temporary roof was planned to secure the ASRS while the building was being reconstructed above it. Before the roof could be completed, however, an early fall rainstorm in late September, 1997, caused some minor water intrusion into the ASRS.

The water damage to stored books then was limited; a handful of us working through the night managed to pull wet volumes and send them to be freeze-dried, with negligible losses. An overnight storm in January, 1998 brought a heavy water incursion into Aisles 5 and 6. Library staff could not pull items immediately due to a combination of contractor activity and a power outage on Aisle 6. We soon understood that we would be unable to salvage all of the wet books. Mold growth occurs within 24-48 hours on wet books if they are not frozen or deep chilled. The area affected was too vast to empty before that much time had passed.

We continued normal operations while also consulting regarding the need for a responsible party to hire a salvage expert to clean the now irrefutably wet and moldy books. As previously noted, DMJM/JGM was the firm in charge of supervising the

FEMA-funded campus recovery construction, including the Library project. As we worked directly with them to solve the problem, DMJM/JGM hired a recovery contractor to clean the ASRS items, bins, and air ducts. An industrial hygienist conducted preliminary tests on February 12, and we closed the ASRS on that date to all persons, based on the most conservative advice of the hygienist after testing.

We consulted with the campus Environmental Health and Occupational Safety Department. They also advised shutting down the facility until the mold could be removed, and they recommended that staff who were sensitive to mold should avoid the facility.

DMJM/JGM immediately hired a recovery contractor who sealed off the area and certified only three Library staff to work there wearing respirators and Tyvek suits. This contractor worked for several weeks to dry the ASRS facility, learn to operate it, set up a system to pull bins and separate wet or moldy books to be sent to be freeze-dried or discarded, and to retrieve and clean items for students and staff on request. A formal bid for the cleanup was issued, and MARCOR, Inc. was hired to complete the job. MARCOR had a similar but even further advanced plan: stabilize the environment and salvage wet items; clean and inspect bins; provide a supervisor and a mycologic technician during each daily shift; provide a HEPA vacuum at each of six work stations; and provide a canopy over each aisle to protect against further incoming water, a constant hazard as construction progressed on the levels of the building located above the ASRS roof.

We would work with MARCOR over several months. We agreed upon a plan of operations and a scope of work, including definitions for all procedures and terms, even words like "freeze dry", "clean", and "complete".

We established a service requirement that our students, faculty, and staff, accustomed to instant access, must continue to have reasonable access to items stored in the ASRS. We agreed to train MARCOR's personnel to operate the ASRS while they cleaned it, thus permitting our students, faculty, and staff needed access within a day of their requests, to a cleaned collection while the mitigation was in progress.

The Library's cooperation with MARCOR was carried out in daily contacts between their project supervisor's staff and my staff, and in frequent, usually daily, meetings between their project supervisor and me. We worked out the details of accounting for and inventorying missing, damaged, and unsalvageable items, and we worked out a plan for the proper environmental disposal of mold damaged items. If this communication had been ineffective, our operation would have faced certain failure. It is crucial to work with companies and individuals who understand your needs, especially the demands of supplying public services, and who can discuss and plan them with you.

It was necessary to keep an accurate record. The online catalog became our inventory and proof of ownership, which is vital for insurance recovery purposes. I was required to provide proof of ownership for every item I reported as a loss in need of replacement or compensation.

MARCOR's workers recorded in a database the bar codes of any items removed from the ASRS for whatever reason. This was later updated to delete those books and journals which were returned to the ASRS after freeze drying. The remaining barcodes represented each item discarded because it was unsalvageable. The barcodes were used to generate from our cataloging database a title and call number list of the ruined items. We used this information as the basis of our plan for replacement, and we also removed these records from our catalog.

Our replacement needs for the majority of our losses in serials and bound journals were best met by Alfred Jaeger, Inc., who quoted the most advantageous prices. Working with Jaeger also saved us from having to coordinate with multiple vendors as we sought to replace 3,000 to 4,000 bound journals dated prior to 1990. Jaeger, with whom we had worked before in water loss instances, gave us a useful estimate of replacement costs and waived the fee for their estimate, which represented their own time devoted to market research. Jaeger also helped to keep costs down by honoring their estimates for as long as possible. This arrangement persists today, longer than two years since they offered their original quotes.

DMJM/JGM, not the University, hired the contractors we needed. DMJM/JGM works directly with the insurance companies representing the building contractors to settle the claim for damages. DMJM/JGM worked with our own campus risk management office to assure the payment of the environmental specialists, MARCOR, and Jaeger from FEMA and other insurance funds.

We are still working with Jaeger to complete the replacement of our journals, and we will work with other vendors to replace the approximately 1100 monographs also lost in this incident. One or more additional firms will be needed to clean and conserve archival and Special Collections items damaged by water.

When people ask me how long it took us to recover from the 1994 earthquake, they are surprised to learn that we are still in the process of recovering, including this disaster after the fact.

The cooperation that you need to establish BEFORE a disaster occurs includes campus police and environmental/occupational health and safety officers, and your campus risk management office. You must have an emergency and disaster response plan which includes current and regularly re-validated information on whom to contact in order to mitigate water, mold, or other damage to collections, and how to arrange recovery of the costs. I recommend getting the campus risk management and purchasing offices to designate approval in advance for your specified remediation vendors before a disaster occurs, in order to avoid the extra work of having to make an emergency hire and then also going out to bid.

You must be able to work with a variety of contractors and jobbers, and there must be a coherent plan, mutually developed, for success to be possible. You must have an officer in the Library who is able to manage these different facilities and collections problems, but who is also sensitive to the service and public relations aspects of these operations. Finally, *you must be able to give your users absolute confidence in your facility before, during, and after any disaster.*

I believe that our Library's mutual operations with MARCOR and Jaeger are a great example of how this works well, and how it allowed us to assure our users of the secure handling and competent treatment of the collection during and after remediation. It takes time and patience, but if you devote these to any disaster recovery operation, your library and its clients will be well served.

Selected Resources

Alire, Camila, ed. *Disaster Planning and Recovery Handbook.* NY: Neal-Schuman, 2000.

Kahn, Miriam B. *Disaster Response and Planning for Libraries.*
Chicago: American Library Association, 1998.

MARCOR Remediation, Inc. *Final Report. California State University Northridge Oviatt Library Mold Mitigation Project.*
Cerritos, CA: MARCOR Remediation, Inc., October 13, 1999.

New England Document Conservation Center, Andover, Massachusetts.
http://www.nedcc.org

Nyberg, Sandra. *Invasion of the Giant Spore.* SOLINET Preservation Program Leaflet No. 5, November 1, 1987.

Price, Lois Alcott. *Managing a Mold Invasion: Guidelines for a Disaster Response.*
CCHA Technical Series No. 1. Philadelphia: Conservation Center for Art and Historical Artifacts, 1996.
http://www.ccaha.org/mold_eng.html .

Stanford University Libraries. Preservation Department. CoOL: Conservation On Line. http://www.palimpsest.stanford.edu

COLLECTION DEVELOPMENT TRENDS AND ISSUES IN HEALTH SCIENCES LIBRARIES

Ramune Kubilius, Collection Development / Special Projects Librarian, Galter Health Sciences Library, Northwestern University

Recap of "Lively Lunch" session:

- The discussion was informal. About 25 attendees participated, representing libraries, publishers and vendors equally. Introductions were made and interest in particular aspects of collection development was expressed.
- Original co-facilitator Julie Garrison from Duke University was not able to attend, but the text of her e-mail about Duke's experience with PDAs at her library was included in the handout.
- It was decided that electronic journal concerns resemble those of other libraries, but that health sciences libraries have particular interest in the following: PDAs (collection development use by librarians and resources that can be mounted on them by users), e-books (beyond products such as the well-established MD Consult, Stat!Ref), and networking/licensing issues particular to medical centers and their libraries. (Not all discussion points in the handout were addressed.)
- One electronic database product vendor asked for some opinions on the feasibility of a spin-off targeted subject product for the biomedical user public. Differing opinions were expressed.
- It was agreed that an annual "roundtable" discussion of this kind is warranted in future Charleston Conferences. The forum provides an opportunity for librarians, publishers, and vendors to meet together, whereas, at other conferences, such as the Medical Library Association, the publishers and vendors are to be found in the exhibit hall, not the conference.

Issues / trends:

Administration

Differing reporting relationships: university library, health education programs, affiliated hospitals
Moral or financial support of administration (university)
Consortial arrangements / agreement
Budget allocations
Health sciences materials costs
Methods / techniques / procedures for decision making

Print versus online

Maintenance / weeding of print
Collection assessment / usage
Print plus online
Online only
Cost differentials

Web-based collections

Definitions, free and fee, individual titles vs collections
E journals, E books
Content / edition concerns
Pay for all, but need only some
Add ons: CD in pocket of print books;
electronic only supplements and updates

Access to online resources

Remote, proxy, firewalls
Web gateway, stand alone, intranet
PC Readers, PDA Readers, dedicated e-book
Licensing agreements & restrictions
Different user populations with different access capabilities, restrictions

The players

Publishers, vendors, jobbers, aggregators
Our home institutions
Our networks, consortia
Libraries, librarians, associations (health sciences & other)
Government: national, state, local

Collection development

Determining depth of collection
Clinical versus basic science versus board review
Areas of excellence
Need to duplicate (within institution, within local area)

Collection management

Processing & cataloging: who should catalog what
Assessment: usage, quality, user demand
Integrated library system versus web site
LinkOut & Open Links; jake and Serial Solutions, etc

Long-term access ownership / access

Conversion, archiving issues
Digital distribution of content
Standards

Projections / Rankings

Only 10 percent of the books sold by 2005 will be e-books (Anderson Consulting Company report projection)

The "Best" Lists: Health Sciences Libraries, Medical Schools, & Where Your are Ranked by All the Lists, Kelly Hensley, MLA 2001 poster session. *From abstract: "...The "best" lists of medical schools corresponds only weakly with lists of "best" health sciences libraries."*

KEEPING UP:

- Web sites of other libraries under "Electronic Books"
- Networks with other health sciences collection development librarians
- Discussions on MEDLIB-L, BLAB (http://colldev.mlanet.org/), MLA-EPUB Discussion List
- Doody's Electronic Journal (Doody's Review Service)
- Professional and publisher literature, press releases÷

Misc. Web sites:

- *Medical Library Management: Collection Development*
  http://nnlm.gov/libinfo/mgmt/colldev.html
  Maintained by the National Library of Medicine National Network of Libraries (NN/LM)
- *Bibliofuture*
  http://www.geocities.com/bibliofuture
  Maintained by Troy Johnson Troy.Johnson@valpo.edu
- *Donation Programs for Books, Journals and Media*
  http://ublib.buffalo.edu/libraries/units/hsl/cms/donationprograms.htm
  Maintained by Pamela M. Rose, M.L.S., Web Services & Library Promotion Coordinator, Health Sciences Library, University at Buffalo

Fee-based providers

BOOKS AND MIXED COLLECTIONS:

Emedicine	http://www.imedicine.com
Harrison's Online	http://www.harrisonsonline.com/
Lippincott Williams & Wilkins	http://www.lwwoncology.com/
	(e.g. Oncology)
MD Consult	http://home.mdconsult.com
Ovid	
http://www.ovid.com/products/books/index.cfm	
netLibrary	http://www.netlibrary.com/
SAM Online	http://www.samed.com/
Stat!REF	http://host1.statref.com
UpToDate	http://www.uptodate.com/

BIOMEDICAL AND SCIENCE ELECTRONIC JOURNAL PUBLISHERS / PACKAGES:

Sampling:

American Chemical Society	*IDEAL (Academic Press & others)*
American Institute of Physics	*IEEE*
American Society for Microbiology	*journals@ovid*
BioOne	*Karger*
Blackwell Science / Synergy	*Kluwer*
Cambridge University Press	*Mary Ann Liebert*
Current Protocols	*Nature Publishing*
EBSCO	*Springer-Verlag LINK*
Science Direct & Web Editions (Elsevier)	

Providers of free resources

E BOOKS AND MISC.

AFP Monographs	http://www.aafp.org/afp/monograph/
Bartleby.com	http://www.bartleby.com/
BMJ Publishing	http://www.bmj.com/collections/
MEDLINEPlus	http://www.medlineplus.gov/
Medscape	

http://cardiology.medscape.com/PCI/public/PCI-about.html

NAP Reading Room	http://www.nap.edu/info/browse.htm
MedicalStudent.com	http://www.medicalstudent.com/
On-Line Books Page	

http://digital.library.upenn.edu/webbin/book/subjectstart?R

PubMed Central Bookshelf

http://www.ncbi.nlm.nih.gov:80/entrez/query.fcgi?db=Books

Virtual Hospital

http://www.vh.org/Providers/Textbooks/MultimediaTextbooks.html

Xrefer.com http://www.xrefer.com

Others: AMA, AAMC, various agencies of the federal government
(besides NLM)...

E JOURNALS

Directory of Electronic Health

http://www.med.monash.edu.au/shcnlib/dehsj/

Sciences Journals

FreeMedicalJournals.com http://www.freemedicaljournals.com

Hardin MD Free Medical Journal

http://www.lib.uiowa.edu/hardin/md/ej.html

HighWire Press http://highwire.stanford.edu/lists/freeart.dtl

Periodici Elettronici Biomedici

http://aib.it/aib/commiss/cnur/peb/peb.htm

PubMed Central/Biomed Central http://pubmedcentral.nih.gov/

HOT TOPICS: PDAs

PDAs for Health Care Providers
http://educ.ahsl.arizona.edu/pda/index.htm

Maintained by Arizona Health Sciences Library. Includes books & texts for
hand-helds, links to library initiatives÷

****

Duke University's experience with PDAs
(From information provided by Julie Garrison, garri008@mc.duke.edu)

Basically, as a Library, we have participated in a number of ways to help support the use of PDAs.

1. LIBRARY ADMINISTRATION

Pat Thibodeau, the Library's director has been active on an administrative level, identifying the number of PDAs being used in the medical center, their varying uses, and working with a group to solve infrastructure issues.

2. EDUCATION

Education Services Librarians developed a one- hour introductory class on PDAs open to all medical center faculty, staff, and students. It was very well attended when we first offered the program. Basically the class covered what a PDA is, what it can do, and demonstrated a few health care programs available for PDAs — e.g. a medical textbook, pharmacology information, and medical calculators. Marlyse MacDonald also created a PDA subject guide to help people get started in finding information.

3. OVID@HAND

We are an Ovid@Hand beta-test site. This program was a little late getting off the ground due to the events of Sept. 11, 2001, however, we finally had our introductory sessions in early October. Basically we have invited a small group of physicians and others in the medical center we thought would be interested in the product to participate in the beta-test along with everyone in the library who has a PDA. We did not open this up to everyone. So far, I think we've found that people would consider this a useful service (getting tables of contents of journals) but that really they want more. Some would actually like to download the entire article so they could read it on the PDA. Also, other information might be well suited to this service - like Cochrane, ACP Journal Club, and Clinical Evidence. I believe Ovid is investigating whether these products would consent to being made available through Ovid@Hand. Participating in the beta-test has been good for us since we can see some areas where improvements are needed and what issues or requests our patrons might have when it comes to offering this product.

4. COLLECTION DEVELOPMENT

Started using Handybase as a collection development management tool. Marlyse MacDonald has created a database for her different sections so she can keep better track of what is in the collection.

****

Point of Care to their Palms: Medical Libraries Provide Critical Knowledge Based Resources, Technology, and Training to Medical Professionals

The OSF Saint Francis Medical Center Library & Resource Center, in cooperation with the University of Illinois at Chicago Library of the Health Sciences (Peoria) have been awarded a $50,220 Library Services and Technology Act Grant from the Illinois State Library, a division of the Office of Secretary of State. The libraries are working together to provide critical knowledge-based resources at the point of care or patient bedside through the use of handheld computing technology. The libraries currently provide the latest information in print and electronic format; this project will assist them in placing important information at the point of care for physicians, residents, medical students, and staff. The grant will provide funding for the libraries to purchase handheld computers for use by medical staff, access to important databases, electronic books, training on how to use the hardware and software, and other resources. Through this grant, the OSF Library & Resource Center and the Library of the Health Sciences-Peoria, will be among the first in the country to pilot the use of Ovid@Hand, a medical database providing up-to-the minute knowledge management resources for the handheld computer. Although handheld computers, commonly known as Palms, PDAs, and so forth have been in existence for several years, they were mainly used as personal information management tools. Now, their capabilities and use have grown tremendously, allowing them to store electronic books, reference works, and to download information from the Internet.

"This "Point of Care to Your Palm" grant provides an exciting opportunity for Library staff to offer new technology and services to our Saint Francis Medical Center physicians and nurses, with the ultimate goal of bringing knowledge-based resources to the bedside," said Carol Galganski, Library Services Manager at OSF Saint Francis Medical Center and Project Director of the Grant.

"The libraries provide the information management expertise to fully exploit the potential of this new information technology," stated Jo Dorsch, Health Sciences Librarian and Associate Professor at the University of Illinois Chicago Library of the Health Sciences-Peoria. "The program outlined in this grant proposal will serve as a model for other libraries introducing PDA technology, positively impact regional medical education, provide ready access to critical clinical information at the bedside and ultimately improve patient care."

Dr. Thomas Foster, Assistant Clinical Professor of Medicine and Pediatrics at the University of Illinois College of Medicine at Peoria said of the project, "I believe this grant will be a part of the process that will direct technology to improve patient care and increase knowledge-based resources at the patient's bedside. Handheld computers will be able to provide critical information to physicians and expand resources that are available to the physician during patient care contacts."

"I predict that from now into the foreseeable future, the dominant relationship between texts and text-bearing devices will be dynamic, rather than static and the dominant type of text-bearing device will be some sort of portable, personally-owned computer, " commented Tom Peters, Director of the Center for Library Initiatives, Committee on Institutional Cooperation, and Project Evaluator. "Health professionals are among the leaders of this ascending form of information portability and access. This LSTA project will explore the potential--and pitfalls--of bringing knowledge-based health sciences library information to the point of information need and patient care."
(Posted on MEDLIB-L, 10/30/01 by Lori Bell, <u>lori.bell@osfhealthcare.org</u>)

This year at the conference we saw many more speakers focusing on the importance of the printed book. It is very important that we serve as stewards of the book, and protect the thing that we love most, which are our libraries. Despite all we hear that the book is dead, it's important to remember that books are still heavily cited in faculty research and that books are continuing to be used at a stable rate. The tragedy of September 11, 2001 was made more vivid by the preponderance of documents used to capture the images of that day. Whereas the electronic environment presents challenges to publishers, they were reminded that they must continue to offer well the traditional services that they uniquely provide. This reaffirmation of the basic underpinning of our profession served in direct contrast to the focus of conference speakers in the previous years.

Books and Publishing

DOCUMENTS AND THE SEARCH FOR STABLE GROUND

David Levy, Professor, University of Washington

The Documents of Sept. 11

Since September 11, we have been bombarded with a steady stream of images, some horrifying, some heartwarming, some stunning, and some simply beyond belief. Of these many images, two stand out particularly vividly in my mind. The first is a photograph of a charred ledger book lying open in the World Trade Center rubble. The second, also a photograph, shows a man standing in the middle of a rubble-strewn street in lower Manhattan. He is staring intently at a single, singed sheet of paper he's just picked up from the ground. Both of these images are documents: small contributions to the documentary record that's been amassed following the terrorist attacks on New York and Washington. But they are also about documents: in one case an accounting book, in the other a page of unknown identity and origin.

Anyone who knows me will hardly be surprised that I've been drawn to these images. For the last two decades my research has focused on written forms of all kinds. First as a research scientist at the Xerox Palo Alto Research Center (PARC) and now as a professor in the Information School of the University of Washington I have been investigating the roles that documents play in society. By documents I mean not just published materials, such as books and serials, but bureaucratic forms (receipts, memos, manuals, etc.) and personal forms (letters, postcards, journals, and the like). And I include within this category digital materials, such as Web pages, as well as materials realized in tangible media, such as paper.

What is perhaps a bit more surprising is that in the aftermath of the September attacks *others too* have lately been focusing on documents — in many cases those as mundane and unremarkable as the two I've just mentioned. At a time when we are all trying to come to terms with these recent events, a number of others have been drawn to written forms, both to visual images of documents and to stories about them. The two images I've just described come from a photography exhibition called "Here Is New York" (www.hereisnewyork.com) that was mounted in lower Manhattan in the aftermath of the attack on the World Trade Center.[1] Called "a democracy of photographs," the gallery on Prince Street has been exhibiting photographs taken not only by professional photographers but by ordinary camera-wielders, who have brought their images to the Prince Street gallery to be selectively accepted, scanned in to digital format, printed, and displayed on the gallery walls.

Walking around the gallery in mid-October 2001, I discovered that many of the images mounted on the walls were of documents. One showed a color photograph of the twin towers lying face up in the rubble. Another showed a couple sitting on the grass in a park reading *The Daily News*, its headline proclaiming (in large capital letters) "THE EARTH FELL ON TOP OF ME." Yet another simply showed a crumpled up newspaper abandoned in an alleyway.

1 These two images have also been published. Joel Sternfeld photographed the charred accounting book. It can be found on page 8 of the 2001 Special Edition of DoubleTake magazine. The photo of the man reading is by Larry Towell and can be found on page 42 of a recently published volume, New York: September 11 by Magnum Photographers.

Not just the Prince Street gallery, however, but newspapers and magazines have been filled with images of and reports on documents. As I watched the news stories appear day-after-day, month-after-month, I noticed that a surprising number of them were about the documents of Sept. 11. The earliest stories were about how documents "rained down on the city." In those first weeks, *The New York Times* reported on "the storm of paper work" and "the airborne detritus of commerce" that blanketed the city. Following these reports came another wave of stories describing the missing posters that began to appear. *The New York Times* explicitly marked this shift when it observed: "The first wave of paper rained upon the city from the World Trade Center like death's disembodied proxy. As if in answer, a second wave rose up from the photo albums and word processors of thousands of desperate families." (Waldman 2001) At first the posters represented hope — that loved ones might still be alive. It wasn't long, however, before the posters were transmuted into memorials to those now believed to have died. And as these posters were rained on, and blown about, some news stories noted, "it seemed . . . as if the tragedy had happened again." (Waldman 2001)

Yet another wave of stories arose as letters laced with anthrax were discovered. Suddenly the normally invisible process by which the post office sorts and delivers the mail was front-page news.

Throughout this whole three-to-four month period, it wasn't unusual to find not just stories about ordinary documents but images of them as well appearing in *The New York Times*, both in the print edition and the online version. Photographs appeared showing a to-do list, a handwritten note, a personal check, a page from a manual detailing emergency evacuation procedures, and a family photo of three young children. One of the more recent stories, dated December 20, 2001, was about a letter that was being mailed from New Hampshire to California and happened to be on one of the jets that crashed into the World Trade Center. The color image of the torn but still legible envelope, which was recovered in Manhattan and mailed back to the sender by a good Samaritan, appeared on the front page of the B section of that day's paper (Belluck 2001) .

Documents as talking things

Why have these ordinary, run-of-the-mill documents been so prominently displayed? In some cases, it's clear enough, ordinary documents have been transformed by extraordinary circumstances. Certainly the anthrax-laced letters, in virtue of the substances they were carrying, should no longer be thought of as "ordinary." How could they be when a medium organized to transmit letters, postcards, greeting cards, bills, junk mail, newspapers and magazines was co-opted to carry instruments of illness and death?

Most of the other materials I've mentioned, however, weren't literally transformed in such dramatic ways. Rather, they seem to have been featured in stories and images not so much because of what they *did* but because of what they *symbolized*. The documents that rained down on the city dramatize and stand in for the lives lost and the many human activities, bureaucratic and otherwise, that were interrupted when the planes hit the towers. The charred ledger book, for example, serves as a concrete manifestation of a set of accounting activities that were torn apart in the attack. In the case of the missing posters, these were first created to represent, or stand in for, the victims of the attack and only later came to memorialize the dead in a visible, tangible, and poignant way. Ordinary documents of all kinds thus came to symbolize life and death, loss and survival, the conduct of ordinary life and its disruption.

That the documents of Sept. 11 could play such roles, I want to suggest, was because documents are inherently concerned with such matters — with matters of life and death, with the attempt to create and regulate "ordinary" life, to create meaning and order. In my recently published book, *Scrolling Forward* (Levy 2001), I say that documents are, at heart, talking things. They are bits of the material world — clay stone, animal skin, plant fiber, sand — that we've imbued with the ability to speak. Our written forms are agents or surrogates for us that we send out into the world to speak for us and to perform all sorts of tasks for us.

In the first chapter of my book, called "Meditation on a Receipt," for example, I take a long look at a cash register receipt for a tuna fish sandwich, a bag of chips, and a bottle of water, showing how its various physical and symbolic features (the letterforms, numeral and punctuation marks; the paper on which it's printed) are marshaled to enable the receipt to act as a witness to a commercial transaction. Each kind of document — each genre — is the marshaling of certain material and symbolic resources to perform a specialized task of some kind. An accounting ledger, a memo, a published book, or a procedure manual is an agent that's meant to perform a limited range of tasks in specific social situations.

Any document we look at, then, will have its own, rather limited circuit in which it travels. Like the receipt, it may seem puny and perhaps even ineffective. But if we look at all our documents in aggregate, at the trillions of them acting in concert at any given moment, we can see them as quite powerful, for they are helping us make and maintain the world: helping us conduct financial transactions, build bridges and skyscrapers, send greetings and express love, run factories and corporations, and so on. Together, our documents are agents helping us to make and maintain a meaningful and workable culture. In this way, they are our helpmates in the ever-ongoing human search for stable ground.

The search for stable ground

What does this mean, the search for stable ground? Let me illustrate with a small, personal story.

I was at work in Palo Alto on October 17, 1989 when the Loma Prieta earthquake struck Northern California. During this time period I had been housesitting for acquaintances in San Francisco thirty-five miles away. Because the condition of the roads was uncertain, I didn't make it back to the house until the next day. As I drove up to the city, I was concerned about what I might find. I was therefore much relieved to discover that the house was still standing and seemed not to have suffered any obvious structural damage. One small detail, however, leapt out at me.

In the weeks preceding the earthquake, I had been studying Biblical Hebrew at Stanford University. Our most recent assignment had been to translate Psalm 104 from Hebrew to English. On the morning of the earthquake, before heading down to Palo Alto, I had translated a single line of the psalm. On entering the house the next day, I saw my notebook lying open on the kitchen table to that line, written out in my own hand in both Hebrew and English:

God has set the earth on a firm foundation so it won't shake.

But there was more. This was a house filled to overflowing with books. Yet hardly a book had fallen from a shelf. When I went downstairs, however, to the study where my computer was installed, a single book had fallen from the bookcase above the desk: Immanuel Velikovsky's *Earth in Upheaval*.

The humor and irony in this juxtaposition was immediately apparent to me. On the surface, here were two directly competing claims: upstairs it said the earth doesn't shake; downstairs it said the opposite. Whether by chance or design, this juxtaposition of messages seemed to pose a series of related questions: Where does our stability come from? Where can be find solid ground? In the end, what can we really rely on?

In his remarkable, Pulitzer Prize winning book written nearly thirty years ago, *The Denial of Death* (Becker 1973) , Ernest Becker argues that all of human life is organized in reaction to the fact of death. Human society or culture, he claims, is the collective attempt to come to terms with mortality by repressing or denying it. Culture, he says, provides human beings with the playing field on which they can strive to stand out, to be special (he calls this "being a hero") in the hope of transcending death.

> "The fact is that this is what society is and always has been: a symbolic action system, a structure of statuses and roles, customs and rules for behavior, designed to serve as a vehicle for earthly heroism. . . . It doesn't matter whether the cultural hero-system is frankly magical, religious, and primitive or secular, scientific, and civilized. It is still a mythical hero-system in which people serve in order to earn a feeling of primary value, of cosmic specialness, of ultimate usefulness to creation, of unshakable meaning. They earn this feeling by carving out a place in nature, by building an edifice that reflects human value: a temple, a cathedral, a totem pole, a skyscraper, a family that spans three generations. The hope and belief is that the things that man creates in society are of lasting worth and meaning, that they outlive or outshine death and decay, that man and his products count. When Norman O. Brown said that Western society since Newton, no matter how scientific or secular it claims to be, is still as 'religious' as any other, this is what he meant: 'civilized' society is a hopeful belief and protest that science, money and goods make man count for more than any other animal. In this sense everything that man does is religious and heroic, and yet in danger of being fictitious and fallible." (pp. 4-5)

In the terms I've just been using, human culture is the collective attempt to find or create stable ground. It is a set of ongoing institutions and practices that provide us with a sense of who we are, where we're going, and what we should do. In our culture in particular, which is so thoroughly infused with written forms of all kinds, documents are major co-conspirators in this work.

The events of Sept. 11 represented a huge tear in the fabric of American society. They reminded us so painfully, much as earthquakes do, that the ground we take to be safe and stable is only relatively so. In light of what I've been suggesting here, it isn't hard to see how the ordinary documents that rained down on the city could come to symbolize the normal workings of culture and its shocking dissolution. Nor is it hard to see how the documents of Sept. 11 could come to symbolize thousands of people who, until the attack, had been living lives of ordinary heroism.

Bibliography

Becker, E. (1973). *The Denial of Death*. New York, The Free Press.

Belluck, P. (2001). One Letter's Odyssey Helps to Mend a Sept. 11 Wound. *New York Times*. New York: B6.

Levy, D. M. (2001). *Scrolling Forward: Making Sense of Documents in the Digital Age*. New York, Arcade Publishing

Waldman, A. (2001). Posters of the Missing Now Speak of Losses. *New York Times*. New York

TREASON OF THE CLERKS

John Smith, President, Total Information, Inc.

I want to address an important subject by first giving a very personal report on the History of Publishing, Bookselling and Libraries over the last thirty years.

Once you have practiced a craft or a profession for more years than you were old when you started, certain privileges accrue. One is the right to spurn footnotes and exhaustive attributions. If I say something that sounds familiar in a half-baked way, the odds are good that at some time we've read the same book. If you think I've got my facts wrong, remember, this is my personal history, not yours.

When I was a child, I remember watching Bennett Cerf on "What's My Line?". To me he has always epitomized the essence of a publisher. Witty and urbane, mildly famous, rich and literary. An example of the "gentleman publisher". He was one of a type that ran the serious publishing houses of the mid twentieth century. (Simon and Schuster, Doubleday, Harper and Row, Farrar Straus, Harcourt Brace, World Publishing, and New Directions are just a few others.) Cerf once revealed that as Random House grew more and more successful he and his co-founder, Donald Klopfer, were urged to insure each other's lives to allow the survivor to purchase the share of the departed in the event, Heaven forbid! that one of them should die. This was, of course, sensible advice that partners in successful businesses do all the time, and provoked little resistance from either of them. However they did, he admitted, have a devilishly difficult time deciding on the amount of the insurance policies. In effect they were being asked to value Random House in such a way that both of them would agree that the amount of the payment was a fair price for one half of the firm. They were able to settle on $500,000 for each of them. A few years later RCA paid sixty-three million dollars for Random House. Everyone in the publishing industry noticed, as did all the conglomerates still operating in the seventies.

At about the same time Carter Hawley Hale was aggressively expanding its B. Dalton Book Chain. S.S. Kressge was doing the same with Waldens. These two early chains were essentially different from any bookselling that had gone before. The Malling of America of the sixties and seventies, drove them, where large retailers with multiple specialty brands would sign group leases for large chunks of new developments. Real estate development was the tail that waged the dog, a phenomenon we have recently seen repeated with the injection of massive Venture Capital into Internet bookselling. In the early seventies the founder sold a small southern California bookstore chain—Pickwick Books—for a sum reported at the time to be five million dollars. The Border Brothers were getting started in Ann Arbor and Len Riggio was aggressively expanding from the original Barnes & Noble he had purchased across the street from Columbia University. Bookselling was changing from the pursuit of the eccentric book lover to the cold-hearted business of retailing. The chains were coming, followed by the Superstores, and finally the Internet. In bookselling, nothing would be quite the same again.

Libraries, and here I am mostly speaking of Corporate and Academic Libraries, have suffered their own devolution. Although free of the pressures influencing bookselling they were captives of the publishers. More and more consolidation in the publishing industry produced two ominous trends that continue to impact them daily. The one given the most attention is the concentration of power in fewer and fewer hands. The other was the continuous inflation of the value of publishers themselves. Benet Cerf dined out, figuratively and literally, on the sixty-three million RCA paid for Random House. How would he have felt about Bertelsmann paying 1.2 Billion? Somebody has to pay for all this.

For Libraries something else was going on at the same time. The special libraries I have worked with entered a period that can only called a crisis of self-definition. They gradually threw off their curatorial and collection development core to turn outward to their near constituency, always keeping an eye on the reaction of management: whether that management was a University Dean who controlled the budget or a Corporate Vice President for Facilities. Driven by the incessant drumbeat of salesmen they wandered through a maze of innovation that took them farther and farther into unknown territory. Most took a turn down the microform alley looking for ways to shrink the bulk of their collection to a vanishing point of pure spirit. Salesmen with equipment that was designed to control the flow of paper through large businesses turned their attention to libraries as a logical extension of their market. Once shrunk and finally digitized these collections were accessible only with the hardware and software that was being sold. Insidiously their budgets were vitiated by ever rising costs of hardware, software, in-library programmers and system administrators. Acquisition budgets for serials and monographs stalled, failing to keep up with the general rise of inflation, not to mention the much greater rise in prices for these materials, and then began to shrink. With a few obvious exceptions the hard money for real books and serials continues to wither. Libraries in general and special libraries in particular were like drunks behind the wheel of a Porsche racing through the night with the lights off. The darker it seemed, the harder they pushed the accelerator. Something bad was going to happen. When the crash came it was called The Internet. Over-hyped, over-sold, over-promised and over-embraced by librarians it gave all the administrators who were chafing at the cost of the Library an opening.

Men and women who if asked for the title of the book that had had the greatest impact on their lives would have answered: "The One Minute Manager" or "Seven Habits of Whatever", were watching as no one contradicted the ridiculous claims for what was, in essence, an under-muscled Wide Area Network that we could all log on to.

There's a lot more to be said about the changes in these three institutions, but this is a prolog and I am going to spread the veil of time constraint over my superficiality.

On the surface it may seem that all I am pointing out is that things change and today is not like "the good ole days". Publishing has been conglomerated and consolidated, bookselling has been "rolled up" and "rationalized", and libraries spend more on technology they do on books. As they might say on Fox: "Get over it!"

If we were talking about industrial fasteners, electric motors or oil drilling equipment I'd agree. But books aren't industrial fasteners, and although we rely on fasteners to hold up our buildings and keep our cars from flying apart, we rely on books to hold up our civilization and keep our society from flying apart. Publishers aren't foundries, booksellers aren't wholesale supply stores, and libraries aren't warehouses. We are the three legs of the stool that is our written record.

I would insist that there is more Rome in Livy and Cicero than in all the ruins and restored frescos of Europe. Buildings and art hint, suggest but, ultimately, merely tantalize. It is the books that speak to us. From our perspective weren't the Peloponnesian Wars most important because they produced Thucydidies?

But if the ancient and medieval librarians chose to devote most of their resources to schemes of classification, we might have been endowed with an empty system for arranging unknown objects. A kitchen filled with recipes but barren cupboards.

If you build a better mousetrap it proves that you can, and that the act and art of mouse trapping can take care of itself. If you write a greater "History of the Peloponnesian Wars", it proves only that you are mad.

By way of explanation let me take a well-known parable from the New Testament: The Parable of the Talents. Everyone who paid attention during Sunday School or Services, or just did the readings for Comparative Religion is familiar with the story of the stewards who, when entrusted with their master's money and left on their own, are judged by how much they earned. When the master returns each is rewarded or condemned. I can categorically attest to the fact that during the fifties and sixties this was the all-subsuming foundation myth of Catholic education, having had it preached to me over and over again. Looking at where I find myself I have a vision of Sister St. Anthony rolling her eyes heavenward and saying: "I'm sure you could do better than that."

Keep in mind that the parable is told twice, once in Matthew and again in Luke. There are three stewards in each, and each telling involves different amounts, different rewards and different punishments. So we really have the stories of two masters and six stewards. Even after those stewards are ranked on the basis of performance, somewhat like the way we evaluate Mutual Fund Managers, something hidden reveals itself: they all returned their original trust intact. (Which would not be like our experience with Mutual Fund Managers.)

We are those stewards, and we are called upon to take the trust of our cultures written, spoken and filmed legacy. Some of us add to the total, some transport it and some guard it. I'm a hod carrier but you are the guardians.

When I was a young man emerging from seven years of undergraduate overheating, it came to me that I would never write great poetry, novels, history or philosophy. But I wanted to be part of that cascading current that I saw flowing out of the distant past through the turbines of modernity and generating the power that sustains the contemporary world. I had to be involved. If I had been in New York City I would probably have sought out publishing, but in Niagara Falls it was bookselling.

I don't know how you all came to your calling, but I know all of you share one important aspect with me: you chose to enlist in the library corps just as I chose to join up with booksellers. Our stewardship is different because it was freely chosen, not imposed. We reached out to take on the task of moving the world project along, and at the same time accepted responsibility for the accumulated value that already existed. What we do together is sustain the world culture while facilitating its advancement. We are committed to making sure that our literature, history, science, music and images will not be lost. We will not be forgotten along with the Etruscans, Mayans, Hittites, Assyrians and untold other cultures that have flourished, faltered, faded and disappeared.

It is not my intention to excoriate Librarians, Publishers and Booksellers for failing to hold back the tide of History. In the end we all must march with change or be swept into its dustbin. But many of us are guilty of easing the weakening of a great cultural institution. By failing to object we conceded the field before the battle was joined. Like an army of amateurs we fled at the first sound of the cannons. By doing so we not only dishonored ourselves, but we gave a false impression of inevitability to the unproven assumptions of our adversaries. Because we failed to question and dispute we allowed the virtual library to triumph without having to confront any serious opposition. By treating the few voices that cried out as unreconstructed reactionaries we betrayed our calling for far less that a bowl of porridge. Because we allowed ourselves to be blinded by novelty we abandoned the rock solid mission of our calling for an empty promise.

It might occur to some of you to characterize me as a bitter loser in the technology wars who wants to freeze our institutions and preserve then intact. That would not be correct.

I realize that **the** "unexamined life not being worth living" comment (which we get from one of those old books) applies with equal force to all our institutions and professions.

The unexamined library becomes "The Library of Babel" overflowing with so much superfluity and redundancy that it is impenetrable. But I also know that the "Chase every Rainbow" library, that robs the serial and monograph budgets to pay the database vendor will resemble the giant machine at the heart of "Forbidden Planet": a whirling, self-repairing leviathan that has no apparent purpose other than to facilitate Internet access.

The unexamined publisher would most likely resemble the GPO, spewing forth thousands of unread and unreadable titles, destined for shelving in the "Library of Babel". But the hip, with-it publisher that characterizes so many of the media conglomerates plops one inanity after another on the public and claims priority of place for itself because "Six Spiritual Laws of Cookie Dough" is also available as an e-book download.

The bookstore that has already been purged of individuality spreads out a never-ending stream of homogenized pap that bears as much resemblance to literature as Richards Wild Irish Wine does to Chateau Margeaux.

The world, and the culture that is the only manifestation we can grasp is a continuous project that blinks out and is reassembled every instant. Like DNA it is vulnerable during duplication. Parts are lost and mutations can insinuate themselves into the chain. John Grisham is swapped for Thomas Mann, Stephen King for Sinclair Lewis. Cells depend on specialized proteins to supervise this duplication and correct mistakes. All of us have taken up that job, and our prime directive must be: "First do no harm."

Duty, loyalty, and stewardship: what do they have in common? How often are we caught in a maze made up of just these urges? Taking up a simple task, a common everyday activity and giving ourselves to it we find ourselves entwined in a mesh that demands more from us than we had intended. Choosing the life of bookseller or librarian it was easy to enjoy the freedom, sense of community and even power that came with it. But that freedom came with a terrible price, the obligation to protect the very thing we love. To nurture it and promote it. To stand strong when we looked foolish to those around us. To resist the inanities that are constantly heaped upon the project we cherish.

It may be the case that we never chose to defend the institution of the library. Certainly our commitment to it meant that we would work to see to it that the project of librarianship would have our support. But somehow, for some of us, we forgot that love means first to keep whole the thing we love. We fell into a trance of novelty, a vigorous embracing of the very thing that was trying to undo the library.

When we picked up this life, the life we chose rather than the life we were born into, we took upon ourselves the same duties that those stewards owed, and we will be judged by not only how well we made it grow and prosper, but also by how well we guarded the talents with which we were entrusted.

This talk is not an obituary. It is at once a diagnosis, an epidemiology and a prescription for action. First: do no harm. Second: stand strong against the snake oil salesmen of novelty. Finally: come home to your commitment to the Library, nurture it, strengthen it and protect it.

THE BOOK IS DEAD

Citation Rates in the Humanities and Social Sciences

John McDonald, Acquisitions Librarian, California Institute of Technology

"The scholarly monograph is dead. Even in the humanities, one look at what authors are citing shows they are no longer using books," said the Associate Director for Collection Development during the Chief Collection Development Officers of Large Academic Research Libraries Meeting at ALA Midwinter 2001. While I expected at least one other collection development officer or at least an audience member to question this statement, all was quiet, no one disagreed, and there was not even a murmur of dissent. General agreement with these types of statements can be easily understood. Electronic resources dominate today's information landscape, with electronic journal and book topics dominating the discourse at conferences and in research journals. Internet resources, electronic journals, ebooks, and database issues dominate the current work roles of librarians and other information professionals.

Many scholars have speculated that we are in the midst of the transition to Lancaster's "paperless office" and witnessing a fundamental shift in how scholars perform their research, how students find and use information, and how scholarly communication is produced and disseminated (Harnad 1998, Ginsparg 2001). Recent studies have shown the tremendous increases in the production of information (McDonald 2000) and rise in use of electronic resources (Porter 2001, McDonald 2000). Similar studies have also noted that the publishing of monographic literature only continues to rise, albeit not at the same tremendous rate as production of journal literature and databases (Bowker Annual, McDonald 2000). Thus, while books are still being written and published prolifically, common assumptions are propagated and persist that scholars no longer use these information resources, at least to the extent that they once did (Bourke & Butler 1996).

Social sciences and humanities rely far more heavily on books and book chapters to disseminate their research results while the sciences rely on journal articles and conference papers (Finholt & Brooks 1999). Therefore the assumption that scholars in the humanities and social sciences are not using or citing books anymore should be examined closely. If it is indeed true it may indicate a fundamental shift in research methodology and information seeking and use.

Are scholars really using books at a declining rate compared to the past? Citation analysis is one possible methodology that may help us understand if books are being cited less frequently. Citations, while not a perfect measure of use, nonetheless have been studied for decades for a variety of purposes. Information professionals have used citation analysis to study aspects of basic library operations like serials management, collection development, and remote storage to other advanced topics like network analysis, invisible colleges, and author reputation (Cullars 1998).

Although there is still no comprehensive theory or model of scholarly citation, Cronin has posited a metatheory for citation (Cronin 1998). This metatheory includes three perspectives on citation: functionalist, normative, and phenomenological. The functionalist interpretation defines citation as being used to provide supplementary evidence, support or refute an hypothesis, or to furnish historical context, as some obvious functions of a citation. The normative interpretation highlights the rules, tacit or codified, which govern the dispensing of credits within the scholarly communication system. The phenomenological perspective rests on the belief that citations are highly individualistic by person and discipline and the patterns associated with citation can appear to be random or systematically biased. Cronin states that citation may mix or incorporate all three perspectives — a citation may provide evidence while formally recognizing the cited authors work or contributions (Cronin 1998).

Citation analysis has its share of proponents and also its share of critics (MacRoberts & MacRoberts 1996, Seglen 1997, Kostoff 1998). Criticism of citation analysis is certainly valid, since the act of citing a reference is still not fully understood (Baird & Oppenheim 1994). Despite these criticisms, the results of many citation studies are still reasonably correlated to other aspects of scholarly quality, prestige, and many measures of use (Baird & Oppenheim 1994). Cronin also believes that citation analysis remains an efficient means of measuring if not perceived quality then perceived usefulness (Cronin 1998). Citation can reasonably be assumed to indicate some measure of use — although those measures and nature of the use are still not fully understood.

Assuming then that citation has always indicated some amount of use and the extent of that use is relatively stable, a current citation analysis by format of cited reference may bear witness to the belief and attitude of the collection development officers — that scholars, even in the humanities and social sciences, are no longer citing books.

Literature Review

Studies of information use by humanities and social sciences scholars are frequent. The current literature review will focus on published studies that explicitly examine cited references by format.

Holsapple, Johnson, Manakyan, and Tanner examined citations in five management information systems journals over five years. All cited references were collected and citations were assigned to a format type category. Theses were included in the book category, while technical reports, working papers, correspondence, and other formats were excluded from the study. They concluded that citations to books have declined over the study time period, agreeing with a study by Hamilton & Ives from the 1970s (Holsapple, et. al. 1993). In addition, citations to proceedings have grown with time (see Table 1 for a complete review). Some argument can be made that their broad assessment that citations to books have declined over time is overstated: the rates they determined were 39%, 37%, 36%, 35%, and then 28% over the 5 years sampled. Although the decline is steady, none is significant until the final year drop from 35% to 28%.

In a citation analysis of anthropology literature, Hider determined that citations to books were actually increasing over a sample of articles from eight volumes of a core journal that encompassed a twenty-five year period. Not only did book references increase, but references to book chapters and grey literature (including theses, correspondence, etc.) increased significantly over time (Hider 1996). Other studies of anthropology literature citation rates by format that were summarized by Hider included Choi (1988b), Aravinda & Pella Reddy (1990), and Rana (1982). Choi found citation rates to books were 45.3% in 1963 and 41% in 1983 while journals were 52.2% in 1963 and 51.8% in 1983. Aravinda & Pella Reddy found 57.5% of references in three years of a single anthropology journal were to books while 37.2% were to journals. Rana found that 51.7% of citations were to books and 33.2% were to journal articles.

Johnson's study of twenty-four environmental and human health publications found that 67% of the cited references were to journal articles, 17% to books, 16% to technical reports, 10% to proceedings, and 7% to thesis. Also examining the dates of cited references showed that the average age of a journal citation was 10.5 years, 9.4 for books, 7.9 for technical reports, 9.4 years for proceedings. Wehmeyer found that psychology dissertation included 23% citations to books, 11% to book chapters, 62% to journals, and 3% to other. Nursing theses citations were to books 19% of the time, book chapters 5%, journal articles were 67%, and other were 8%. Biomedical Sciences were 3% books, 6% book chapters, 89% journals, and 2% other (Wehmeyer 1999). Cullars (1998) found that 85% of citations in philosophy materials studied were to books, which agreed with Buchanan & Herubel (1993) finding of 81.3% of citations in philosophy dissertations were to books. Clemens (1995) summarized 6 studies in Sociology from 1940 to 1971 (Broadus 1952,1967; Lin & Nelson, 1969, Brown & Gilmartin 1969, Baughman, 1974). Citations to books ranged from 42% in 1940 to 62% in 1970. Citations to journals in the same period ranged from 40% to 39% from 1940 to 1970.

Table 1: Previous Citation Studies focusing on format of cited references

	Clemens (1940)	Cullars (1996)	Holsapple (1987-1991)	Hider (1966-93)	Johnson (2000)	Wehmeyer (2000)	Wehmeyer (2000)	Wehmeyer (2000)
Subject area	*Sociology*	*Philosophy*	*MIS*	*Anthropology*	*Environmental Health*	*Psychology*	*Nursing*	*Biomedical Sciences*
Books	42-54-62-64-54-62%	85%	34.8%	42%-50%	17%	23%	19%	3%
Book Chapters	40-46-39 36-40-39%	——	——	13%-24%	——	11%	6%	6%
Journal articles	——	——	53.7%	43%-27%	67%	62%	67%	89%
Grey literature	——	——	——	1% - 5%	——	3%	8%	2%
Conference proceedings	——	——	11.5%	——	10%	——	——	——
Theses	——	——	——	——	7%	——	——	——
Technical Reports	——	——	——	——	16%	——	——	——
Total citations	569 – 11,130	——	27,543	——	1650	4779	3267	10,073

Current Study

A model of monograph use by humanists and social scientists includes heavy citation of books, book chapters, archival evidence, and journal articles. While scholars in other disciplines rely to a great extent on journal literature, those in the humanities and social scientists cite more resources per publication, cite more books, and cite a wider variety of material formats in general than do scholars in the hard sciences (Nordstrom 1987, Walcott 1994, Cullars 1998). Citation rates by format of cited material vary widely among disciplines but also remain rather static over time. The current study focuses on the formats of cited references by faculty authors in the humanities and social sciences at an academic research institution.

The California Institute of Technology is a world-renowned university that focuses heavily on the natural and hard sciences. Faculty or alumni have won twenty-nine Nobel Prizes, but only two from the humanities or social sciences (Linus Pauling for peace in 1962 and Robert Merton for economics in 1997). Although Caltech's humanities and social science departments are not extensive, many of the faculty are active researchers and authors.

This study examined the publications produced by forty-six faculty members in the humanities and social sciences. The sample included thirteen economists, twelve historians, seven literature faculty, six political scientists, six philosophers, and one each in law and anthropology.

A literature search was performed on these forty-six authors and 173 publications were identified and selected to be included in the study. The publication dates ranged from 1994 to 2000. Not all publications identified for these authors could be included in this study because they fell outside the date range, the full text of some publications could not be found during the study period, or the publications were editorials, book reviews, etc. that contained no citations. The publications included 148 journal articles, 15 books, 5 book chapters, 3 theses, and two working papers. Each publication was assigned a designation of book or journal article. The two working papers and five book chapters were of journal article length and cited references ranged from 20 to 80 cited references making them more consistent with journal articles and were thus added to the journal category. Three extensive review articles and the three theses were more consistent with the length and cited references of books were included in the book category. The sample breakdown by discipline included 65 publications in economics, 36 in political science, 30 in history, 21 in philosophy, 13 in literature, 5 in law, and 3 in anthropology. Of the twenty-one items assigned to the book category, history faculty, five by literature, and three each by philosophers and economists wrote ten.

The total number of cited references for these publications equaled 11,852. Each cited reference was assigned a material type based on its format. Initially, there were nine cited format categories: book, book chapter, journal article, conference proceeding, working paper, technical report, government document, thesis, and other. After reviewing these cited references, they were aggregated into the 'book', 'journal article', and 'other' categories, since the frequency of these formats were so low. Conference proceedings, working papers, technical reports were assigned to the 'journal article' category. Theses and book chapter were assigned to the 'book' category. Newspapers, interviews, government documents, and other grey literature were assigned to the 'other' category.

Citation Numbers

Table 2: Cited references by publication type

Type	Publications	Cited References
Journal Article	152	5112
Book	21	5521
Total	173	10633*

Table 3: Cited references by year of publication

Year	Publications	Cited References
2000	24	1305
1999	32	1944
1998	31	3116
1997	22	1316
1996	23	1378
1995	21	928
1994	20	648
Total	173	10633

Table 4: Cited references by format of cited material

Cited Format	Citations	%
Book	5178	49%
Journal Article	4907	46%
Other	548	5%
Total	10633*	

Table 5: Cited references by year and format

Cited Format	2000	1999	1998	1997	1996	1995	1994	1994-2000	%
Book	47%	50%	50%	45%	58%	43%	39%	5178	49%
Journal Article	48%	49%	43%	47%	39%	50%	57%	4907	46%
Other	5%	2%	7%	8%	3%	6%	4%	548	5%
Total	1305	1944	3114	1316	1378	928	648	10633*	

Table 6: Cited references by format in two year blocks

Cited Format	2000-1999	1998-1997	1996-1995
Book	49%	49%	52%
Journal Article	48%	44%	44%
Other	3%	7%	4%
Total	3249	4430	2306

Table 7: Cited References by format in two time periods

Cited Format	2000-1998	1997-1994
Book	49%	48%
Journal Article	46%	47%
Other	5%	6%
Total	6363	4270

Table 8: Cited references by citing publication and year

Cited format	2000		1999		1998		1997		1996		1995		1994	
	Book	Journal	Book	Journal	Book	Journal	Book	Journal	Book	Journal	Book	Journal	Book	Journal
Book	56%	37%	62%	39%	50%	51%	53%	36%	85%	33%	56%	42%	78%	26%
Journal Article	39%	59%	37%	59%	43%	44%	39%	55%	14%	62%	29%	52%	21%	69%
Other	5%	4%	1%	3%	7%	5%	8%	8%	1%	5%	14%	6%	1%	6%
Totals	697	608	898	1046	2345	769	689	627	651	727	78	850	163	485

Table 9: Cited references by discipline

Cited Format	Anthropology	Economics	History	Law	Literature	Philosophy	Political Science
Book	64%	29%	57%	13%	78%	44%	35%
Journal Article	36%	63%	39%	76%	16%	54%	60%
Other	0	8%	4%	11%	6%	2%	5%
Totals	200	2374	4035	281	1377	1326	1042

Table 10: Cited references for economics faculty (a discipline that cites journals heavily)

	2000	1999	1998	1997	1996	1995	1994	1998-2000	1994-1997
Journal Article	69%	68%	58%	39%	82%	78%	77%	65%	60%
Book	26%	30%	25%	48%	14%	17%	14%	28%	30%
Other	5%	2%	17%	13%	4%	5%	9%	7%	9%
Totals	260	584	361	550	205	132	282	1205	1169

*In tables 2 — 10, two outliers were excluded from the statistical compilation of the "other" category. A 1999 book about voting rights that included a preponderance of citations to government documents accounted for 80% of the citations assigned to the "other" category (372 citations), and a 1998 book, focusing on a legal case about scientific fraud whose citations were mainly legal documents and interviews, included 80% (845) of the citations in the other category.

Discussion

This citation analysis of Caltech's current humanities and social sciences faculty publications shows that they are still citing books in their research. They even appear to be citing and therefore presumably using books at a relatively stable rate over the time period of the study. In addition, the results of this citation analysis closely match the results of other citation analyses in the humanities and social sciences.

In aggregate, humanities and social sciences faculty cite books, journals, and grey literature at the same rates as reported by Clemens, Holsapple, Hider, and Wehmeyer in the comparable disciplines they studied. The aggregate citation rate for all publications studied (49% citation rate for books, 46% for journals) well within the ranges reported by Clemens for Sociology and by Hider for Anthropology that spanned years ranging from 1940 through 1993. The citation rates, by discipline, for Caltech authors also closely mirror the rates in previous studies. Caltech's Economics faculty heavy citation of journals is similar to Holsapple's review of management information systems journals and Wehmeyer's study of psychology. Caltech's anthropologist's citation rates are similar to the report of studies by Hider, although one faculty member and only three publications are too small a sample to be conclusive.

Citation rates by format over time have also remained stable for Caltech authors. Neither books as a cited format nor journals as a cited format have varied much over the aggregate statistics over the study period. Books were cited 49% of the time and journal articles 46% of the time from 1994 to 2000. The lowest one year total for books as cited format was in 1994 with a 39% rate, followed by 1995 with a 43% rate. These two years also represented the largest percentage of cited references from journal articles. Citations to journal articles were also closely clustered around the aggregate rate of 46% for the entire sample, aside from the sample years of 1994 and 1995.

Citation rates aggregated into two-year blocks from 1995/96, 1998/97, and 1999/2000, also show that there was little difference based on format. Books were cited 52%, 49%, and 49% while journal articles were cited 44%, 44%, and 48%. This low variability shows that publications from 1995/96 cited book and journals in relatively the same proportions as were cited in 1999/2000. Using large aggregates from 1994 to 1997 and 1998 to 2000 shows the same low amount of difference in citation rates. Books were cited 48% of the time in works published from 1994 to 1997 and 49% of the time in publications from 1998 through 2000. The journal citation rates also remained the same, as seen in Table 7. Scholars, at least in this sample, are still citing materials in their publications at the same rate over this time period.

The type of material that the academic researcher is publishing also seems to follow stable citation rates for format of the cited material. Books cite books more frequently than they cite journals, while journals cite other journal articles more frequently than they cite books. The format of the publication type does indicate the format of the cited material. This measure is also stable over time during the years studied, despite large outliers for 1996 when one book citing books accounted for 67% of the citations in that category.

In addition, specific disciplines also seem to be citing materials at the same rates as they have in the past. For example, faculty in the economics department at Caltech cite journal articles at a stable rate nearing 65%. Publications from 1994 to 1997 cited journal articles 60% of the time, while those published from 1998 to 2000 cited journal articles 65%. Economics is a social science that is heavily dependent on journal literature, so this rate is not unexpected. The rates that they are still citing books may surprise some, from 1994 to 1997 they cited books 30% of the time and from 1998 to 2000 they cited books 28% of the time. This is surprising since their use of monographic literature does not seem to be dependent on the type of publication. Economics publications in the same totaled 62 journal articles and only 3 books. The fact that those journal articles still cite books at such a high rate, and with little variety over a seven-year period, show that these faculty still use books when writing articles for publication.

The original purpose of the study was to examine citation rates of humanities and social sciences faculty to determine if citation rates by format have changed over time. More specifically, are books being cited less and therefore can be assumed to be used less today than in the past? The comments by the collection development officer reported at the beginning of the article can be safely said to be incorrect, at least for academic scholarly research publications. The publications included in the study still cite books at the same rates that they have over the recent past. Citation of formats by publication types (books or journal articles) also remains stable over the time period studied. Citations of specific formats, while discipline specific, do not seem to be changing in aggregate percentages over time either. While electronic resources dominate the responsibilities of information professionals, scholars are still using books, as evidenced by citations in their academic publications.

Bibliography

Baird, Laura & Oppenheim, Charles. (1994). Do Citations Matter? *Journal of Information Science*, 20(1), 2-15.

Bourke, P. & Butler, Linda. (1996). Publication types, citation rates and evaluation. *Scientometrics*, 37(3), 473-94.

The Bowker Annual of Library and Book Trade Information. (1991-1996). ed. Dave Bogart, New Providence, NJ: R.R.Bowker.

Choi, Jin M. (1988). Citation Analysis of intra-and interdisciplinary communication patterns of anthropology in the USA. *Behavioral & Social Sciences Librarian*, 6, 65-84.

Cronin, Blaise. (1998). Metatheorizing citation. *Scientometrics*, 43(1), 45-55.

Cullars, John M. (1998). Citation characteristics of English-language monographs in philosophy. *Library & Information Science Research*, 20(1), 41-68.

Finholt, T.A., & Brooks, J. (1999). "Analysis of JSTOR: The impact on scholarly practice of access to on-line journal archives." In R. Ekman and R.E. Quandt (Eds.) *Technology and Scholarly Communication* (pp. 177-194). Berkeley: University of California Press.

Ginsparg, Paul. "Creating a global knowledge network," *Proceedings of the Second ICSU-UNESCO International Conference on Electronic Publishing in Science*, February 2001, http://associnst.ox.ac.uk/~icsuinfo/ginspargfin.htm

Harnad, Steven. (1998). For Whom the Gate Tolls? Free the Online-Only Refereed Literature. *American Scientist Forum*.
http://amsci-forum.amsci.org/archives/september98-forum.html
http://www.cogsci.soton.ac.uk/~harnad/amlet.html

Hider, Philip M. (1996). Three Bibliometric Analyses of Anthropology Literature. *Behavioral & Social Sciences Librarian*, 15(1), 1-17.

Holsapple, Clyde W., Johnson, Linda Ellis, Manakyan, Herman, and Tanner, John. (1993). A Citation Analysis of Business Computing Research Journals. *Information & Management*, 25, 231-44.

Johnson, Bill. (2000). Environmental Impact: a preliminary citation analysis of local faculty in new academic program in environmental and human health applied to collection development in an academic library. *Library Philosophy and Practice*, 2(2)
http://www.uidaho.edu/~mbolin/lppv2n2.htm

Kostoff Ronald N. (1998). The use and misuse of citation analysis in research evaluation - Comments on theories of citation? *Scientometrics*, 43(1), 27-43.

MacRoberts, Michael H. and MacRoberts, Barbara R. (1996). Problems of citation analysis. *Scientometrics*, 36(3), 435-444.

McDonald, John (2000) E vs. P: A use statistics comparison. Presentation given at the Charleston Conference, November 2.
http://library.caltech.edu/john/evsp.htm.

Nordstrom, L.O. (1987). Applied Versus Basic Science in the Literature of Plant Biology: A Bibliometric Perspective. *Scientometrics*, 12(5-6), 381-93.

Porter, George and Sponsler, Ed. Online Journals: Utility of ToCs vs. Fulltext. *Crossing the Divide: Proceedings of the Tenth National Conference of the Association of College & Research Libraries*, March 15-18, 2001, Denver, Colorado, 110-19,
http://library.caltech.edu/publications/acrldenver/

Seglen, Per O. (1997). Citations and journal impact factors: questionable indicators of research quality. *Allergy*, 52(11), 1050-56.

Wehmeyer, Jeffrey M. (1999). The comparative importance of books: clinical psychology in the health sciences library, 87(2), 187-91.

PROBLEMS IN THE BOOK PIPELINE

Robert Birch, Director of Sales, Greenwood Publishing Group

At the risk of sounding like a besotted starlet on Oscar night, I would like to begin by thanking a few people—not my third grade teacher, I promise, though she did have a formative influence... but that's another story. There were eight of us who wrote the articles that appear in this issue of *Against the Grain*. In addressing the growing and changing problems in the supply pipeline of academic publishing, I wanted to ensure that there were voices from the three partners in that pipeline, publishers, distributors, and libraries. My co-authors put a lot of themselves into their articles and were patient with my various editorial and deadline pressures. To all of them, I am deeply appreciative, and two are joining me on this panel. And thanks (I think it's thanks) also to Katina, who has a seductively sweet way of getting one to do most anything she wants, sometimes without one even knowing they are doing it. No, seriously, thanks Katina for your patience and support.

On this panel are a publisher, a distributor, and a librarian. Niko Pfund of Oxford University Press had hoped to join us, but could not attend for a number of personal reasons. So I will be attempting to do justice to both of us from the publishing world. It's important to note who is not represented—the authors and patrons who begin and end the flow of ideas that constitute our business. This omission is not intended to suggest a relative lack of importance—far from it, for authors and patrons are the ultimate deciders of every course we take. However, publishers, distributors, and libraries are the ones who connect the authors and patrons through what I have called a pipeline of ideas. Traditionally, the three of us have functioned as partners, though at times our relationships have been more 80's dysfunctional than 50's Leave It To Beaver. However, of late there have appeared to be a growing number of problems in the pipeline.

A few years ago I was on another panel at Charleston that was also addressing issues facing publishers, distributors, and libraries. In my talk, I like the others raised some of the problems we faced. But I tried to stress the need for us to continue to function as partners, for as the dissemination of academic information changes in our increasingly "e" world, the value of our roles within that world is enhanced when we continue to draw from each other's strengths.

Since then, the changes and pressures of which we spoke have not only continued, but have actually accelerated. The extent to which this is true was borne out to me earlier this year when separately two heads of acquisitions of major research university libraries approached me about buying all of Greenwood's titles directly. Obviously, I was intrigued by the opportunities such offers represented. But I also wondered what were the implications, for in effect the proposals, in bypassing distributors, completely altered the pipeline as we know it.

There have always been pressures on the three of us, as constantly threatened library budgets and precariously thin margins for distributors and publishers lead to what often seems like a singularly unattractive form of mud wrestling: we all push and pull each other, but in the end we not only get nowhere, but we are covered with mud. If libraries demand better discounts from distributors, distributors will in turn do the same to publishers, who if they concede on discount may simply raise prices, leaving only an illusion that anything has changed. This has basically been true for all of the traditional pressures we place on each other.

However, of late pressures have begun to seem a bit darker and more problematic. In the face of increasing demand from patrons, libraries are finding their material costs and required breadth of professional skills escalating at a pace that taxes their budgets. Distributors are expected not only to provide discounts, but also to provide an ever wider array of services. Publishers are asked to ease their terms while simultaneously developing more flexible publication strategies. The results of these and other pressures have been obvious: a staggering amount of consolidation that has left fewer publishers, fewer distributors, and fewer voices from individual libraries as they join consortia.

The greatest pressures have come with the advent of e-publishing. E-books from the outset seemed to offer wonderful opportunities for all—publishers could reduce inventory, distributors would not have to deal with material transfers, libraries could increase access. Print on demand has been equally seductive, as publishers can reduce print runs, distributors can become publishers, and once again libraries can increase access, here to formerly hard to find books. With e-publishing, all would change for all time.

Well, needless to say, it hasn't worked out that way. Where once we heard from Microsoft that more e-books would be published by 2004 than print, now we are told that they always meant that it would be eight to ten years before e-publishing began to equal that of print. We hear from people such as Sterling Lawrence, editor in chief of WW Norton who said, "If e-books were the only thing to buy in a 'bookstore', I would buy a lot fewer books. I am glad I will be dead by the time they take over the business." I even brought along a prop—a cap from bigwords.com, which has died and come back to life. I have made a habit of collecting t-shirts, caps, and other assorted giveaways from the .coms. It's a growth industry—think of the value of such artifacts in years to come. On a more serious note, there was a chill that went through the pipeline at the news a few weeks ago that not only was netLibrary for sale, but that all employees would lose benefits and be paid only $360 a week. The nervousness and uncertainty that resulted has been heard throughout this conference.

Why have e-books not taken off as expected? As Niko pointed out in his article, most of what he called the "hysteria" over e-books arose not out of reason, but rather from emotion. There was a stunning influx of venture capital into the .coms and this made publishers, distributors, and librarians feel they had better get with it and soon or be left behind as anachronisms. However, it was soon found that the technology wasn't there yet, nor was there a developed market for these products. So, now, as before with cd-roms and multimedia, hysteria has been replaced with a far more sober view.

However, e-books are not going away. Their share of academic publishing will increase, albeit more slowly. Though admittedly they are free, the 3 million downloads of e-books from the University of Virginia Library's Electronic Text Center point to a very real interest in the medium. And for me the most telling support for e-books comes from my father-in-law, a crusty old Virginian who vowed that he'd never read an e-book until he found you could enlarge the type for easier reading. Now, he is thinking of asking for a reader for Christmas.

And the pressures that come with e-publishing also aren't going away. Costs to change from old operating systems to new ones that can handle this technology are large and endless as the technology keeps changing, and this especially threatens smaller publishers, distributors, and libraries. And some even foresee a radical vision of the future, a cataclysm of disintermediation in which publishers will vanish as authors publish and vett their books, distributors won't distribute but will provide only services, and libraries will be websites with animated paperclips for librarians.

Now, I don't believe this will happen. We all, though at times in our anxieties might forget it, have value. Publishers edit and market, as well as produce. Distributors consolidate orders as well as provide services. And librarians will always be far better guides in a world of ideas than on-line help. Recently, a distributor I know attributed the problems of the .coms to the fact that their decision makers were the wrong people, coming too often from the tech not academic worlds. He said all that was needed for e-books to take off were people who knew and understood this rather peculiar world of academic publishing.

And that is where we three come in, for academic publishers, distributors, and librarians do know that world. The pressures remain and will grow. However, I retain what some may think a wistful conviction that the pipeline works and that all three partners are needed and should work in concert, not against each other. And this was my goal in both the *Against The Grain* articles and this panel: to shake things up a bit, get people talking, with the hope that the problems we individually face may be seen in the broader context that affects us all. For as Niko concluded in his paper, we had better continue to offer and offer well those services that we uniquely provide, individually and collectively, or we may find our value and reason for being will have vanished.

The existence of a library consortium forces the member libraries of that consortium to work in collaboration. What collaboration entails at various levels and a various times is a theme that runs through two of the following papers. The third paper discusses the impact of multiple library consortia within a state.

consortia

STONE AGE CONSORTIA, NEW AGE CONSORTIA—THE PLACE FOR COORDINATED COOPERATIVE COLLECTION MANAGEMENT

Cathy Doyle, University Librarian, Christopher Newport University; Christopher Millson-Martula, Director, Knight-Capron Library; and Steve Stratton, Social Sciences Librarian, Virginia Commonwealth University

Good afternoon. My colleagues, Cathy Doyle and Steve Stratton, and I welcome you to this afternoon's session. Before we begin, let's do some unscientific polling by a show of hands in response to the following questions:

1. Who believes in patriotism and the flag?

2. Who believes that motherhood and apple pie are good?

3. Who believes in the value of coordinated cooperative collection management?

Your affirmative response to the third question surprises us a bit. We have found that coordinated cooperative collection management, or CCCM, remains an unknown or elusive commodity for many librarians and library staff. While there has been a good deal of rhetoric in support of it, its successes haven't been broadly publicized and the typical library staff member isn't rushing to undertake or participate in such projects.

What do we plan to cover today? First, we'll briefly discuss CCCM in general and also within the context of collaboration. Following that, we'll mention examples of key projects. Next, we'll describe in detail two case studies—one from over ten years ago, in the stone age, the other contemporary. Then, we'll provide some analysis of factors that are either barriers to or conducive to or critical for the success of such programs. Lastly, and perhaps most significantly, we hope to start up a dialogue with you in which we all share our experiences with CCCM thus far as well as our projections for its future.

CCCM IN GENERAL

To insure that we're all on the same playing field, let's begin with a definition that we can all accept for the purposes of today's session. We define CCCM as the joint development or management of collections by two or more libraries based on a formal agreement for this purpose. What are some manifestations of CCCM? A representative listing includes:

- Coordinating the purchase of expensive items
- Assigning primary subject-collecting responsibility
- Providing funds for a central agency to purchase materials
- Cooperative digitizing of resources
- Cooperative selection and retention of materials
- Cooperative selection and storage of little used materials
- Collaboration in the area of preservation
- Providing financial support to libraries with the best subject collections so that they can continue to collect intensively.

Why should a library undertake or participate in CCCM projects? We suggest that the key goal or benefit should be to provide enhanced service to users by providing greater, faster, and easier access to an expanded range of resources, particularly those materials of secondary value to an institution. Other benefits and goals could include: sharing bibliographers, preservationists, and other staff; eliminating undesirable and unnecessary redundancy; establishing new relationships based on interlocking collections and closer relationships with faculty and administrators; and sharing storage facilities. Some projects result in a better understanding and monitoring of collection management performance and greater selectivity in acquiring non-core titles, while other projects could yield more economical and cost-effective patterns of collection management; planned, rather than haphazard, cost reduction; advantages derived from consortial licensing agreements for electronic resources; and coordinated pruning, canceling, or storing of materials.

The most successful CCCM projects are likely to thrive in a collaborative environment. Thus, let's take a few minutes to consider the concept of collaboration.

COLLABORATION

We can define collaboration as an activity that involves people or institutions coming together for the long term to realize mutually agreed upon goals or objectives based on interdependent planning, implementation, and support. Collaboration requires persuasion since followership is voluntary. In addition, it's extremely important to focus on the benefits, not the features, of an activity.

Collaboration requires four essential elements:

- Vision and relationships—the full commitments of organizations and their leaders
- Structure, responsibilities, and communication—characterized by clearly defined roles, the development of joint strategies, a focus on the activity's impact on users' needs, and many levels of communication
- Authority and accountability—leadership is dispersed, with control shared and mutual
- Resources and rewards—resources are pooled or jointly secured and there are meaningful rewards for the participants.

KEY CCCM PROJECTS

Let's now shift gears and look at some of the major CCCM projects from the past. This is not an all-inclusive listing, nor is it in any order of significance. While I won't indicate the degree of success for each project, I will highlight the project's key activities or goals. If any of you are or have been a participant in any of these programs, please feel free to share your perspectives or experience with all of us.

1. Triangle Research Libraries Network

Duke and the University of North Carolina Chapel Hill established the network in 1933, and they were later joined by North Carolina State University and North

Carolina Central University. Network goals were to increase the range of research materials available, assign areas of collecting responsibilities at the research level, and avoid unnecessary duplication. The network adopted the principle of mutual exclusivity regarding subjects of interest to only one institution. Members have formulated agreements based on area studies or categories/formats of materials such as government documents and newspapers.

2. Center for Research Libraries

Established in 1949, the center has implemented programs involving the coordination of collection policies based on area of the world or publication format, centralized cataloging, cooperative storage of little used materials (books and microforms), and cooperative acquisition of rarely held serials, newspapers, and foreign dissertations, with heavy reliance on microforms.

3. University of California Shared Purchase Program

Begun in 1976, this program uses the funds of each campus library to purchase items costing more than $1500 that are related to the programs of more than one campus. The program's goal is to prevent the unnecessary duplication of expensive, low-use materials among the campuses.

4. Ohio LINK

Yesterday we learned a good deal about Ohio LINK and it currently is one of the most well known consortia in the country. However, in the early 1990's, it consisted of fewer than twenty institutions, and it was mandated by the state's board of regents to develop programs for cooperative storage and collection management. Members initially planned to develop a collection management module for its online system, measure collection use, and assess individual and collective strengths and weaknesses in terms of collection gaps, overlap, and uniqueness. Members aimed to develop the ability to make decisions on cooperative storage, weeding, and preservation.

5. Research Libraries Group

RLG is the last project that I'll include in my review. Collection assessment is undoubtedly the cornerstone of successful CCCM programs, and this is the area of RLG's most significant contribution.

RLG developed the conspectus as not simply a systematic description of collections but rather a means to communicate and share information about collections—a common language. The conspectus allows for collection evaluation based on subject descriptors or classification numbers. It identifies existing collection strengths and current collecting activity using collection levels ranging from out of scope to comprehensive, and it includes notations regarding the language characteristics of the collections. While it theoretically incorporates both qualitative and quantitative elements, in my opinion, the latter tends to outweigh the former in that assessment is usually made based on title counts or shelf list measurement (from the stone age). Thus, what appears as a quite objective tool can actually be greatly subjective and impressionistic. Having said this, however, I would still maintain that the conspectus is a valid and viable instrument for collection assessment.

CASE STUDY 1—GREATER MIDWEST REGIONAL MEDICAL LIBRARY NETWORK

Let's now examine our first case study, that of the Greater Midwest Regional Medical Library Network, affectionately known to some as Gremlin.

Acting as one of the National Library of Medicine's regional networks, Gremlin served more than 500 libraries, mainly academic, hospital, and special, in a ten-state region extending from Kentucky in the southeast to North Dakota in the northwest from a management office at the University of Illinois at Chicago.

Gremlin first became involved in CCCM in 1983 with awards, funded by contract money, for the purchase of serial subscriptions, monographs, and media. Full involvement in CCCM resulted from a five-year contract with NLM covering the period 1985-90.

The program's goals were to improve the quality, quantity, depth, and breadth of the regional collection, optimize the use of monetary resources, and increase the region's self-sufficiency by improving the regional interlibrary loan fill rate. The program had four components:

1. **Resource analysis**—We modified the RLG conspectus to fit our needs, which required us to maintain balance among the clinical, academic, and research arenas. In 1987-8, 42 libraries (all 21 resource libraries—mainly medical school libraries plus special libraries such as the John Crerar Library and the libraries of the American Medical Association, the American Dental Association, the American Hospital Association, and the Mayo Clinic—plus 21 hospital libraries) evaluated their collections. Our conspectus had 223 standard subject descriptors plus 10 that we added dealing with the socio-economic aspects of the health sciences. For each descriptor, evaluators provided existing collection strength and current collecting intensity for serials (numbers of retrospective and current serial titles) and monographs (number of monographs and the number added during the most recent year). Based on this data, evaluators assigned one of six collection levels (out of scope, minimal, basic information, instructional support, research, and comprehensive), and they also provided for each descriptor the mean age of the monograph collection and its general physical condition as well as language characteristics of the collection.

How did we attain a reasonable degree of consistency among the assessments? Did we use verification studies or hire consultants? No. Instead, we compared a library's monograph holdings to NLM's monograph holdings for each descriptor, the monograph titles added by NLM in 1986, and, for serials, we compared holdings to the list of journals indexed by Index Medicus. We also randomly selected 24 subject descriptors, or roughly 10% of the total, sorted the records using dBaseIII Plus, and compared the numbers of serial and monograph titles reported. As a result, we found about 150 instances of overassessment.

2. **Resource development**—We had as our goal the identification of serial titles to be purchased and subject areas where the monograph collection contained gaps or needed greater depth. We tended to emphasize the current collecting activity and desired to have three research level collections in the region for descriptors identified as significant. Program participants competed for awards ranging from $3000 to $5000 to fill gaps and develop new core collections. As a result, we awarded $17,000 to six libraries for the purchase of 21 serial titles and monographs in the area of health care administration, which was the only gap chosen for development.

3. **Resource retention**—Members made commitments to retain serial titles for as long as practicable.

4. **A regional collection development policy manual**—This was not intended as a typical full-fledged policy statement, but rather a map of the 42 collections that would constitute the regional collection. We produced a microfiche set based on the conspectus evaluations. In addition to one comprehensive compilation, we also sorted the data by elements such as collections at the comprehensive level, those with foreign language materials, descriptors with fewer than three research level collections in the region, descriptors with no collections, and, for each state, collections at the research or comprehensive levels.

Did the project succeed? While we satisfactorily fulfilled the obligations of the contract, the project unfortunately had no visible long lasting effects. The program failed to be replicated by other regional medical library networks across the country, and the program's components did not continue past the end of the contract.

FACTORS IMPEDING SUCCESS

What can we identify as obstacles or barriers to the success of CCCM projects? As the list that follows indicates, the barriers are numerous and generally quite formidable. Thus, individuals who desire to implement successful CCCM projects must persevere in the face of adversity.

1. **Low levels of commitment**—At least moderate levels of commitment by those with the authority to make decisions as well as by those who will implement the decisions are necessary. In addition, there should be a reasonable degree of balance between the two groups. Supporters and advocates must address and overcome resistance from faculty and library staff.

2. **Multiplicity of consortia**—This is most definitely a fact of life for virtually all of us. The Gremlin medical school libraries didn't feel that Gremlin was the consortium of greatest importance to them, and this had a direct effect on their degrees of involvement, enthusiasm, and support.

3. **Communication**—Communication must be regular, but not necessarily constant, and despite the use of technology, the need for human in-person interaction remains.

4. **Limited free choice**—While the Gremlin program was developed by a committee representative of the membership, some nonetheless felt that it was imposed upon them. This, of course, affected their level of support for the program.

5. **Lack of balance between local interests and consortium interests**—People didn't always see it as a win-win situation in that they felt that they had to sacrifice self-interest for the greater good. While virtually any cooperative project is likely to involve the loss of autonomy, independence, or prestige, at the same time, staff must feel that they and their customers are deriving significant benefits or gains as well.

6. **Competition among participants**—The Gremlin medical schools tended to compete with each other for students, faculty, and research grants. Many felt that sharing information about their collections, no matter how innocuous that seemed, was like revealing state secrets.

7. **Geographic factors**—The Gremlin region was quite large.

8. **Lack of an efficient delivery system**—While some states had statewide delivery systems, there was no single system crossing state lines in the region. Thus, there was a reasonable degree of difficulty in providing physical access to materials.

FACTORS PROMOTING SUCCESS

What environmental factors are conducive to cooperation or should motivate individuals to collaborate? Virtually all of us are facing budget pressures in the form of rising costs of materials, shrinking budgets, and increasing costs for storage and retrieval. In addition, new technologies for information management expand the universe of information sources, thereby making it increasingly difficult for libraries to handle all formats successfully. In many institutions, access is finally replacing ownership as an acceptable situation, and, lastly, interinstitutional cooperation is occurring in areas other than libraries.

Before moving on to our second case study, let's first recap things by mentioning preconditions or requisites for successful CCCM activities. While I have already mentioned some of them, their importance bears repeating.

- The need to share bibliographic data
- An efficient document delivery system
- The need for leadership—Somebody must be in charge and must demonstrate enlightened and persistent leadership.
- Individuals and institutions must buy in to the process.
- Categorical and item-specific knowledge of collections
- Trust that partners will maintain their cooperative commitments, and trust that exists between institutions
- Reasonably high utility or value of the materials upon which agreements are based and the belief that the agreements will meet user needs
- The ability and willingness to see a picture bigger than that of an individual library
- Adequate training for participants
- Programs that are responsive and minimally threatening to local priorities and programs and that should protect and recognize the substantial institutional program commitments by building on them.

Now, Cathy will give us a behind the scenes look at VIVA, the Virtual Library of Virginia.

CASE STUDY 2—VIVA (VIRTUAL LIBRARY OF VIRGINIA)

In 1994 the Virginia General Assembly gave academic libraries a one-time increase in their acquisitions budgets. The Library Advisory Committee (LAC) of the State Council for Higher Education in Virginia (SCHEV) decided to pool this money to create VIVA, the Virtual Library of Virginia. VIVA was designed to create a uniform set of electronic resources for all state supported institutions, support the prompt delivery of materials via interlibrary loan and create a central area on the internet to find information about member libraries. While state funding could not be used to purchase resources for private institutions, contract negotiations for all products allowed private institutions to receive discounts comparable to public institutions, should they choose to purchase products that VIVA purchased.

Previously, actions on the state level had not been coordinated, except for stand-alone projects, such as union listing and local consortiums to promote borrowing within a specific area (for instance, the Tidewater Consortium for Higher Education, which has a library subcommittee to promote lending in academic institutions from Williamsburg south to Virginia Beach). Member libraries had different integrated library systems and were often in competition at an institutional level for students. Changing to a more cooperative approach was a great change in mind-set for many members, who had previously been in competition with each other for students and resources.

The first year of VIVA involved setting up an infrastructure, which included hiring a half-time executive director (donated by a member institution), purchasing servers to run the VIVA website, supplying member libraries with state of the art computers to access VIVA materials, adding staff to the Interlibrary Loan departments of doctoral institutions and developing a mechanism to reimburse libraries for lending books in-state. The initial VIVA products were the *Encyclopedia Britannica* and FirstSearch. These products were designed to give benefit to the greatest number of libraries to build support for VIVA across the Commonwealth. These goals were met, and VIVA advanced.

One of the reasons that VIVA was so popular with the Virginia legislature was the fact that the project did not call for the establishment of a huge bureaucracy. While the half-time director is now full time and has secretarial assistance and a technical support line has been added, most of the work of VIVA is done by committees composed of staff from member libraries. However, the founders of VIVA had promised the legislature that VIVA would show savings from cost reduction (cancellations) as well as cost avoidance (reduced prices). Our sub-committee was established to keep this promise.

COMMITTEE DECISION-MAKING

In 1995, the Collections Committee of VIVA established three sub-committees to plan for and build confidence in the development of collections in three subject areas: science, technical and medical journals; business and economics; and nursing and allied health. A wide variety of libraries contributed members, including private colleges, doctoral institutions, comprehensive colleges and community colleges. Members volunteered for the committee, creating a group that was committed to the success of the mission. The chair of the group was also a member of the Collections Committee and facilitated communication with the full committee. The group worked well together, despite the occasional personality conflict.

Our first meeting took place during a two-day brainstorming session in Charlottesville attended by all three sub-committees and members of the Collections Committee. George Soete facilitated this meeting, introducing us to the concepts of cooperative collection development and outlining past projects in this area. Each committee then proceeded to develop a plan of action to complete its task. We decided that our task was to insure that academic libraries throughout the Commonwealth had access to information in nursing and allied health literature, that core collections for study would be maintained on each campus, and that participating libraries would have the confidence to cancel titles of lesser interest, reassured by the fact that they could obtain information via interlibrary loan in a timely fashion. The recent development of a VIVA interlibrary loan agreement added confidence that materials could be delivered within a reasonable amount of time.

The existence of the Brandon-Hill lists of journals in both nursing and allied health made our work much easier. We had lists validated by an external source, respected by faculty, librarians and accreditation agencies which saved us a great deal of time in developing such a list ourselves. As a further measure, selected libraries reviewed their interlibrary loan records for FY 1996 and 1997 to see if any further titles appeared that were not covered by in-state holdings. There were none.

The committee chair developed a database of titles in both Brandon-Hill lists and holdings were gathered via OCLC. The committee made decisions on retention based on the facts of sole holdings, longest backfile and equitable distribution of holdings throughout the state. Although most of the decisions were made for libraries represented at the table, a number of titles was assigned to other public and private institutions. The average number of titles retained for a non-doctoral institution was seven.

Now that you have a sense of the context in which the project existed, let's focus on the project itself.

THE PROJECT ITSELF

One thing about CCM projects is that they definitely require maintenance and evaluation, much as a physical collection in your own building would require. The first step for me was getting to meet some of the participants in the project. Because of our diverse institutions and the distance between the participants, the meeting was going to be held in Charlottesville. Charlottesville is home to none of the participants, but not too far from them to make a day trip impossible for any except the folks at Mountain Empire Community College. But then everything is a long way from Big Stone Gap, Virginia. Cincinnati is actually closer than Charlottesville.

Since there is such a distance between project members, e-mail was often the best way to maintain communication. Use of the phone was also necessary after too much time passed between communication at some institutions. The phone was often where I would turn to learn that librarians in the project had left their jobs, or moved to other responsibilities. One call I made to a particular institution resulted in learning that the director and the lone librarian were both new to their jobs and had no idea the project existed. They had already cancelled one title that the previous administration had agreed to maintain because they were unaware of the agreement to not cancel the title. With a little convincing, another institution agreed to add the title to their list of retained publications.

Maintain agreement among project participants

As time moved along, changes to our base list resulted in changes to the holdings of some institutions. The Brandon-Hill lists are updated biennially. When the new editions reached my desk I did a quick poll of participating schools and, across the board, they thought it was important to maintain our list of holdings with the list produced by Brandon-Hill.

This prompted me to check holdings in OCLC and local catalogs of the participating schools to locate holdings for these new titles. An e-mail was sent out to project members asking for volunteers to agree to add these new titles to their holdings and retention lists. Three new titles were added as well as a title that had been overlooked the first time around in the process and the title that had been inadvertently dropped by one of the project members. The project members responded fairly quickly. Several schools responded for each of the titles.

The next step was to send out new agreement letters to the schools that added new titles. This process took a few months as verbal agreements were received and followed up by agreement letters to the library directors involved. The whole process actually went rather smoothly, considering the project was new to two of the directors involved. This process of adjusting was repeated in a few months when one of the project schools was forced to cancel a title due to a journal cancellation project.

Project Evaluation

The final piece of the project was an evaluation at the end of the initial expiration of the agreements. The three-year run of the agreements ended at the end of 2000. The evaluation was discussed among members of the project via e-mail. Several questions were written which would make up a survey of VIVA members to gauge the usefulness of the project. Questions asked about the knowledge of the project, local CM decisions made because of the project, views of AHN journal coverage because of the project, and success in meeting the stated goals of the project. After approval by the Resources for Users Committee of VIVA, the survey was sent out to the VIVA listserv, Vavirtua-L, twice, once in June 2000 and again in October 2000. The message indicated that "anyone is welcome to read and complete the survey". In particular, the survey was directed to the people responsible for collections at the VIVA libraries.

The survey was disseminated to the 413 people who subscribe to the list. Of that number 20 completed and returned the survey.

RESULTS OF THE PROJECT

Reaching agreement on holdings lists

Reaching agreement between 16 colleges and universities, both public and private, across the state of Virginia was a big success. At the time the project was initiated, there was little in the way of electronic journal titles in these fields. The project assured the state an ongoing access to the 150+ titles selected by Brandon-Hill as the most useful for collections in these areas. In a time of drastically increasing journal costs, using this method of assuring access was deemed important and was acted upon with a good deal of time and effort by the participating schools.

Ongoing revision of list

The ability to revise the lists indicated the importance of the project to several of the member schools. Keeping up the interest in the project despite the distance in miles and time proved to be a success

Importance of AHN journal titles

The view of nursing and allied health journal titles improved in VIVA during the term of the project. One of the first purchases of current full text journals by VIVA was in those areas. Recently, more titles in these areas were secured through the purchase of subscriptions to all Lippincott, Williams and Wilkins journal titles for VIVA. I work at a large university where the medical collections are very important to our work. So with the increasing cost of titles, I think the project displayed that access to these titles was important for many of the schools. I know that participation in the CCCM project was important to us. In the survey, 75% of the respondents indicated that their school had made journal cancellation decisions based on access to the collection.

Lack of knowledge of the project

Obviously the lack of knowledge of the project was a big disappointment. Although the project had been in existence for three years, not many people were aware of it. Of the responses received in the evaluation survey, only 25% felt they were well aware of the project and what it encompassed. The project had its own Web pages on the VIVA Web site, and had been discussed at the Collections Committee, later the Resources for Users Committee, on a regular basis. Library directors were supportive and aware of the project, so the lack of knowledge was surprising.

Lack of survey response

Lack of response to the survey was a great disappointment. It surely indicated that people were uninterested in the continuation of the project, or simply lacked knowledge of it. Given the knowledge at the collections and director level, the lack of survey response was indicative to me of the low importance of the project at that time.

State of Limbo

The largest disappointment for me was the lack of response the project report and evaluation received from the Resources for Users Committee of VIVA. This committee was the successor to the original collections committee that had initiated and authorized the work of the project. But to this date the RUC has yet to respond to the report we issued. Yet, this project possesses value and relevance for my university due to our size and number of journals we subscribe to currently. By leveraging our holdings with other statewide institutions, it gave us some options in the area of print cancellations. However, the project has not been re-authorized, nor has it been closed officially.

CONCLUSIONS

The project succeeded in its objective of organizing holdings of nursing and allied health journals around the Commonwealth of Virginia. It succeeded because the plan developed was well focused and had a committed leadership, both at the level of our sub-committee and on the Collections Committee. VIVA was a new enterprise and people were willing to work hard and try new ideas. Also, the project did not ask members to cancel their journal holdings in favor of a remote source. Libraries certainly had the option to cancel subscriptions (and some did take advantage of it), but the project's goal of making journals available throughout the Commonwealth was seen in a positive light. Accreditors from the State Board of Nursing accepted the idea readily during a site visit to one co-author's library. The fields of nursing and allied health are not central to the mission of many of the participants' institutions; directors may have been more willing to accept off-site access for journals in this area, as compared to fields such as business.

On the other hand, the project hasn't had the visibility we initially sought. In the follow up survey to evaluate our progress, we found that many VIVA members had no idea that the project existed. As personnel changed at libraries, we found that the institutional memory of the project needed to be refreshed. While there is still interest in cooperative collection development throughout the state, it seems to be moving to the electronic field, as libraries form buying consortiums to obtain better prices on electronic material that VIVA cannot purchase.

What of the future for the larger picture of CCCM? As the conference theme indicates, the times are changing rapidly and frequently. We believe that the new environment will make more of us willing to at least take a look at CCCM, and, perhaps even take the plunge into a project.

WHAT A STATE WE'RE IN! LEARNING ABOUT LIBRARY CONSORTIA IN NEW YORK

Penny Bealle Collection Development and Management Librarian, Swirbul Library, Adelphi University

Introduction

At the Charleston Conference, I presented my preliminary reflections regarding some of the complexities of New York State library consortia. Because I am a newcomer to the library profession and employed as a collection development librarian, library consortia have caught my attention. And what a lot I have learned about the state that I am in!

New York State has a complex library consortia landscape that I am interested in for numerous reasons, some practical and others theoretical. On the practical side, although library consortia offer diverse services, as a collection development librarian my main focus is how consortia can assist with the licensing of electronic resources. While coordinating Adelphi University's electronic information resources with the consortia in my region, I realized that an important link was missing. Numerous guides aid librarians in selecting and licensing electronic resources, in addition, online directories identify library consortia, but less attention has been given in the literature regarding how librarians can learn about library consortia. There is so much diversity and change, that this information is largely conveyed by word of mouth, but a written guide could provide librarians who are learning their way some tips about where to start. No doubt this is easier in regions where one or two library consortia dominate the arena, but in New York with numerous library consortia, what's a new librarian to do? I feel like the architect in Thomas Cole's painting, *The Architect's Dream* (Toledo Museum of Art, 1840), as he gazes at a wonderful bevy of choices — Greek temples, Gothic cathedrals, Egyptian pyramids and more. All these choices are available, but where to begin? Therefore, my goal is to provide a brief overview of some New York consortia, as well as some thoughts regarding the current state of affairs and what the future might bring, particularly for academic library consortia. At this stage my discussion, while primarily descriptive, includes some speculations that will be analyzed in future publications as I examine efforts to develop an influential statewide consortium in New York.

The creation of an influential statewide consortium in New York is a long-term goal shared by many New York library professionals, including me. Gaining an understanding of current New York consortia provides the knowledge base to explore what channels might be open to establish an influential statewide consortium. Some statewide activities have been coordinated in New York, however a lack of centralization, especially for academic libraries, means that no single consortia has the bargaining power of an entity like the highly successful OhioLINK.

In addition to the practical reasons, just discussed, I was also motivated to learn about library consortia because I have a research interest in the dissemination of technological innovations. Everett Rogers' theories, regarding the diffusion of innovations, provide a conceptual framework to understand why conditions in the 1990s were ripe for the proliferation of library consortia.[1] Simply stated, the timing, technology, and desire to license electronic resources in the most economical and efficient manner were all present and library consortia could expedite the process. A study of the New York consortia landscape requires evaluating the effect of these factors.

A Centralized Approach — Factors for Success

The extensive array of New York library consortia prompted me to ask why we couldn't be more centralized like Ohio with OhioLINK, or Georgia with GALILEO, or the United Kingdom with JISC (Joint Information Services Committee). Tom Sanville, executive director of OhioLINK, when describing its success cited an alignment of the planets that allowed OhioLINK to be born over a decade ago.[2] Elements that were in alignment included: state funding, timing, participation, and cooperation. State funding was adequate and sustained. The timing was ideal because expensive electronic information resources and the technology to deliver these resources became widely available at the same time that the Ohio library network was receiving state funding for extensive cooperation. Participation of the most influential higher education institutions in the state was automatic because in Ohio most of the influential higher education institutions are state rather than independent institutions. Statewide library cooperation was also firmly established in Ohio.

New York has extensive consortial activity, but rather than having all the planets aligned, I view it as a universe with numerous solar systems. In theory, the diverse solar systems are interested in merging for the good of all, but numerous practical obstacles have prevented the coordination of this universe to create one solar system. To compare the factors that made a statewide consortia possible in Ohio, with the same factors in New York will emphasize the importance of funding, timing, participation, and cooperation.

Whereas Ohio had a state-funded mandate for library cooperation, New York has not received adequate state funding targeted for an extensive statewide project for licensing electronic resources. Some statewide initiatives are present in New York, but the bottom-line is that with multiple solar systems the available resources are not pooled into one fund that would have the potential of attaining the most favorable terms.

Whereas OhioLINK began at a time that was ripe for the extensive networking of electronic resources, during this same period New York was developing several initiatives. Now that New York has multiple efforts to create a unified statewide initiative, it is more difficult to unite diverse solar systems than it may have been to create one from scratch at an earlier stage.

Whereas in Ohio the most influential higher education institutions were on board from the beginning, because they were state institutions, New York's situation is different. New York has an extensive statewide university network, SUNY, but the most prestigious academic institutions, and thus huge customers for electronic resources, Cornell, Columbia, NYU are independents - thus not part of the state system. They have more affinity with large research libraries than with SUNY institutions and smaller independent universities, so naturally purchase some of their electronic resources through NERL (Northeast Research Libraries). They are also interested in statewide initiatives and have participated in the statewide licensing of electronic resources through initiatives such as the New York Consortium of Library Consortia (NYCOLC). Yet their licensing of some high-priced electronic resources from a multi-state research library consortia, while clearly a logical place to shop when no comparable state initiative exists, is another factor that dilutes the ability of New York to coordinate a statewide initiative. This is significant because, as William Potter discussed the involvement of the most influential university libraries plays an important role in the success of statewide academic library consortia.

Ohio was able to turn its history of extensive statewide cooperation to advantage in developing a procedure for one integrated approach to the statewide licensing of electronic resources. New York, in contrast, has not yet turned its history of some statewide library cooperation and funding into an influential statewide initiative. A more thorough analysis of how the development of library consortia in New York compares with that in other states is a topic that I am continuing to research.

New York Library Consortia

There is no shortage of library consortia in New York. Nor is there a shortage of ambitious statewide plans. What is lacking, as the following description of New York consortia demonstrates, is a single statewide consortia that has the bargaining power of a state system such as OhioLINK.

EmpireLink is a pilot project of the New York State Library (NYSL). It provides the people of New York free access to full-text, online, commercial databases through their libraries. It was launched in January 1999 as a three-year pilot project. This sounds like the type of project that librarians in New York dream about, but while it has provided good resources, they have been few in number.

NOVEL (New York Online Virtual Electronic Library) is coordinated by NYSL and New York State Education Department. A Regents Commission on Library Services recommended the creation of NOVEL to deliver high-quality, reliable digital information to all New Yorkers. NOVEL is designed to complement existing partnerships among libraries of all types and to build on existing networks such as EmpireLink. The July 2000 remarks by the co-chair of the Regents Commission on Library Services to the New York State Board of Regents proposes that NOVEL represents:

> "...a commitment to propel New York to the top ranks among the 37 other states that have already begun to provide their residents with a statewide digital library. ...The economies of scale and benefits to all ... make the case for NOVEL truly compelling."[4]

These are wonderful goals, but of course they require funding and extensive cooperation. The future holds promise, but considering the current economic situation in New York, progress towards these goals could be slow.

SUNYConnect is the electronic library initiative that serves the statewide SUNY system, which consists of numerous universities, colleges, and community colleges. The goal of SUNYConnect is to provide access to basic online reference tools and full text databases.

Nylink was established in 1973 as the SUNY/OCLC Network and serves New York State and the surrounding areas. It offers many services, including consortial prices for electronic resources. As an important participant in the New York consortia scene, it has been speculated that, "Nylink - which is reviewing its affiliation with the state university - could emerge as an independent library network akin to OhioLINK. New York lacks such a statewide organization..."[5]

New York's 3Rs are nine regional library consortia that were created by the New York State Board of Regents and the State Legislature in the 1960s. Each geographical area has a 3R; for example, on Long Island my library belongs to LILRC (Long Island Library Resources Council). These regional systems were chartered to improve reference and research library resources throughout the state. They provide many services including negotiating consortial prices for electronic resources.

With the existence of initiatives like those discussed above, New York library services have had statewide components for a long time, but this statewide system has not translated into a centralized approach to electronic resources. As I view it, one factor contributing to this lack of centralization is that the regional 3Rs have partially satisfied their regions' requirements for electronic resources. However, now that electronic resources are such an important part of the information landscape statewide licenses would be preferable. This brings to the forefront the notion of Rogers' theories that, need stimulates acceptance of innovation. Initially the regional councils could satisfy demands, but with the greater prevalence of electronic resources a more centralized approach would increase efficiency. Indeed, current events are bearing this out. Since I presented this discussion in Charleston, the 3Rs have formed an Electronic Resources Advisory Group that is considering an initiative to pool some state funds for a statewide licensing of electronic resources.

In addition to the initiatives discussed above, New York also has other consortia that are not state initiatives, although they often work closely with state initiatives such as the 3Rs or the New York State Library. WALDO (Westchester Academic Library Directors Organization) has been highly successful at negotiating consortial pricing for electronic resources that are available to libraries throughout the state. Pi[2], which was founded in 1995, is a consortium of independent academic libraries in New York State and surrounding environs that has negotiated licenses for electronic resources. One of its founders, Loretta Ebert, co-initiated NYCOLC (New York Consortium of Library Consortia) to coordinate disparate consortia on a statewide basis. Tony Ferguson, Associate University Librarian at Columbia University, representing the New York Comprehensive Research Libraries, said in support of NYCOLC that "New York represents a tremendous marketplace for electronic resources. It is critical that libraries and library consortia in New York collaborate together to aggregate their buying power. Everyone will benefit..."[6] In this spirit, a new initiative has recently been announced: The New York State Higher Education Initiative has been formed as a collaboration of academic libraries to cost effectively enhance academic library resources. Naturally there is extensive overlap between the various consortial initiatives; for example, some of the advocates from NYCOLC and other consortia initiatives are also active participants in the NOVEL and the Higher Education Initiative.

Concluding Remarks and Future Directions

My desire for a more streamlined approach was motivated by what I experienced as a newcomer navigating the New York consortial landscape. In the January 2001 *Charleston Advisor*, Tom Peters discusses how the existence of so many library consortia result in overlap and competition for too few products.[7] With too many consortia doing similar things, some consortia leaders recognize that some consortia will disappear, others merge, and all consortia must evaluate the types of services that they should offer to their members. In this regard, one library director stated, "As members of multiple consortia, we're all looking at streamlining, not supporting multiple groups trying to do the same things."[8]   My experiences in New York affirm that overlapping consortia result in duplication of effort for consortia employees and for librarians. Consolidation would have benefits, but there could also be a downside as competition could disappear.

My examination of New York consortia has stimulated me to think about some projects that would help information professionals who are trying to navigate this complex network. As I look at what I have learned, I realize that a concise guide to New York consortia would have been a valuable tool for me. Therefore, I intend to expand this initial discussion of New York consortia into a practical online guide. In addition, fueled by my background as an art historian and my interest in the dissemination of innovations, I am enthusiastic about the prospect of writing a history of consortia in New York.   I began my examination of New York consortia because of practical needs, but my explorations led me to realize the extent to which the workings of New York consortia are a case study in how innovations are diffused. I'll be working on aspects of these projects for a special issue of *After the Grain* on Consortia and will be inviting submissions for other consortia topics.

With numerous statewide initiatives in place, it seems that extensive coordination should be in New York's stars for the future. Hopefully the financial and governance issues can be resolved so that instead of several separate solar systems, New York's planets can become aligned into a single solar system. It is reassuring to me that there are many efforts from diverse constituencies advocating for statewide coordination. Perhaps the statewide coordination could include subsets that would serve different constituencies — for example, one for public and school libraries, another for academic libraries, to name just two. Whatever form it takes, the need is there and it will stimulate the development of this critical resource for New York - an influential statewide consortia to change the state we are in. And, dare I dream, perhaps the future will also continue to yield ambitious multi-consortia licenses, or perhaps wider-reaching regional, or even nationwide, academic consortia that could enhance efficiency.

REFERENCES

[1] Everett Rogers, "The Diffusion of Innovations Model," in, Ian Masser and Harlan J. Onsrud, ed, *Diffusion and Use of Geographic Information Technologies*, (Boston: Kluwer Academic Publishers, 1993) p. 9, 15 synthesize the salient points of Rogers' theories. For a more complete discussion see: Rogers, Everett M, *Diffusion of Innovations*. 3rd edition, (New York: Free Press, A Division of Macmillan Publishing Co., Inc.), 1983.

[2] Norman Oder, "Consortia Hit Critical Mass," *Library Journal*, 125, no. 2 (Feb. 1, 2000): 48-51.

[3] William Gray Potter, "Recent Trends in Statewide Academic Library Consortia," *Library Trends*, 45, no. 3 (Winter 97): 416-34.

[4] This statement is in Appendix K, of the "Final Report of the Regents Commission on Library Services." http://www.nysl.nysed.gov/rcols/finalrpt.htm, (Accessed Oct. 2001).

[5] Oder.

[6] NYCOLC, 10/22/97 Press Release. http://www.lib.rpi.edu/about/consortia/nycolc/documents.html , (Accessed Oct. 2001).

[7] Tom Peters, "Overlap and Competition Among Consortia for E-Resource Agreements," *Charleston Advisor*, (January 2001): 57-58.

[8] Oder.

IS COLLABORATION AN UNNATURAL ACT?

Tom Peters, Director, Committee on Institutional Cooperation, Center for Library Initiatives

INTRODUCTION

My goal this morning is to address the question posed to me by the conference planners: Is collaboration an unnatural act? This is a new experience for me. Rarely do I discuss unnatural acts in private, and certainly this is my first public address on this topic. I feel like I should be speaking to a group of theologians, sex therapists, or possibly animal rights activists--not to publishers, vendors, aggregators, and librarians.

Rather than open with the obligatory joke, I want to tell you a true story about a Google search I performed as I prepared for my talk. I entered three keywords into the basic search window: collaboration, unnatural, and act. The results of my Google search were very interesting—but for unanticipated reasons. Rather than find prurient or salacious sites dealing in various ways with collaboration and unnatural acts, I found basically a series of PowerPoint presentations (how disappointing), covering a wide range of disciplines, in which collaboration is declared to be an unnatural act. The general thesis is: Collaboration is an unnatural act, normally practiced by non-consenting adults, usually around a table. The first few screens of the results of my Google search revealed variations on this general thesis is articles in and presentations to: The Journal of Chemical Education, the National School Board Association, the National Labor Management Association, the Michigan Society of Association Executives, the U.S. Dept. of Health and Human Services, and the Johns Hopkins Institute for Policy Studies.

Based on this exhaustive research, my tentative conclusion is that there is a widely held belief--at least among the more highly educated sections of the populace--that collaboration is indeed an unnatural act. This widely held belief jars against the other apparently widely held belief that collaboration is a good thing that should be encouraged in civilized societies and organizations. Evidently, we have ambivalent attitudes toward collaboration.

Collaboration needs an apology—in the sense of a formal, eloquent justification and defense. I cannot do that in the next 20 minutes or so, but it needs to be done.

The question posed by the conference organizers is both interesting and challenging—in part because it gets to the heart of what consortia are about. I must confess, however, that I find it much more interesting to explore the potential meanings of the question than to attempt boldly to answer it. Our collective goal (as speaker and audience) is to collaboratively explore what this question means (i.e., its facets, nuances, underlying assumptions, history, etc.), then take a stab at answering the question--because all questions yearn for an answer.

SOME ERGO ASSUMPTIONS

It seems to me that lurking inside the question are some "ergo" assumptions. For example, we could assume that, if the answer to the question were yes, most people would conclude that collaboration therefore is either not worthwhile or downright bad. Another possible "ergo" lurking behind the question is that, if collaboration is an unnatural act, then competition must be part of the basic human condition. By extolling the virtues of collaboration, we collectively deny our basic human instinct to be competitive animals.

MY DEFINITIVE ANSWER

Before we delve into the issues associated with this simple—yet profound— question, let me throw out my definitive answer: Yes and no. (It depends on how you interpret the question.) Let me explain.

DOES COLLABORATION EXIST IN A STATE OF NATURE?

First, if we assert that collaboration is unnatural, we may be implying that collaboration does not exist in a state of nature. Experience seems to offer contrary evidence. Even lowly creatures, such as barnacles and bees, seem to engage in some rudimentary forms of collaboration. To better understand how collaboration works in the natural world, consider our feathered friend, the goose. When geese migrate, they collaborate in at least two ways. First, their characteristically beautiful v-formation flight pattern evidently is not primarily an aesthetic statement (although it is beautiful to behold), but rather an exercise in group aerodynamics. The geese fly in that pattern in order to reduce the wind drag for everyone involved—except the lead goose. Similar collaborative drafting can be observed in some human sporting events, such as the Tour de France and the Daytona 500. Goosey collaboration is natural to geese, and sometimes we mere mortals practice this type of collaboration. Second, the point goose rotates. Each goose knows that he or she will be in the point position for only a short period of time.

So, collaboration clearly exists in a state of nature, and apparently it works for geese. Note that, when it comes to goosey collaboration, the geese have two unwavering, unchanging foundational aspects to their collaborative efforts: a strong, communally shared objective, and prevailing environmental conditions, based on the laws of nature, that do not vary much from year to year. As a group, the geese have a clear objective—to get from Canada to the Caribbean. The geese also carefully studied the prevailing environmental conditions to learn what types of collaboration work best. The V-formation was victorious over all other possible formations—the box kite formation, for example. In some ways, then, goosey collaboration seems to be both natural and learned.

Fortunately, humanity does not exist in a state of nature. We are civilized. Almost by definition, the civilized human competencies we value and encourage all are unnatural. These competencies must be learned. For example, probably no one would claim that reading is a natural act, but few would claim that, because it is an unnatural act, it is therefore bad and not worth pursuing. The first "ergo" argument noted above is becoming suspect.

Collaboration in Context: Good, Bad, and Ugly C-words

Like most things in life, collaboration gains meaning from its context. One context is a cohort of related words—all curiously beginning with the letter C—that can be categorized as good, bad, and problematic.

GOOD C's

> Cooperation
> Collaboration
> Consortia
> Culture
> Civilization
> Caribbean
> Charleston (of course)

Note that historically the value of "collaboration" has risen tremendously in the last 50 years. During WW II, especially in France, a collaborator was a bad person.

BAD C's

> Coercion
> Collusion
> Cartels
> Cabals
> Canada (just kidding)

FENCE-SITTING C's

> We're not quite sure whether they are good or bad—it depends on the situation.

> Competition
> Change
> Cajoling

LIBRARY CONSORTIAL COLLABORATION

Because I work for an academic consortium, my primary experiential base involves collaborative efforts among librarians at the 13 major research libraries in the CIC, but hopefully what I have to say today can be extrapolated to other types of human collaboration. What type of collaboration is practiced, or at least extolled, by library consortia? Is collaboration among publishers, vendors, and aggregators potentially more fruitful than collaboration among libraries?

Are we looking solely at institutional behavior, or at individual behavior as well? Frankly, I don't see much difference. When it comes to collaboration, individual behavior is the bedrock of institutional behavior. If you dig deep enough into even the largest global collaborative efforts, you eventually will find mere mortals collaborating. We need to note that, at the core of many major collaborative efforts is a small group of committed individuals. The dynamics of collaborative efforts among individuals are inextricably linked with the processes of inter-organizational collaboration, at least for the foreseeable future.

COLLABORATION AS AN IDEA

Collaboration is a powerful, glorious idea, particularly in these high-tech, post-modern times, when online environments and our own anxiety conspire to cry out for deeper collaboration among individuals and organizations. Despite the numerous PowerPoint presentations my Google search revealed that—perhaps tongue-in-cheek—collaboration is an unnatural act practiced by non-consenting adults seated around a table, collaboration usually receives high marks as a social and cultural value. Collaboration now has a positive social value, ever since we received our marks in the early elementary grades concerning our ability to play well with others. Positive social values often run into the buzz saw of reality. It is one thing to be in favor of motherhood, apple pie, and the American way, but quite another to collaborate with a group of people to set up and sustain an apple pie business. Reality quickly intrudes and overwhelms the core value (apple pie is good).

THE REALITY OF COLLABORATION

If we examine the Latin roots of the word collaboration, we see that it means to labor together. Alas, real collaboration is hard work, and collaborators often become mired in the Slough of Despond. The overhead and resource costs of collaborative efforts remain largely unknown, hidden, and attenuated. Another nettlesome aspect of collaboration is that the results and outcomes often are a long time coming, and often they are difficult to perceive directly and measure.

One purported advantage of collaborative efforts is that they create projects and programs that can be scaled up more easily or quickly, and that the sustainability of collaborative efforts is higher than for other types of efforts. Back in 2000 when Richard Lucier was the Director of the California Digital Library, he gave a speech at NC State University during which he noted the following assumption behind the CDL: "Collaboration among universities is essential for scaling and long-term sustainability, and worth the overhead inherent in collaboration."

There are several very practical reasons to collaborate, including:

- Expertise mining
- Risk sharing
- Sharing the resource investments
- Quality assurance
- Co-branding possibilities
- Creating greater impact on the broader environment

DO ELECTRONIC ENVIRONMENTS PRIVILEGE THOSE WHO COLLABO-RATE?

Collaboration is a form of linking. Information providers (including publishers, aggregators, vendors, and libraries) should collaborate because linking content is so much easier in digital, networked environments than it is in the world of print. Information may or may not want to be free, but it certainly gains from being linked.

LEADERSHIP IN COLLABORATIVE SITUATIONS

What type of leadership is needed for good, useful, worthwhile collaborative initiatives? Often those who attempt to foster and facilitate collaboration have no authority over their fellow collaborators. Usually there is no daily interaction among the collaborative team. It can be difficult to sustain the energy and enthusiasm necessary for successful collaboration. When something goes awry, the leader may become despondent or angry. Wylie and Yeager (1999) suggest that institutional collaboration is a good way to make epiphanic discoveries—about the collaborating institutions, their relationships, the information marketplace, and the promise and reality of digital information.

CREATE A CULTURE OF COLLABORATION

In conclusion, let us tentatively conclude that collaboration is both natural and unnatural, not necessarily bad, and not necessarily at odds with competition. The challenge for dedicated professionals and organizations is to create a culture of collaboration—a carefully tended seedbed in which collaboration can grow and bear fruit. This is what we have done in the CIC, the academic consortium of the Big Ten universities, plus the U. of Chicago. Fostering a culture of collaboration can take years, if not decades, but having the culture in place makes current and future collaborative efforts easier. The CIC has been successful in nurturing and sustaining a culture of collaboration.

CONCLUSION

Possession is nine-tenths of the flaw.

We are all surly Alexandrians. We still want and prefer to have all information collocated in one place.

Collaboration is a blind leap of faith.

References

Lucier, Richard. 2000. "eScholarship: Scholar-Led Innovation in Scholarly Communication." Speech given at Reinventing the Knowledge Wheel: Leading the Revolution in the Ownership and Management of Scholarship, a colloquium organized by the Scholarly Communication Center at the North Carolina State University Libraries, October, 5, 2000. PowerPoint Presentation available on the Web at http://www.lib.ncsu.edu/scc/colloquium.html

Wylie, Neil R., and Yeager, Tamara L. 1999. Library Cooperation. In New Directions for Higher Education, no. 106, pp. 27-35. [place]: Jossey-Bass.

Contact Information

Tom Peters
Director, Center for Library Initiatives
Committee on Institutional Cooperation
302 East John Street, Suite 1705
Champaign, IL› 61820-5698
Phone: (217) 244-9239
Fax: (217) 244-7127
Email: tpeters@cic.uiuc.edu
Web: http://www.cic.uiuc.edu/

How to find and develop staff and how to implement system changes with existing staff are two major challenges facing supervisors in academic libraries. Several of the following papers offer suggestions on how to tackle each of these issues based on the personal experience and knowledge of the presenters. The remaining presentation discusses the personal experiences of a librarian who decided to move from South Carolina to Dominica and the challenges she faces at the library of the medical school there.

Personnel Development

WHERE HAVE ALL THE ACQUISITIONS LIBRARIANS GONE?

Barbara B. Moran, School of Information and Library Science, University of North Carolina at Chapel Hill

The title of this session might have been phrased a bit more broadly—"Where Have All the Academic Librarians Gone?"— because the scarcity of acquisition librarians is a reflection of a larger problem affecting all types of jobs in academic libraries. I realize, as all of you do, that there is a shortage of librarians of many kinds—school, children's and others—but one of the types of libraries that is experiencing the most acute shortage of librarians is the academic library. It is rare to visit an academic library today without hearing about the difficulties of attracting qualified applicants to fill vacant positions. More and more academic librarians are reporting instances of extremely small applicant pools and failed searches. This is quite a change from the situation a few years ago when there were often hundreds of applicants for each opening. It can certainly be argued that having hundreds of applicants for each opening is just as troubling as having only a few. It is certainly more upsetting to the job applicants. But, right now we appear to be going through another one of those periods of discrepancy between labor supply and demand. In an ideal world, we would be able to avoid these wild swings between too many applicants for positions and not enough. What we would like is to ensure that there is always a good balance between the number of positions that are available and the number of qualified applicants to fill those positions. But we don't live in an ideal world, and librarianship like all other professions sometimes suffers from an imbalance between the number of applicants and open positions. At the present time, we are confronting the problem of too few applicants so we need to find a way to attract more people to academic librarianship, and specifically to the field of acquisitions.

Eleanor [Cooke] and Peter [George] are going to speak specifically about filling acquisition librarian positions, but I am going to begin at the stage before. How do we attract talented people to the profession? How do we get them in the pipeline so that when a library has a need for an acquisition librarian there will be someone there to fill the position? The problem of recruiting has become a critical issue for the profession as a whole. It is especially important for academic librarians because of the demographics of the academic library workforce. I know that many of you are familiar with the work of Stanley Wilder. He looked specifically at ARL librarians but his findings are applicable to most librarians. Overall, librarians are significantly older than most other professionals. Relative to comparable professions, librarianship contains one third the number of individuals aged 35 and under and almost 75 percent more individuals aged 45 and older (Wilder, 1995). Similar results have been reported in academic libraries as a whole, and indeed in the whole field of librarianship.(St. Lifer, 2000). This skewed age distribution is a result of many factors, but primarily is the result of the large number of librarians who were hired in the 1960s when higher education burgeoned. It is compounded by the fact that for many people librarianship is a second profession so that even "new" librarians are older than most. So our profession is confronted not only with a shortage of librarians now, but with a potentially more serious shortage soon when the waves of baby boomer retirements begin. If we want to be sure that there will be people to replace us when we are ready to retire, we need to begin working on this problem immediately. We need to attract new people to the profession as a whole and to acquisitions librarianship specifically. What are the most effective ways to do this?

Recruitment to librarianship is complicated because for many people librarianship is a career choice that is made relatively late in life. How many of you wanted to be a librarian when you were in elementary school? In high school? As an undergraduate? Later? How many of you had another career before you became a librarian? There is no one specific time period when individuals decide to become librarians. This makes it difficult to target recruitment efforts because people make the decision to enter the profession at so many different points in their lives. If we want to draw people to the profession we need to consider a broad range of recruitment tactics. Today, I would like to discuss some of the techniques that are being used to attract people to librarianship as a whole with a specific emphasis on recruitment to academic librarianship and acquisitions work.

Interestingly, as a profession we have done little to reach out to attract pre-college students to the field. I know some librarians who regularly go to high school career fairs to talk to teens about becoming librarians. I am sure that there are many school library media specialists who try to get students to consider librarianship as a career. And in the past, ALA has designed some materials aimed at high school students. But, nonetheless, there have not many formal efforts targeted to this age group. This has been a neglected opportunity and one that we should give more thought to as we try to increase the number of new librarians. The younger individuals are when they commit to a profession the better opportunity we have to help them shape their preparation for their future careers. In addition, attracting students to librarianship as a first career would lower the average age in the profession.

There are more organized efforts to recruit undergraduate students to the field of librarianship. For example, some liberal arts colleges where undergraduate student assistants are an important element in the functioning of the library have special programs to mentor these students and to try to get them interested in librarianship as a career. In my opinion, the undergraduate years are perhaps the most fruitful time to attract new professionals to the field. This semester I am teaching the seminar in academic librarianship that I teach almost every year at Chapel Hill. Every single person in that class worked as a library assistant in their undergraduate library. About a third of the students in the class came directly from undergraduate studies to SILS—the rest had worked briefly in other fields. But they all said it was the undergraduate library assistantship that drew them to librarianship, and specifically to academic librarianship. So it often is that first job as a library assistant that makes a person decide to consider librarianship as a career or conversely to decide that he or she would never be a librarian.

In the U.S. almost every academic library has a large number of undergraduates working in it. Think about the type of work experience these students get. Are they experiences that will lead the student to conclude that work as a librarian would be stimulating and mentally challenging? Often the work that students are given to do is the dullest in the organization. If our undergraduates are spending 15-20 hours a week in mind-numbing work—shelving books and periodicals for example—is it any wonder that they don't see themselves pursuing librarianship as a career? Admittedly this is work that has to be done, and I am certainly not advocating that the students not to it. But in those libraries where student work consists only of tasks that are tedious and dull, perhaps the job could be restructured so that some duties that are a bit more interesting could be included? Perhaps more responsibility could be added as students get more experience? Perhaps more varied tasks could be put in the mix? Perhaps student assistants could be used on an advisory committee? There is no one "right" way to use undergraduates who work in the library, but librarians should consider whether the work being assigned to student assistants is allowing them to gain a perspective on the profession that would make them want to enter it. Do the student assistants have any ideas of what professional academic librarians do? Are they aware of the challenges and the opportunities associated with working in an academic library? Are they only allowed to see the trees and not the larger forest? If not, is it any wonder that these student assistants won't be lining up to apply to get an MLS degree.

This leads me to the point that I think is the most important factor in recruiting. Librarians —all of you in this audience —are the very best recruiters we have. Most of us are librarians today because of a librarian who at some time in our lives made an impression on us and made us think that we might also like to be a librarian. This may have been in our childhood, in the local public library or in a school library. But likely it was later. And it is in the undergraduate years when most students are seeking a career that this influence can be the strongest. If among the students who work in your library or among the students at your institution in general there are some who have the characteristics that make you think they would be good librarians, talk to them about your profession, mentor them, and help them learn more about what being a librarian means. And in a similar vein, reach out to those support staff who would be natural candidates to become professionals. These support staff members are the people who already know the work environment of academic librarianship and who feel an affinity towards the work. Some libraries have helped support staff make the progression to the professional ranks by providing some sort of financial assistance or leave time for them to pursue the MLS. But whether we are talking about attracting students assistants or support staff, practicing librarians are the best recruiters we have. So please continue your individual recruiting efforts, and I think it would be completely appropriate if you tried to attract aspiring librarians to the field of acquisitions.

Once a student has decided a pursue a master's degree, this is where the faculty in the Library and Information Science (LIS) schools can play a part. Each year new students arrive at our schools, and many of them don't know what kind of an environment they want to work in after graduation All the schools try to provide an opportunity for students to gain knowledge and experience about the various environments in which they might eventually work. I recently checked the catalogs of all the ALA accredited schools, and almost all of them offer a course in academic librarianship. Fewer of them offer specific courses in acquisitions, but that topic is often covered in courses dealing with technical services or collection development. So if students are interested in acquisitions work in academic libraries they should be able to find coursework to introduce them to the field.

But students don't depend on coursework alone to gain knowledge about a subfield in librarianship. Most of them try to get practical, on-the-job knowledge about a potential career destination while they are MLS students through work experience in that setting either as a graduate assistant or as an intern. These students choose to work in an academic library and perhaps in an acquisitions department to see if there is a good fit between their career aspirations and that particular environment. This is where they compare what they have been learning in class with reality. Each year I talk to large numbers of LIS students who are working as graduate assistants in academic libraries. In some work settings they are treated as junior colleagues; they are allowed to attend department meetings and their opinions are solicited and respected. In other settings they are given the most mundane work and are treated as "hired help." It is critical that students are exposed to the joys and the challenges as well as the frustrations of working in academic libraries. I have known too many students who thought they wanted a career in academic libraries until they started working in one. The influence of librarians at this stage can't be overstated. If students are placed in an environment where they are never allowed to experience any of the challenges of librarianship or where the librarians themselves denigrate the profession, they often decide they have other options and go elsewhere.

Some libraries are taking steps to ensure that student assistants have a chance to gain a broad perspective on the profession. At UNC-Chapel Hill, the Academic Affairs Library has joined with the School of Information and Library Science and started a program that we are calling the Carolina Academic Library Associates (CALA). CALA is designed to be an enhanced pre-professional experience for students who want to prepare for careers in academic librarianship. The graduate assistants are required to work 20 hours a week. They do real work, necessary for the delivery of library services, but in addition, the CALA students receive mentoring, they take part in a series of presentations about current issues in academic librarianship, and they are given the opportunity to attend conferences, etc. This program is just in its second year, but we are already seeing results. As it becomes better known, we expect it to draw excellent students to UNC-CH and to academic librarianship. We believe it can help these students develop a commitment to academic librarianship based on an informed and realistic view of what such a career entails and, at the same time, give them some of the experience not available in their academic studies needed to become effective beginning librarians. So the CALA program provides an example of one way that academic libraries are making efforts to recruit new students to the field. The post-master's fellowships such as the ones at Michigan, NC State, and the University of Illinois at Chicago are other good examples of ways that academic libraries are attracting new graduates to the field of academic librarianship.

The libraries and the LIS schools need to work in partnership in this effort. I realize that the LIS schools are often blamed for the shortages of librarians in certain areas, and I agree that we haven't done all that perhaps we could do. The schools and the libraries need to work as partners if we are to succeed. But unfortunately, the force that is sometimes stronger than both is the market force. I know I am preaching to the converted by mentioned low entry level salaries to this group but there is no doubt that money speaks in a loud voice. Students talk to each other and have a good sense of the market forces. They know that their fellow graduates entering the corporate field regularly receive entry level salaries $10,000 to $15,000 more than those going to libraries. The most recent *Library Journal* salary survey showed that the average beginning salary of 2000 LIS graduates is $34,871 (Terrell and Gregory, 2001). If that figure is compared to the salaries of graduates of other professional programs it is nothing to brag about. Unfortunately, that survey also showed that the average salary of those entering the acquisitions area was $31,286—an average beginning salary that surpassed only two others—those in ILL and youth services. So one reason that there is a shortage of acquisition librarians is because of the pay scale. Working in libraries provides other benefits that cannot be measured in money, but many of the best students decide they will go for the larger salaries. Whatever libraries and acquisitions departments, can do to increase salaries will help in the competition for the best and the brightest of the MLS graduates.

There are not good statistics available about how many acquisitions librarians or even academic librarians are being produced each year. We do have statistics about the number of ALA accredited MLS graduates per year. The last ALISE statistics showed that just under 5000 MLS degrees were awarded in 2000 (Daniel and Saye, 2001, p. 122). The only source of information about placements is the *LJ* survey that I just mentioned. In the survey, the number of recent graduates who reported a first position in an academic library was down substantially from last year. And only 19 reported a first position in acquisitions.(Terrell and Gregory, 2001) So, unless you are from one of those 19 libraries with an acquisitions department that hired a new graduate last year, it is no wonder that you are wondering where all the acquisitions librarians have gone. It is obvious that as a profession we need to do more in recruiting new librarians to the field, and we need to learn from one another what recruitment tactics are most successful.

I hope that we will be able to discuss other recruitment techniques after the panel is finished. Right now I want to turn the program over to my colleagues for their perspectives on this topic.

References

Daniel, E. H., & J. D. Saye (Eds.). (2001) *ALISE library and education statistical report 2001*. Reston, VA: Association for Library and Information Science Education.

St. Lifer, E.(2000) The boomer brain drain: The last of a generation. *Library Journal*. 125(8), 38-42.

Terrell, T., & V.L. Gregory. (2001) Plenty of jobs, salaries flat. *Library Journal*. 126(17), 30-36.

Wilder, S. J. (1995) *The age demographics of academic librarians: A profession apart*. Washington, DC: Association of Research Libraries.

MERGERS IN ACQUISITIONS: IMPLEMENTING FASTCAT PROCESSES IN ACADEMIC LIBRARIES

Rebecca L. Mugridge, Head of Cataloging Services, Pennsylvania State University
Robert B. Freeborn, Music/AV Cataloging Librarian, Pennsylvania State University

The Pennsylvania State University, like many other large academic libraries, began to implement FastCat processing of monographs in the mid-1990s. Our definition of FastCat is cataloging that is 1) usually LC copy; 2) completed upon receipt; 3) usually, but not necessarily, completed by acquisitions staff; and 4) completed with little or no editing. Others have defined FastCat in a more restrictive manner. Nancy Slight-Gibney tells us that FastCat is "the process of cataloging by exporting a record from a bibliographic utility into a local system without editing or review". What this paper attempts to do is examine the implementation of FastCat processes at large academic libraries, explore the reasons behind the implementation of FastCat processes and evaluate the success of the efforts.

Background: FastCat at Pennsylvania State University

Penn State's Technical Services in a nutshell: Technical Services at Penn State has gone through much reorganization in the 1990s. The current organization includes three departments. Cataloging Services is the largest unit, with 30 faculty and staff making up five units. There are four self-directed, format-based cataloging teams (Monographs, Music/AV, Maps, and Special Collections) and the CatMarking Team, which is responsible for labeling, stamping, and targeting. Cataloging also includes the Department Head, the Assistant to the Head, a secretary, and six faculty librarians who serve as resource people, but not supervisors, for the four cataloging teams. Acquisitions Services consists of three self-directed work teams, the Department Head, and one trainer. The Serials Department consists of a department head, one faculty cataloger, one trainer, and three self-directed work teams (Cataloging, Ordering/Invoicing, and Receiving).

Penn State made an attempt to implement FastCat in the early 1990s. This involved having part time staff and people from the CatMarking unit do cataloging with very little or no editing of records. This attempt was not successful and quickly fizzled. A later attempt was made in the mid-1990s, which was much more successful and lasting. This second attempt fits our definition of FastCat, and is performed by Acquisitions staff. The reasons behind the implementation of FastCat at Penn State were many. First of all, Penn State was at the time planning on implementing PromptCat. With the implementation of PromptCat, we knew we were going to have to compromise on some of our cataloging standards. For example, series titles in which our classification practice differed from the Library of Congress' would no longer be able to be separated out during the cataloging process, because we would be accepting the records as they were delivered to us by the PromptCat service. Since we were already planning on making an exception for PromptCat materials, we decided that we should make the same exception for all materials with Library of Congress cataloging. The second reason behind our implementation of FastCat was that the Acquisitions department was already importing records from a MARC file into the catalog so that they could attach an order. Since these records were Library of Congress cataloging records, many of them full level, we decided that they should be able to finish the cataloging on them upon receipt. However, there were many exceptions to this, which will be touched on later. Other reasons behind the implementation of FastCat at Penn State include reducing handoffs and getting rid of the backlog.

FastCat worked successfully for several years at Penn State. In 1999, the Libraries' new Assistant Dean for Technical and Access Services set up a task force to examine whether monographic acquisitions and cataloging should be combined, so that even more cataloging could be done upon receipt. The process of benchmarking, examining our processes and making recommendations has been documented elsewhere, but some points are worth mentioning here. First of all, since Penn State's Acquisitions department is organized based on customers served, but the Cataloging department is organized according to formats, this would have been a significant change to both departments, not just a matter of merging two units. Further impediments to a merger of the two departments included the fact that the acquisitions staff, whose work is very routinized, were very interested in increasing their responsibilities and broadening their job duties. However, the cataloging staff were not at all interested in learning acquisitions functions, many of them thinking that it was "below" them. After benchmarking with other large academic libraries and querying listservs about the pros and cons of reengineering monographic copy cataloging, the task force made recommendations that included redistributing one staff member from the Monographs cataloging team to one of the teams in Acquisitions, and increasing the categories of materials that is handled by FastCat. In particular, acquisitions folks are going to be upgrading Cataloging in Publication (CIP) material, which they had heretofore referred to Cataloging for completion.

Implementing the recommendations of the task force raised several questions to the authors of this paper. First of all, why do libraries implement FastCat processes? Has the implementation of FastCat process met the expectations of the libraries? What has been successful or unsuccessful? A search of library literature revealed several articles that shed some light on why FastCat is implemented in some organizations and what the advantages and disadvantages are. Nancy Slight-Gibney discussed the implementation of FastCat at the University of Oregon Library System and how it was used to increase production without increasing staff. FastCat was implemented at the University of Oregon in order to address ongoing backlogs of uncataloged materials, while the presence of good quality cataloging records and the opportunity or need to increase efficiencies provided further impetus. Technical services at Stanford University were reorganized with the goals of creating a flatter organization and reducing handoffs of decisions and processes. Sue Neumeister and Judith Hopkins reported on the reorganization at the State University of New York at Buffalo. The goals of the reorganization were to reduce movement of materials between technical services departments, to achieve a faster turnaround time for copy cataloging, to free some staff up in cataloging to work on projects, and to deal with an overall decrease in staff size.

FastCat Implementation Survey

After studying the Monograph Task Force's report and searching the professional literature for relevant articles, the authors then sent out a new survey focusing specifically on FastCat procedures. The survey was sent to the Autocat (cataloging and authority control discussion forum), MLA (Music Library Association), and OLAC (Online Audiovisual Catalogers, Inc.) electronic discussion lists, and included our definition of FastCat and the following questions:

1. Based roughly on our definition, does your library perform FastCat?

2. If your definition of FastCat differs significantly from ours, would you please state your definition?

3. What precipitated your decision to implement FastCat? (e.g., desire to increase efficiency, presence of a large backlog, need to address staffing or personnel issues, etc.)

4. What has been the outcome of your implementation of FastCat? Has it met your expectations?

5. If you've documented the categories that you include in FastCat and/or your FastCat procedures, would you be willing to share them with us (a URL is fine)?

6. In order to maintain the highest level of professional scholarship, may we cite your institution in our presentation? If you'd prefer that your responses remain anonymous, please let me know this as well.

7. How has your Public Service Personnel reacted to those materials receiving FastCat treatment?› Positively?› Negatively?› Have they even noticed? Can you give examples of their reactions? [NOTE: This question was sent directly as a follow-up email to those individuals who had responded to our initial survey.]

There were seven institutions that identified themselves in their responses, and the authors would like to publicly thank them for assisting us with our survey: the University of Alabama, the University of Buffalo, the University of Georgia, Massachusetts Institute of Technology, the University of Oregon, the University of Tennessee, and the University of Washington.

The majority of the responses stated that their definition of FastCat either agreed completely with ours, or differed on just a few points. One institution said that Cataloging staff rather than their Acquisitions counterparts performed their FastCat functions, while another stated that student assistants, database maintenance staff, or new copy catalogers undergoing training handled the processes. One institution said that cataloging was not done as part of the receipt process, but was handled immediately afterwards.[1] Other institutions excluded certain materials, such as multi-volume works and books with accompanying materials, or particular call-number ranges from the FastCat treatment.

In one instance, FastCat was just one distinct part of a process called QuickCat. This process was used only for books published in Roman and Cyrillic alphabets, in which the items were completed upon receipt by Acquisitions with little or no editing. The FastCat procedure dealt with LC copy only, and required that Acquisitions staff edit any obvious typographical errors and indicate the item's cataloging location. AcceptCat was the other part of the QuickCat process, and it dealt with full-level member copy containing an LC classification number and one or more LC subject headings. In addition to correcting obvious typos and indicating the location, Acquisitions staff checked the series statement and verified the form of heading for series. Name and subject authority work was done post-cataloging for both procedures, while series authority work was also done post-cataloging for FastCat materials.

There were multiple reasons that institutions decided to implement FastCat procedures. The most common responses included increased efficiency by reducing handoffs and improved cataloging turnaround times. Others focused on the presence of large backlogs and the continual reduction of technical services staff. One said that the implementation of FastCat had freed up Cataloging staff to both tackle the more difficult current receipts and undertake retrospective conversion projects. An interesting reply stated that advances in computer technology, namely the macro feature in OCLC's Passport for Windows, had made FastCat a viable option at their library. The macros both allowed them to automate the sorting process to determine which materials were eligible for FastCat treatment, and increased the speed and accuracy of the overall editing process.

When it came to whether or not FastCat implementation had met their expectations, the majority of responses stated that the process had met or exceeded them. One institution did qualify their reply, however, by stating that FastCat only became successful once there had been several key retirements to their Technical Services staff.

Public Service reactions to materials receiving FastCat treatment were almost as positive as their Technical Service counterparts. One institution stated that their Public Service personnel were making fewer rush-material requests due to the new procedure. Another said that, while their Public Service cohorts hadn't noticed any change in processing times, they were very pleased that Cataloging staff now had the time to take on special projects (e.g., the retrospective conversion of their government documents).

Of course not everyone was satisfied with FastCat's results. One anonymous respondent stated that, in terms of music and art books, the procedure created too many mistakes that had to be sent back for correction. Their major complaints were that call numbers were not thought out, and that there was no attempt made to be consistent with their local practices. They felt that accepting whatever was present in OCLC without any further considerations was detrimental to the collection. They also felt the procedure was fostering poor public relations with their patrons by providing misleading information.

Finally we'd like to present a collection of FastCat Common Practices that are based on Penn State University Libraries' model: [ii]

A. Items to be completed in Acquisitions

   1. English language monograph books having full LC or OCLC copy, except for:

      a. Certain shelf locations
      b. Certain call number ranges
      c. Books with accompanying materials
      d. Rare books

2. Monograph books and surrogates having LC CIP copy, except for:

   a. Sets
   b. Conferences
   c. Series
   d. Facsimiles, reprints or translations

3. PromptCat books, except for:

   a. Books lacking full copy
   b. Non-English language books
   c. New set titles and new added set volumes

4. Added locations for monograph books and surrogates, previously-cataloged set volumes, and video recordings.

B. Items to be referred to Cataloging

   1. Exceptions listed above
   2. Computer files/Electronic resources
   3. Geographical atlases
   4. Maps
   5. Microfilm/Microfiche
   6. Scores
   7. Sound recordings
   8. New video recordings
   9. Serials

References

1. Neumeister, Susan M. and Judith Hopkins. Copy cataloging in an acquisitions department (at SUNY Buffalo). *The acquisitions librarian* 12 (1994): 81-94.

2. Propas, Sharon. Rearranging the universe: reengineering, reinventing, and recycling. *Library acquisitions* 21 (1997): 135-140.

3. Slight-Gibney, Nancy. FastCat. *The acquisitions librarian* 13/14 (1995): 121-140

.,>>>>>>>>>>>>>>>>>>>>>>>>>>>>>

[i] Presumably Acquisitions staff was still doing the cataloging work, but the respondent did not state this in their reply.
[ii] http://www.libraries.psu.edu/iasweb/techserv/cat/FastCat/FastCat.htm

LOW COUNTRY YANKEE
BECOMES PALM TREE LIBRARIAN

Elizabeth Connor, Ross University School of Medicine, Portsmouth, Commonwealth of Dominica, West Indies

The May 14th issue of Forbes referred to Ross University faculty and future physicians as Palm Tree M.D.'s.

In April 2001, I left the Medical University of South Carolina Library in Charleston to work at an offshore medical school. My mission is to build electronic collections and a student-centered Library.

I'd like to start by illustrating the geographic location of Dominica, explain the history and mission of Ross University within the academic setting, discuss the challenges of my mission, share some future plans related to resources, services, staff, facilities and technology, and while answering specific questions, show the gorgeous flora and fauna of the island also known as the Nature Island.

Dominica is the largest island of the group of Windward islands, part of the lesser Antilles, and is not to be confused with the Dominican Republic. Discovered by Columbus on a Sunday, Dominica was once inhabited by Carib and Arawak natives. Dominica was the last of the Caribbean islands to be colonized by Europeans, due chiefly to the fierce resistance of the native Caribs.

France ceded possession to Great Britain in 1763, which made the island a colony in 1805. Dominica gained independence in 1979. From the wild east coast on the Atlantic ocean, to the calmer beaches of the Caribbean Sea, Dominica is home to Ross University School of Medicine. The school's mission is "to prepare highly dedicated students to become effective, successful physicians in the United States."

Ross University was founded in 1978 and over time has developed an accelerated course of study for students unable to gain acceptance at American medical schools, offering a second chance for persons wishing to practice medicine in the United States. The rigorous course of study includes three semesters per year, year-round with incoming students each semester. At any given time, more than 800 students are on campus, with hundreds more in the United States at more than 100 clinical sites located in ten states.

Fifty basic sciences faculty teach introduction to clinical medicine, pharmacology, physiology, behavioral sciences, anatomy, pathology, microbiology, immunology and the neurosciences. Most faculty have American educational backgrounds or have completed postgraduate training in the U. S.

During the orientation for new students, I administer a brief informatics knowledge and attitudes survey. For May 2001, I have survey results from 130 students. For September 2001, I have survey results for 168 students.

Of the students who own computers, 12.5% of the May class own PDAs and 17% of the September class own PDAs. For the question as to whether computing is an integral part of their daily routines, 84% and 85% agreed or strongly agreed with this statement.

Students insist that they know how to perform database searches of the scientific literature as indicated by these numbers in the 70s.

I surveyed the faculty at the end of May and June 2001, receiving just 18 completed surveys after many weeks of reminding. I'd like to mention just three specific questions from the survey. When asked whether faculty agreed or disagreed with the statement, "Libraries are all about access," 83% agreed and 17% did not answer the question.

Faculty were asked whether they agreed with this quotation from an article by Widdicombe. [Eliminating all journal subscriptions has freed our customers to seek the information they really want and need: the result - more access, not less *Sci Technol Libr* 1993; 14(1) <http://www.lib.stevens-tech.edu/general/staff/article2.html>] "We expect that as technology improves, our users will not even want whole articles but kernels of ideas properly noted with author and ownership tags." Forty four per cent agreed and 56% disagreed.

When asked whether they agreed or disagreed with a statement about students knowing more about technology than they did, 61% agreed and 39% disagreed.

The library's focus is on students, teaching faculty, best evidence, and new and emerging technologies. I try to develop and maintain a student-centered service unit that provides a wide range of resources (books, journals, multimedia, databases), services and facilities designed to enhance self-directed learning,group collaboration and academic excellence.

The library features 19 FTE, a 16,000 square feet building, 72 Internet-accessible workstations, 200 journal subscriptions and 5000 books.

Challenges include improving staff, resources, services, facilities, and technology within the context of an accelerated curriculum in a geographically isolated location.

Since joining the university, I have developed a series of staff workshops related to planning, cataloging, biomedical journal, interlibrary loan and reference. I have promoted some staff to supervisory positions, developed job descriptions and helped to improve staff morale by purchasing a microwave and small refrigerator for the staff room.

For the first time in months, we had new books on the new book shelf, and I developed a detailed plan for electronic resources needed in the short-term.

As an academic chair, I was named to a number of committees related to the curriculum and case-based learning. In a short period of time I have shared my vision with as many students and faculty as possible by being attentive, focused and energetic.

Two initiatives presently underway include installing EOS Q Series as the new integrated library system, and choosing Knowledge Finder as the common interface for UltraMED and Cochrane Library databases. The original plan included two other databases (PsycLit and EMBASE Alert) that have since been dropped by Aries Knowledge Finder from their suite of databases. Knowledge Finder facilitates the linking of bibliographic citations to full text content.

Immediate plans include conducting a retrospective conversion, providing access to aggregated, full-text biomedical resources, developing and delivering more staff training, and working with faculty to integrate informatics into the curriculum.

Strategies include using do-it-now and evidence-based approaches, working closely with students and faculty, and developing white papers to convince and persuade others.

Personal challenges include shopping, transportation and housing. The flora and fauna of Dominica promote rain forests, eco-tourism, and simple, healthy lifestyles. Dominica is known for the world's largest concentration of persons over 100 years of age.

In conclusion, I hope you have enjoyed this snapshot of living and working on a beautiful Caribbean island. I welcome your comments and questions.

Additional PowerPoint slides from Ms. Connor are available on the Charleston Conference website.